Praise for

"Flowerevolution *both pleases the eyes and touches the soul. Louie Schwartzberg doesn't just capture the beauty of flowers with his photographs—he makes you fall in love with them. And Katie Hess's evocative stories, rituals, and reflections show that flowers can truly transform our lives in concrete ways, helping us to connect more deeply with the planet, with others, and with ourselves.*"

— **Arianna Huffington,** co-founder, president, and editor-in-chief of *The Huffington Post*

"*A simply stunning book.* Flowerevolution *is about to revolutionize the way we think about and use flowers. The author invites us to catalyze our own personal flower evolution and create a positive worldwide ripple effect. And then she sets out to show us just how to do so in and through our relationship with flowers. Gorgeously illustrated with photos by well-known photographer Louie Schwartzberg.*"

— **Rosemary Gladstar,** herbalist and author of *Rosemary Gladstar's Medicinal Herbs: A Beginner's Guide: 33 Healing Herbs to Know, Grow, and Use* and *Herbal Healing for Women*

"Flowerevolution *is utterly enchanting. Everyone likes flowers. But few of us know how well their essences serve our evolution and well-being. Once you are introduced to the depths of flower power, you'll begin to see them differently. More deeply. And with more appreciation.* Flowerevolution *is one of those books that you just have to have. And after diving in and reading the testimonials, I can't wait to bring more flower power into my life— starting with eating more edible flowers and taking flower essences. Bravo, Katie. Beautiful work.*"

— **Christiane Northrup, M.D.,** *New York Times* best-selling author of *Goddesses Never Age*

"*A stunning, beautiful, and courageous book.*"

— **Stephen Harrod Buhner,** herbalist and author of *The Lost Language of Plants, The Secret Teachings of Plants, Sacred Plant Medicine,* and *Herbal Antibiotics*

"*Katie Hess has written a beautiful and groundbreaking work that blows open the doors on a little-known tool for transformation—flowers. She shows us how easy it is to tap into the power of flowers to heal and support our bodies and lives.I'm thrilled to learn the inside story behind the marvelously talented Katie and her magical elixirs. Joyful, fun, and deeply insightful—*Flowerevolution *will be a lifelong companion.*"

— **Kris Carr,** *New York Times* best-selling author of *Crazy Sexy Juice*

"*This book has ignited something deep inside of me, reminding me of being a little girl who took flowers and made elixirs, and knew the power of plants. So much has been lost in this modern world, but the revolution is here. And Katie is at the forefront, with her kind and gentle soul, educating and inspiring us with the medicine and healing of plants. The world may appear in peril, but after holding this book in your hands you will feel a sigh of relief that healing is here and always has been. We just forgot what we knew as children—flowers feel good.*"

— **Carrie-Anne Moss,** actress and founder of Annapurna Living

"Since I met Katie Hess many years ago, I've put my attention on flowers in an entirely new way. Her flower elixirs give me a moment of self-care that resonates throughout my day, reminding me to slow down and listen. Now, flowers come home with me all the time; they meet me on walks wherever I land, and enhance my life with the lessons of their very existence. They teach me about connection, communication, vibration, and color. They lend me their fragrance, their intelligence, their beauty, and their majesty. Thank you Katie, for creating this book to show us how this magic happens."

— **Elena Brower**, author of *Art of Attention*

"Katie's beautiful words and Louie's brilliant photographs teach us that flowers not only contain the ability to heal our wounds, but they also swarm with power and purpose. We are fortunate to have Katie as our guide to explore the deepness and richness that flowers behold."

— **Kristin Meekhof**, author of *A Widow's Guide to Healing*

"As a holistic/integrative psychiatrist, I search for safe tools to support healing and recovery. This book provides a glorious path to think about flowers and healing in vibrant new ways. Katie Hess offers a deep resource for supporting your path to healing. I highly recommend this beautiful book that blossoms like a flower within as you read it."

— **Scott Shannon, M.D.**, psychiatrist and author of *Parenting the Whole Child*

"What a magnificent journey! This book delights at every turn, with a passionate story by Katie and a visual celebration by Louie. No matter what you know (or don't) about flowers, these master crafts(wo)men deliver something special and surprising at every turn. Brimming with personal experience, cultural history, and practical application, the book reminds us that flowers are energy and we can use them, accordingly. The result? A radiant read that elevates flowers from 'taken for granted' to 'take for a rich plus vibrant life!'"

— **Stephanie Marango, M.D., RYT**, founder of i.m.body, and author of *Your Body and the Stars: The Zodiac as Your Wellness Guide*

"I firmly believe that flower remedies will be the next frontier of holistic health, and Flowerevolution will be the book that elevates them into the public consciousness. If you care about wellness but have yet to explore the power of flowers, Flowerevolution is a must-read. It has completely changed my daily health routine."

— **Max Goldberg**, founder of Living Maxwell and Pressed Organic Juice Directory

"The shared perspective of Louie and Katie is both uplifting and inspirational. They show such a connectedness that becomes a powerful metaphor for life and our sustainability on this planet in the most beautiful collaborative presentation. I could not recommend it more."

— **Oliver Luckett**, technology entrepreneur, philanthropist, and author of *The Social Organism*

EVOLUTION

ALSO BY LOUIE SCHWARTZBERG

Books

*Mindful Intentions**

A Good Day: A Gift of Gratitude

America's Heart & Soul

DVDs

Majestic Nature

Breathing Spaces

Inspiration

Moving Art

America!

Chasing the Light

Wings of Life

Mysteries of the Unseen World

America's Heart & Soul

*Available from Hay House

Please visit:

Hay House USA: www.hayhouse.com®
Hay House Australia: www.hayhouse.com.au
Hay House UK: www.hayhouse.co.uk
Hay House India: www.hayhouse.co.in

flower EVOLUTION

BLOOMING INTO YOUR
FULL POTENTIAL
WITH THE MAGIC OF FLOWERS

Written by Katie Hess

Photography by
Louie Schwartzberg

HAY HOUSE, INC.
Carlsbad, California • New York City
London • Sydney • Johannesburg
Vancouver • New Delhi

Published and distributed in the United States by: Hay House, Inc.: www .hayhouse.com® • *Published and distributed in Australia by:* Hay House Australia Pty. Ltd.: www.hayhouse.com.au • *Published and distributed in the United Kingdom by:* Hay House UK, Ltd.: www.hayhouse.co.uk • *Published and distributed in the Republic of South Africa by:* Hay House SA (Pty), Ltd.: info@hay house.co.za • *Distributed in Canada by:* Raincoast Books: www.raincoast.com • *Published in India by:* Hay House Publishers India: www.hayhouse.co.in

Indexer: Jay Kreider • *Cover design:* Michelle Polizzi • *Interior design:* Nick C. Welch • *Photos on pages 152, 157, 175, 329, 330:* Courtesy of Katie Hess • *Photos on pages 111, 212 (Banana Yucca), 122 (Date Palm Flower), 158, 163, 206, 228, 233, 314, 356:* Taylor Rico • *Photos of Katie Hess and page 41:* Thea Coughlin • *Photos on page 73:* Jennifer Paul • *Photo on page 170:* Sally Hess-Samuelson • *Photo on page 195:* Jennifer Erlys • *Flower icon illustrations pages 126–358:* Kylee Jaeger • *All other photos courtesy of Louie Schwartzberg*

The authors of this book do not dispense medical advice or prescribe the use of any technique as a form of treatment for physical, emotional, or medical problems without the advice of a physician, either directly or indirectly. The intent of the authors is only to offer information of a general nature to help you in your quest for emotional and spiritual well-being. In the event you use any of the information in this book for yourself, the authors and the publisher assume no responsibility for your actions.

To protect the privacy of others, certain names and details have been changed.

Names: Hess, Katie, author.
Title: Flowerevolution : blooming into your full potential with the transformative power of flowers / written by Katie Hess ; photography by Louie Schwartzberg.
Description: Carlsbad, California : Hay House, Inc., [2016]
Identifiers: LCCN 2016028078 | ISBN 9781401948252 (hardback)
Subjects: LCSH: Flowers--Therapeutic use. | BISAC: HEALTH & FITNESS / Alternative Therapies. | SELF-HELP / Personal Growth / General. | HEALTH & FITNESS / Herbal Medications.
Classification: LCC RX615.F55 H47 2016 | DDC 615.8/515--dc23 LC record available at https://lccn.loc.gov/2016028078
Hardcover ISBN: 978-1-4019-4825-2

10 9 8 7 6 5 4 3 2
1st edition, October 2016

Printed in the United States of America

That you may fall in

love with flowers.

Again.

And spark your life.

CONTENTS

A SHARED VISION: COLLABORATING WITH LOUIE SCHWARTZBERG

PART I: THE TRANSFORMATIVE POWER OF FLOWERS

PART II: THE SECRET TEACHINGS OF FLOWERS

Flower Profiles **116**

A SHARED VISION: COLLABORATING WITH LOUIE SCHWARTZBERG

We nearly walked right into each other—Louie Schwartzberg, with his huge friendly smile, Sara Jeane, his gorgeous partner and photo editor, and me. Arriving at the exact same moment at a theater in downtown Boulder, Colorado, we had all come for the LOHAS (Lifestyles of Health and Sustainability) conference.

I was deeply touched by Louie's work. Weeks before, nestled in my bed, I had watched Louie's film for Disney called *Wings of Life*. I was delighted by the fierce and joyful hummingbirds he captured midhover, their emerald wings slowed to a speed that our human eyes could perceive. I was in awe of the desert scene at night: tall cactuses exploding with white flowers while mama bats, carrying their babies, fluttered around them, slurping nectar from the juicy flowers in the starlight.

Louie and I hit it off at the conference; it was a joy to hear him speak and watch his films.

I fell in love with his unique expression of the language of flowers and was impressed by how his team supported and expanded his artistry. Louie couldn't believe there was someone else out there as passionate as he was about flowers, celebrating them from a different perspective.

Louie's path to becoming a cinematographer was unique. After graduating from UCLA he moved to Northern California. He wanted to shoot high-quality video on high-resolution film, but he didn't have much money, so he shot one frame every 20 minutes. Placing all those images together revealed what happened over a trajectory of time. Seeing flowers move toward the light was a transformational experience, filling him with wonder. He hasn't stopped since; he now has over three continuous decades squeezed into about 15 hours of film. You've likely seen his work in movies like *American Beauty, E.T., The Bourne Ultimatum, Crash,* and countless

Every time I watch his films, I am touched somewhere deep inside and get choked up. It's a phenomenon many people experience when they see his work: tears spring to their eyes. When we see the beauty of nature so intimately, it reminds us of how precious everything is. Then the truth of impermanence is inescapable: that we are all sprouting, blossoming, and wilting; being born, living, and dying, together.

Only a few months after our first meeting, Louie, Sara, and I found ourselves together again in the land of miracles and magic: India. The scent of rose petals, spices, and incense wafted in the air at the Global Spa & Wellness Summit. In a collision of brilliant minds, Louie and his films preceded the keynote speaker: His Holiness the Dalai Lama. We were at the right place at the right time, with blessings abounding. The crowd was supercharged with joyous energy and aspirations to benefit the world.

During the summit, Bonnie St. John, the emcee of the event, a dear friend who is an Olympic medalist and author of five books, casually suggested, "You guys should write a book together!" As Louie says, "She planted a seed in fertile ground." It was a natural alliance.

The similarity of our vision—saving the world through flowers—is undeniable. We just express it in different ways. Louie shoots exquisite footage of flowers, landscapes, and people. He even hangs out of helicopters for Hollywood, National Geographic, and IMAX films, and creates visual

others. You've also probably seen some of his viral videos on YouTube and TED, with more than 50 million combined views.

With our normal vision, we see flowers as stationary, motionless; but with time-lapse photography, Louie shows us how flowers lean into the light, how they wiggle and dance into full bloom. As Louie puts it, he captures anything that moves too slow or too fast for the human eye to see. With film as the medium, he opens a portal into the hidden worlds all around us. He makes the invisible visible—revealing whole universes that would normally go unseen.

healing systems for spas, resorts, and other spaces worldwide. I go into the wild in many countries to collect the essences of flowers, make elixirs, blend them into custom formulas, and infuse them into spa experiences and tools to help us thrive in our crazy everyday lives.

I've spent the last five years creating an international business with the intention of making flower elixirs known and accessible throughout the world. This has involved uniting a courageous community of people who want to change the world from the inside out; I write about flowers, meditation, and mindfulness on our blog. I have also created an interactive website and smartphone app that helps people figure out which flowers will most efficiently accelerate their personal growth, along with a system to track their results.

After I saw Louie in India, he went on to be interviewed by Oprah on Super Soul Sunday, was invited by TED to do another talk, and was given the honor of creating a short film to open the United Nations Climate Summit Talks.

Louie's work is quite radical in our current culture. Most filmmakers entertain us with fictional stories, whereas Louie dives deep into what's real, filming the miracles that are happening all around us. He gives us a lens through which to see the extraordinary world that we live in. His work illuminates the very preciousness of life itself.

Deeper than the how of what Louie does is the why. If you ask, he'll tell you that his motivation is to heal and awaken people through his films. He calls it visual healing. His aspiration is to elevate consciousness and help us fall in love with our planet, so that we protect it by making decisions that sustain life.

During the writing of this book, I went to visit Louie and Sara at their home in Southern California. I met their dog, Wally, took a tour of their garden, and even snuck a peek at Louie's time-lapse studio aglow in violet lights, the flower buds unfolding on center stage with the camera lens focused on them.

Louie told me that when he heard about the colony collapse disorder among bees, it moved him to create a film about them, which expanded his appreciation for flowers beyond their beauty into what he calls the love story that feeds the Earth. He studied and filmed the intelligence of flowers: how they devise strategies for attracting pollinators to help them reproduce and thus survive. This intersection between the plant and animal world that happens billions of times every day is the foundation of life—the ordinary miracle that enables all of us to flourish on this planet. "Without the flowers," Louie says, "we wouldn't be here."

Not only are flowers the foundation for all life on this planet, they are quietly working their magic on us. When we spend time around flowers they transform our lives. Even by just looking at photographs of flowers, as research shows, we feel better and heal faster. They awaken within us a deeper kindness, a true generosity, and a sense of being part of a community. Paging through the flower images in this book will inspire, enliven, and soothe you. To quote Louie, "The flowers only live for a week. This book will live in your heart forever and that's our gift to you."

Artist's Statement: "Plants had a problem: they have no legs. In order to reproduce, they blossomed. The beautiful flower seduces a messenger to them, to move their DNA forward. This perfectly choreographed dance is the foundation of life. It happens billions of times each day. Flowers dazzle pollinators and humans with their beauty, appealing to our senses of smell, taste, touch, and most importantly sight, with their spectacular visual display. Beauty and seduction are nature's tools for survival because we protect what we love. And I will never get tired filming flowers. The pollination of flowers is a love story that feeds the Earth, and it's an affair that has been going on for 50 million years."

Louie Schwartzberg

INTRODUCTION: *SEEDSPARK*

My Life in Flowers: Coming Alive in Petals & Nectar

I remember walking with my mother in the woods when I was a child. She would point out special plants, like wintergreen. We'd gently pick one leaf from the wintergreen plant, tear it down the middle, and breathe deeply—the crisp, cool wintergreen scent—from the juices of an unassuming leaf! If you didn't know about it, you'd walk right by it. It was a treasure to me, a miracle. My mother recited plant names so I would learn to identify them. Early meadow rue was my favorite, not only for the way the name rolled off my tongue but also for its array of delicate leaf patterns.

I learned to appreciate endangered flowers like the lady's slipper, a wild forest orchid of the upper peninsula of Michigan. On rare occasions we'd see one, its precious yellow or pink slipper hanging from the stem alongside tendrils that spiraled downward like ribbons. Lady's slippers grew in a very solitary way—one plant all alone. You'd never see bunches of them together, not like the abundant neighboring communities of white trillium flowers that looked like popcorn sprinkled onto the forest floor.

At school during recess, it was never the jungle gym or the swings that called us kids out to play—it was the woods, the shaded forest of cedar trees that reached for the sky, their rough bark coming off in strings. We'd make up elaborate dramatic scenes and play them out for the trees. Nature was just as much a classroom for us as the one indoors full of desks and no. 2 pencils under the fluorescent lights.

Even in my early preschool years, when I still lived in Minneapolis, my best memories include climbing the huge pine tree in our front yard, its golden resin oozing from the trunk and sticking to my fingers and clothes. I would run through the alleyways to find wild honeysuckle and tenderly bite down on the tiny bulbs of nectar. I explored my mother's garden, full of big, ruffled pink peonies that I would bury my face in. I watched the ants roam frantically around the big, round peony buds for what seemed like hours. I lay in the grass, peering up into the tiny bells of the lilies of the valley, dangling bleeding hearts, and hanging pots of bright-colored fuchsia. I would peer into wooden barrels of water hyacinths, admiring the leafy green bulbs floating in the water next to reflections of sky.

Along one side of our house was a stone wall with a beautiful green vine whose tendrils curled around the stones. The vine had dark blue berries, and if you squished them between your fingers, the berries oozed a bright red juice that looked like blood. You can imagine our stories: "Look, look, I'm bleeeeeding!" The berries were poisonous, but somehow we knew not to eat them.

The world was full of petals, dirt, nectar, fresh air, and pure fun. The last thing we wanted to do was go into the house for a bath or a nap. Our discoveries never got old. The world was ours—it belonged to us. We were totally in it. We tasted and touched things. There was nowhere we couldn't go, and nothing we couldn't do—like the dandelions that pushed their way up through the cracks in the concrete, the same dandelions whose soft, fuzzy seeds we'd blow into the wind to carry our wishes.

We all still have that child inside us. By now, since you're reading this, your own free child may be rising to the surface again, remembering the richness of this miraculous world that we live in. In this book, you'll discover how flowers can be powerful healers and guides in your personal growth. For example, did you know that your favorite childhood memories of flowers can give you useful information about your strengths and the gifts you came here to share?

Explore: Your Flower Guides

Let's explore your connection with flowers when you were a child. Close your eyes.

Go back to a time in childhood when you played in nature or around flowers.

What were you doing? Who were you with?

What was your favorite flower?

What three words best describe the personality of that flower and how it made you feel? Go ahead and write them down in the space below if you wish.

Flower: _____

Personality: _____

Feeling: _____

What is your favorite flower today, and what three words describe that flower's personality and how it makes you feel?*

Go ahead and write them down in the space below if you wish.

Flower: _____

Personality: _____

Feeling: _____

Now here's the surprise! The way you describe the personality of your favorite flower from childhood usually describes YOU, your essence, how you are at your best, and how you offer your gifts to the world. (If you wrote down more than one favorite flower, then they reflect the different facets of your personality.)

* If you happen to choose words that don't evoke positive qualities, flip the word to the positive aspect of that quality; for example, if one of your words is *stubborn,* then switch it out with *determined* or *persevering.*

Think for a moment: Does the description fit your personality? What are some of the ways you embody those three qualities you ascribed to your flower?

The second part of the exercise signifies something slightly different. The way that you describe your favorite flower right now represents aspects of your personality that want to grow.

How are these aspects of yourself manifesting in your life right now?

_____

_____

How do they differ from or compare with your childhood flower?

_____

_____

Think about your life today and what you are accomplishing.

_____

_____

What are you focusing on right now in your life?

_____

_____

What qualities might you want more of to support you and your endeavors?

_____

_____

What You'll Get Out of This Book

This book is packed with information, stories, reflections, and rituals designed to wake up your connection with flowers, trees, yourself, and your loved ones. It offers a powerful way to experience a heightened interconnectedness with everything around you. Using flowers as teachers, you will discover how to accelerate your personal growth and delve into new insights about yourself every day through flowers.

Flowers and plants are in service to us in profound ways that often go unnoticed. By sharing what I've learned about flowers and flower elixirs over the last 15 years, my aim is to open a window into a fresh new world—one that is full of magic and possibility.

Most people would never suspect that quiet, unassuming flowers can be highly effective at amplifying our positive qualities and awakening new joy in everyday life, but, in fact, flowers can spark us to reach our greatest potential—one that is likely bigger than we can even imagine.

How to Read This Book: Choose Your Own Adventure

This is an interactive book. You can read it from cover to cover or skip around and read only the parts you're most interested in. Think of it like the Choose Your Own Adventure books we read as kids.

If you just landed on this page and haven't read the previous part of the intro, you may want to backtrack a little to find out what your favorite flowers mean about you. If you have read up to here, by now you're probably eager to dive in.

Here's the scoop. There are two major sections of the book. Part I explains why flowers are special, how they affect our lives, and how we can tap into them to transform the world from the inside out. Part II tells you all about the flowers themselves, how the ones you're drawn to reflect insights back to you and show you which qualities want to be expressed within you.

Part I: The Power of Flowers

Chapter 1 walks you through everything you already know about flowers, but didn't know you knew. You'll have aha moments and be reminded of the tremendous value that flowers offer us personally, culturally, and spiritually. We'll activate your right brain to show you how *you* interpret the language of flowers.

If you're intrigued by the scientific superpower of flowers, turn to Chapter 2. Discover how plants are psychic, how flowers emit energy, and how energy is captured in water. We've even included photographs of the water crystals of flower elixirs.

In Chapter 3, discover the ways in which flowers have been used around the world, from meditation pills in the Himalayas to healing dew drops in Europe. Or, if you're curious to know more about how I stumbled upon flower elixirs, you'll be taken from the streets of Mexico to a lush, remote forest in British Columbia, Canada.

Interested in reading real stories from real people who have taken flower elixirs? Chapter 4 describes the most common experiences that people report from regular, daily use of flower elixirs, ranging from a few days to ten years of consistent use.

If you're intrigued by what could happen in your life as you start to use flower elixirs, check out Chapter 5. It leads you through the three phases of transformation that occur and prepares you for what is possible for *you*.

If you've already heard of flower elixirs, but have burning questions, Chapter 6 answers the top 10 most commonly asked questions. Or if you want to know how to use them during a specific stage of life, check out Chapter 7, which recommends specific flower elixirs for support from birth to death and everything in between.

Chapter 8 tempts you with the big picture. It's possible that simply by using flower elixirs we can transform the world we live in. Learn how we are powerful beyond our imagination and what we can do to exponentially multiply our impact.

At the end of each section is an exercise or ritual designed to give you immediate insights about yourself, perhaps inspiring a profound experience that may reconnect you with what is most deeply important to you in life.

If you already know all about flower elixirs, and you simply want to know which flower to start with, skip Part I and go directly to Part II. Or, if you want an immediate reflection of what aspects want to be revealed within you in this moment, you can also go directly to Part II.

Part II: The Secret Teachings of Flowers

The second part of the book features 48 of the flowers and trees whose remedies are the most pertinent, powerful, and essential for our modern-day lifestyle. Use this section daily or weekly as an inspiring practice of allowing flowers to mirror back to you what aspects most want to flourish inside you.

Here's how: Go to page 119 and look at the images of all of the flowers that follow. Choose the flower you're most drawn to; look up what it's for and what it means about you right now. You're always drawn to those flowers that benefit you most.

Use this part of the book to refine your intuition, recognizing that you're attracted to those flowers that soothe, inspire, and activate you most right now. Dig into the exercises, reflective questions, and action steps, because they will evoke specific qualities in you that want to expand and grow. Sprinkled throughout this section are flower-powered DIY projects and recipes to inspire your daily life with flowers.

Finally, if you are looking for a specific antidote for a feeling you currently have, turn to the Master Key to the Elixirs at the back for indications of flowers that either dissolve or magnify specific states of mind or life situations.

As you're reading, if you reach a point where you want to put the book down and get yourself some flower elixirs, you're in good company. I've personally gone out into the wild and collected all of the flowers in this book—if you're curious to know more, visit www.lotuswei.com. If you're inspired to share insights, photos, or your flower-powered projects with the Flowerevolution community, hashtag them: #flowerevolution

Let's Start a Flowerevolution!

We are vastly more powerful than we think we are.

With a little support from flowers, we can recognize how deeply we affect others with our own energy and presence. We can cultivate a sharper awareness of our impact in the world.

By tapping into flowers and their elixirs, we have a method at our fingertips that helps us be our happiest, clearest, and most loving selves. With this book I invite you to catalyze your own personal Flowerevolution and create a worldwide ripple effect of positivity—transforming the world from the inside out.

If you're a person who loves nature and feels an inexplicably profound interconnectedness with the Earth, keep reading. If you believe that life is short and worth being the best human being that you can possibly be, read on. My dearest friend—this book is for YOU.

Bloom, baby, bloom! It's only the beginning.

Love & flower petals,

Katie

PART 1

THE TRANSFORMATIVE POWER OF FLOWERS

CHAPTER 1

WHAT YOU ALREADY KNOW ABOUT FLOWERS, BUT DIDN'T KNOW YOU KNEW

> *To what does the soul turn that has no therapists to visit? It takes its troubles to the trees, to the riverbank, to an animal companion, on an aimless walk through the city streets, a long watch of the night sky. Just stare out the window or boil water for a cup of tea. We breathe, expand, and let go, and something comes in from somewhere.*
>
> JAMES HILLMAN[1]

My Life in Flowers: Nature as My Refuge

Had I known when I was child that there was a way to bottle up all the wonderful feelings I had when I was around flowers and trees, I would have done it. If I had thought for a minute that I had stumbled on one of the oldest secrets of healing the human psyche and spreading happiness in the world, I would have gotten to work right then and there.

Instead, I started school and eventually lived in three different states. As I moved around, from Minnesota to Michigan to Wisconsin, I always felt like the "new kid" and never totally fit in. Whenever I needed peace I would turn to flowers and trees to soothe me. They gave me perspective and reminded me of who I was. Whenever life got tough, confusing, or lonely, nature was my refuge.

As I got older, I traveled even more: At 16, I spent a year in Germany as an exchange student, and later, a year in Spain. I explored different languages, cultures, and customs, but no matter what country I was in, I never felt at home—unless, of course, I was in nature. Spending time around flowers and trees continued to be a touchpoint that brought me back to my center, reassuring me that no matter where I went or what language I was speaking, at my core I was the same.

During that time the healing power of flowers and nature was solely a personal refuge. Being in a field of flowers or a forest would pull me out of mental turmoil and into a world of petals, leaves, vast landscapes, and a blue sky that went on forever. It reminded me that what was in my mind was small, and that there was a huge world flourishing outside of my head. Most of all, it would reconnect me with the real me.

Flowers Reconnect Us to Our Own Essence

When we're in nature, we move toward what elicits our best qualities. When we need a boost of confidence, joy, courage, or love, we're attracted to those flowers that evoke those qualities within us. After spending time around trees and flowers, we actually feel different; we can feel all kinds of positive qualities rising up within us. Those qualities are already within us, but it's being in nature that wakes up those feelings inside us and remind us—with a visceral experience—of who we are. Flowers reconnect us to our own beautiful and unique essence as human beings. They wake up our positive qualities so that we feel them and they begin to emanate from us, just as each flower radiates its own unique quality.

Flowers Remind Us of Impermanence

When we're young, nature has a way of giving us a direct experience of interconnectedness with everything around us. As we grow older and spend less time in nature, we may forget about that feeling we had as children. However, for most of us, flowers make cameo appearances at crucial moments in our lives, serving as a point of connection between ourselves and other people.

All cultures use flowers to denote important occasions. In the U.S., for high school proms, corsages are crafted with special flowers and ribbons and stored in the refrigerator until the moment comes to pin them on lapels or wrap them around wrists, an adornment that makes us feel special and marks a memorable moment of passage.

At weddings, flowers are found on every table and in the bride's and bridesmaids' bouquets, and petals are often strewn before the couple as they walk down the aisle. In India, the flowers in weddings are even more dramatic—made into huge mandalas, or garlands of red roses and orange marigolds, including a garland that gets looped around the couple, connecting them together in ceremony. Each time the couple walks around the mandala, the guests reach their hands into baskets of fragrant flower petals and throw them up in the air—like an offering—showering the petals down on top of the smiling couple.

In many spiritual paths and religious traditions, offering flowers is an expression of devotion, love, prayers for others, and wishes for self-actualization. In Asia, Hindus, Buddhists, and Taoists have elaborate altars for making offerings, in which there is an abundance of lotus flowers, jasmine, and roses. In Mexico, for *Día de los Muertos*, or Day of the Dead, massive altars with bright orange marigolds are created for loved ones who have passed.

When people we love are sick in the hospital, we bring flowers to cheer them up. Studies show that patients heal faster when they have flowers around them; even simply having images of flowers on the walls in hospital rooms helps patients heal faster![2]

Culturally, flowers almost always play a role at times of profound transition: at a birth or after a death, when we fall in love, marry, or when a loved one is sick. These are all times that remind us how precious life is—and that it is always changing. Flowers appear during these key moments to remind us of the evanescent beauty of the world we live in.

Flowers Make Us Feel More Connected to Others

According to a study conducted at the University of Rochester, being exposed to flowers and nature inspires more compassion, generosity,

and sense of community. Dr. Richard Ryan led the study, in which more than 370 people were exposed to either natural or man-made settings, and then were tested on their values around close relationships, community, fame, and wealth.

The scientists' findings? Natural environments increased the participants' caring for others and their generosity. They noted that spending time around flowers and plants changed people's attitudes, better connecting them with their authentic selves and with the world as a whole. As a result, people were more likely to be concerned with the needs of others, and therefore more generous. In the exercise, the participants who spent time in natural environments gave away more money than those who were in man-made environments.

As a result, one of the scientists, Netta Weinstein, remarked that if we spend less and less time in nature we may lose connection with each other: "We are influenced by our environment in ways that we are not aware of. Because of the hidden benefits of connecting with nature, people should take advantage of opportunities to get away from built environments. When inside, they should surround themselves with plants, natural objects, and images of the natural world."[3]

The study also showed a direct relationship between spending time in nature and how deep our connections are with each other. Dr. Ryan commented, "A lot of times we don't take the time to really immerse ourselves in nature, to really appreciate the surroundings and the green living things that exist everywhere around us. We're pretty busy. We're rushing through life and we're not in touch with those things. What these scientific findings show is that to the extent that you pay attention to the living things around us, that connects you more deeply with the human race."

Flowers Act as Messengers

Flowers connect us with our loved ones. Giving flowers to someone involves far more than putting a pile of petals, pollen, and green stems into their hands. We're giving them not only the miracle of life—something that is literally *alive*—but also a profound expression of a particular essence or feeling that cannot always be expressed in words. When we buy flowers for other people, we consider them as we choose the flowers. We access that "feeling" part of us to see what kind of flowers suit them or embody the particular feeling that we want to convey.

Each flower embodies a unique quality. Irises, for example, evoke an elegant and wild creativity, with their royal purple, paintbrush-like tips that ruffle out into full bloom and the bold streak of yellow in the center. Gerbera daisies, on the other hand, are all joy; they're expansive, radiating liveliness and vitality with their radial shape like the sun. Orchids are an entirely different story, otherworldly in their exquisite sophistication and beauty.

Imagine for a moment giving an orchid to someone. Now visualize giving the same person a bouquet of peonies. Next, see yourself giving them a bouquet of sunflowers. How does it feel? Each gift of flowers feels totally different, right? And they will likely provoke different responses from the recipient.

There are some flowers that we wouldn't think of giving to certain people. For instance, you'd never give your grandmother the long-stemmed red roses that you would give a lover. These are things that we know intuitively. We may not be able to put it in words, but it's a wisdom that we possess.

Even when you buy cut flowers or a potted plant for yourself, your choice expresses or brings out a certain quality in you. Some flowers you feel particularly drawn to, and others you simply don't. More often than not, the flowers you are drawn to are not the same as the flowers the next person is attracted to. Based on our internal landscapes, we gravitate to specific flowers for the way they make us feel.

These preferences are not based on traditional symbolism; they come from understanding the flowers through our hearts. We already speak the language of flowers, without knowing it. The flowers that we are most attracted to are those flowers that have qualities we want to embody or that dissolve, shift, or awaken something inside us.

Flowers Magnify Specific Qualities

A rose feels different from a daisy, an orchid, or a lily. And a water lily has a very different quality than a tiger lily. This is something that we know on a deep, intuitive level—so deep we may never have stopped to acknowledge it.

Let your mind go free and, without thinking too much, write down the first word that comes to mind as you look at each flower below:

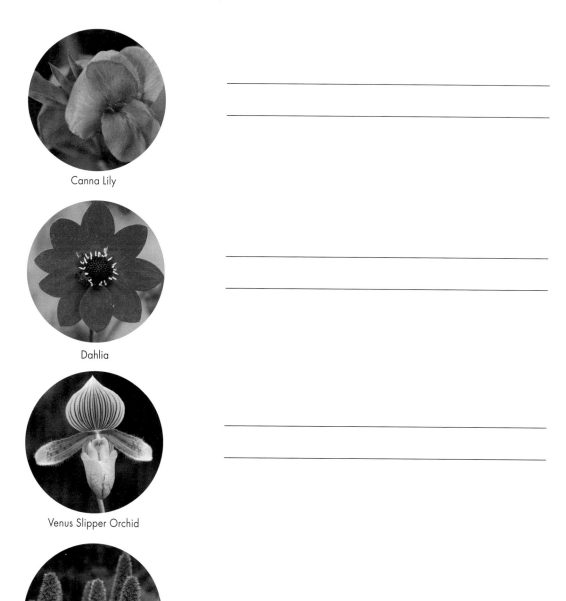

Canna Lily

_____

_____

Dahlia

_____

_____

Venus Slipper Orchid

_____

_____

Pride of
Madeira

Each flower makes us feel different, because each flower has specific qualities. When we are attracted to a flower, we connect with the essence of that plant and those special qualities are evoked within us.

Interestingly, with the same flower, other people may feel the qualities but express them in a slightly different way, or tune in to one aspect more than another. Ask a friend or family member to write the first word that comes to mind with each of the flowers above and compare lists. As you're comparing notes, notice how happy it makes you to talk about flowers with another person.

Flowers magnetize us with their beauty and reflect back to us our own essence. Their qualities magnify positive aspects of ourselves. They serve as messengers to remind us of the preciousness of life at the most crucial times of our lives. Flowers are doing this for us all the time, and all we have to do is pay attention.

Torch Ginger

Cattleya Orchid

Snapdragon

_____

_____

White Iris

_____

_____

Explore: Buy Someone & Yourself Flowers!

Buy someone flowers! Or go out into the wild and pick flowers for someone. Stand in front of all the flowers and think about the person you're getting flowers for. Spontaneously choose the flowers. Reflect on the quality of the flowers and how they make you feel. What insights arise about your relationship?

Then pick out flowers for yourself. Notice what qualities they have. What aspects of your personality are you seeking to express more of right now? If you decide to put the flowers in your office or house somewhere, when you enter that room, what's the first thing you see? You will probably find that your eyes go straight to the flowers, magnetized by their vitality.

CHAPTER 2

FLOWERS RADIATE ENERGY THAT TUNES OUR BODY

The fact that we lack the skills to communicate with nature does not impugn the concept that nature is intelligent. It speaks to the inadequacy of our skill set for communication.

PAUL STAMETS

My Life in Flowers: Bees Outside My Window

In my office, I have a large closet where I keep our mother flower elixirs in sealed jars. There is nothing with a scent—no essential oils or aromatics—just the flower elixirs. During the few weeks each year when we can have our windows open, the bees line up at my window screen and hover for long periods of time, as if there were something inside they were interested in.

We used to open the office doors when the weather was pleasant, but we'd spend so much time catching the bees and putting them back outside that leaving the door open was no longer feasible. It was as if the bees could sense the flower elixirs. The same thing happens every year.

Flowers Radiate Energy

If the above sounds strange, consider some of the most recent scientific studies coming out about flowers and bees. Until recently most people believed that bees were attracted to flowers for their bright colors or fragrances. However, recent research demonstrates that bees are attracted to the energy in flowers, not their fragrance or color. Flowers emit electrical impulses in the form of vibrations, and the bees are able to detect the electrical fields of different flowers.

Research led by Professor Daniel Eric at the University of Bristol in the U.K. demonstrated that bumblebees and flowers communicate through electrical fields. The researchers placed electrodes inside the stems of petunias, and they found that each flower's electrical charge changed after a bee had visited. It stayed that way for several minutes, alerting other bees to the fact that a bee had already been there. They also found that flowers emit different electrical impulses when they are full of nectar and pollen versus when they have none left, communicating to bees whether or not to alight.

Researchers surmise that bumblebees are able to sense the different electrical fields through the hairs on their legs, which may move in a way similar to how our hair moves with the presence of static electricity. "The ubiquity of electric fields in nature and their integration into the bees' sensory ecology suggest that E[lectric]-fields play a thus far unappreciated role in plant-insect interactions."[1]

Remember the highest-grossing movie of *all time*? *Avatar*, a science fiction movie in which humans land on Pandora, a lush moon in outer space, shows plants and flowers that glow and emanate energy.[2] Now we know that the *Avatar* depiction of flowers is not far off from how flowers operate, if we could perceive them as

they truly are. Each flower on the Earth radiates energy in its surroundings.

Flowers Purify Us & Make Us Happy

Humans cannot save the Earth. Only trees can.

KARMA SANGYE RAPTEN

One of my spiritual teachers explained to me years ago that trees and plants absorb people's poisons. The "poisons" he was referring to were toxic moods and attitudes, stress and static, disturbing emotions, and disharmonious energies.

In some cultures, this has been common wisdom for centuries. When traveling in Taiwan, I would often see large groups of people practicing tai chi in the parks. Practices like tai chi and qigong, as well as some Eastern styles of meditation, involve consciously infusing one's body with the energies of the Earth and plant life to develop one's "chi," or life force.

In Japan, there is a practice called "Shinrin-yoku," literally translated as "forest bathing." This is the practice of walking through forests and allowing your body to become revived by the energies of the trees and wildflowers. The idea is to "bathe" your body and "wash" your mind in their regenerative life force.

Japanese doctors prescribe Shinrin-yoku and studies at the Nippon Medical School show that it reduces stress, reduces cortisol levels, and lowers blood pressure within 15 minutes, as well as increasing immune-boosting white blood cells. Forest bathing also reduces adrenaline,

relaxes the nervous system, dissolves tension, and increases vitality and happiness.

Tokyo-based researcher Qing Li, M.D., Ph.D., found that after subjects spent only one day in the forest, the positive immune-boosting effects lasted for one week. The benefits were exponential; for those who spent an entire weekend in nature, the immune-boosting and emotional benefits lasted for an entire month.[3]

In Japan, there is such great respect for forest bathing that the Japanese Forest Service has certified 44 national forests for the purpose of focusing on stress reduction and improving health and wellness.

Forest bathers become aware of all their senses: what the air smells like, what touching a flower feels like. They look at all the different shades of green and listen to the sounds of the forest. They savor the experience without rushing or having any agenda other than to just be in the forest.

Plants Are Psychic

Late one night while working alone in his lab, Cleve Backster got curious, and hooked up his polygraph machine to the leaf of a potted plant. His findings surprised him.

Cleve Backster worked for the CIA as an expert in the lie detector machine. He taught at the Polygraph Examiner School and had 25 years of experience with the polygraph, which among other measurements, works with Galvanic Skin Response, or GSR. GSR measures changes in electrical resistance in the skin through electrodes connected to the machine, which has a needle that draws on a scroll of paper. When the machine detects stress, the needle shows those variations on the paper.

Cleve hooked the machine up to the plant and wondered if it would register stress in the same way stress would register for humans. He dipped one of its leaves in a cup of hot coffee. The machine showed a merely slight stress response, comparable to boredom in humans, so after a while he thought to himself that he would get a match and set one of its leaves on fire. Immediately upon just having that *thought*, the plant registered a high level of stress. Cleve had not yet even left the room for the pack of matches. He had only thought—and intended—to set the plant on fire. When he came back with the matches, the high level of stress was still registering on the machine. He put the matches down. After this experience, he could no longer harm the plant.

He also conducted a series of studies demonstrating that houseplants attune to their caretakers and sympathetically feel their stress. At precisely the moment the plant's caretaker experiences stress, the plant also registers stress on the polygraph reading.

What's more, plants can even perceive their caretaker's stress when they are miles away. Cleve found this out by hooking up the plant to his machine for hours at a time. His office colleague, who also had a relationship to the plant they were testing, left on a trip to a neighboring state. The colleague was unaware that his friends had planned a surprise party for him. At precisely the moment he was startled by his friends shouting "Surprise!" the plant also registered the stress.[4]

Botanical & Floral Communication

Hundreds of millions of years before the Internet, Mother Earth developed her own "world wide web"—a mycelial network. This network consists of a single-cell layer of mushroom cells within the first layer of the Earth. The network is so fine that if we took a walk in an old-growth forest, under each footstep would lie enough mycelial cells to stretch 300 miles.[5] These tiny, subterranean fungal strands connect plants and trees together, sharing nutrients and helpful substances to protect them from pathogens and harmful insects. This is the same network used by "mother trees" to pass along nutrients to smaller trees—even of a different species—who cannot reach the same resources as the older, taller trees.

Communication between trees, plants, and flowers does not require a brain, and they do not experience themselves as separate from their ecosystem, as we humans do. Through this mycelial network, plants are inseparable from one another and pass along information in a series of subtle electrical impulses; it could be said they speak in waves of energy. Additionally, the entire communication network is a giant living organism that grows several inches daily and recharges itself, no outlet needed.

Similarly, every day humans use technology to stream invisible waves of energy through space to receive texts on cell phones, listen to music on the radio, or watch moving pictures on a computer or television. Different sizes and frequencies of energy waves are translated into a form that we can use, depending on the medium used to translate the information from within the wavelength.

Just as technology transmits information through space, so do flowers. Each flower emits subtle electricity that is invisible to the human eye, as are the waves of technology. However, in the case of flowers, we human beings are the sophisticated technology that translates the information and knows what to do with it. We may not yet understand how information or energy is transmitted between flowers and human beings, but universally we know that the feeling we get from a Rose is totally different from the feeling we get from a Daisy.

Sympathetic Resonance

If you hold two tuning forks of the same key and you hit one of them, it will vibrate invisible—and mostly inaudible—sound waves into space. When the second tuning fork picks up on the sound waves, recognizing that they are in the same key, it starts to vibrate sympathetically with the first tuning fork.

If you have a guitar on your lap and you sing the note E, the E string on the guitar will start to buzz in resonance with the sound waves coming from your vocal cords. The e-string recognizes that note, says, "yes that's me," and starts to vibrate in sync with your voice. In Indian classical music, instruments like the sitar have 18 to 20 strings, but only a third of them are plucked. The remaining strings are not played; their job is only to resonate sympathetically with the other strings, creating an exquisitely beautiful sound.

Sympathetic resonance happens among people too; for example, if you go to a party with lots of people you don't know, there are some people you want to move closer to, meet, and talk with—you resonate with them—and there are others you prefer not to engage with. We've all experienced it. Sympathetic resonance is even part of our everyday language, as when we say, "That really resonates with me," or "That struck a chord with me."

With musical instruments, it's easy to understand sympathetic resonance because it's audible. The same goes for dissonance, or lack of harmony. If we listen to an orchestra play music with instruments that are out of tune, it strikes us as chaotic or painful. Once the instruments are perfectly in tune with each other, it once again feels harmonic.

In the human body, lack of harmony is experienced as stress, mental fatigue, negative emotions, or physical imbalances. It's like having static in the body without the noise. Spending time around flowers or trees uses the power of sympathetic resonance to dissolve static and tune the energy of our bodies like retuning the orchestra. This explains why nature makes us feel better when we are "out of tune," "out of sync," or full of stress. Flowers emit a subtle energy that gives our bodies and minds a tune-up, bringing us back to our own natural balance.

Water Records Flower Energy

Graphite and diamond, respectively, are some of the softest and hardest materials we know. Yet each is made *entirely* of the same substance—carbon. What makes them so different is the way the carbon molecules are bonded together.

Similarly, water may appear to be homogeneous, but its structure—particularly how the molecules are organized into clusters—can differ significantly according to the energy it is receiving.

Professor Rustum Roy of Penn State University investigated the lesser-known qualities of water, with surprising results. "People do not think that when they turn on the light water is changing, but we have seen in our experiments that it does." In his scientific experiments, Professor Roy found that the structure of water, similar to a nervous system, reacts to any vibratory wave form, and instruments revealed that within each of water's clusters there are 440,000 information panels, each of which is essentially capable

of recording and storing information. Roy concludes, "It may be the single most malleable computer. It is like computer memory."[6]

Dr. Masaru Emoto, a professor and scientist from Japan, became well known for his work capturing the changes that occur in water with his world-famous water crystal photographs. Dr. Emoto's team used sophisticated equipment to take high-speed photographs of water just as it is approaching its freezing point. They conducted extensive research on water, which had been subjected to different thought forms, intentions, emotions, music, and prayers, as well as to words taped to the outside of the container.

If the word, *intention* or *music* was harmonic and benevolent, the water crystals took form in beautiful and symmetrical shapes similar to snowflakes. If words like *hate* or other negative feelings or intentions were written on the container of water, the water crystals appear sludgy, disjointed, and disturbingly incoherent. This confirmed that water has a memory, the ability to retain information. The coherence, symmetry, and beauty of the water crystal depended on whether the water was subjected to positive or negative energy.

I had never seen any photographs of water crystals related to plants or flowers, so I sent Dr. Emoto's team some samples of flower elixirs to see what the crystals would look like. The photographs show that the water retains the energy of the flowers, which manifests in highly organized and harmonized structures, each one slightly different from the others. Take a look at the photos and notice how they make you feel.

Crystal of water infused with flower elixirs that inspire creativity.

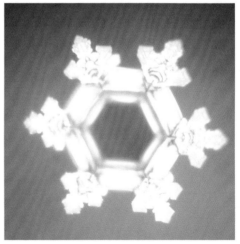

Crystal of water infused with flower elixirs that elicit joy.

Explore: Infuse the Earth's Life Force into Your Water

Charge water with the life force directly from the Earth and see how it affects you! Here's how: Put purified water in a glass jug or mason jar of any color, and place it outside directly on the ground overnight. Drink the water the next morning. You may find that the water has a pleasant, smooth, and almost slippery quality, and seems to taste better than the water you usually drink. Drink water that has been supercharged by the Earth for 30 days and see how you feel. You'll likely retain more vitality and feel more in tune with your surroundings.

CHAPTER 3

CAPTURING EACH FLOWER'S ESSENCE

> *Plants do talk to us and teach us. Their language is accessible, or I should say languages, as they speak in many tongues. It is not a lost language, nor is it accessible to only a few. Children hear it best, but are often discouraged. And like any language not spoken often, after awhile it begins to fade. By middle school most children have forgotten the exquisite language of the plants.*
>
> ROSEMARY GLADSTAR[1]

My Life in Flowers: Auspicious Messenger

I had no idea that there was a sophisticated system of collecting these energies from flowers, or that they could be used to bring people happiness, until I graduated from college and left the country for the third time, this time for Mexico. I went to Querétaro, a beautiful colonial city about three hours from Mexico City, to do a year of full-time volunteer work. The city was a magnet for natural healing, and in my free time I studied aromatherapy, Reiki, yoga, and other wellness therapies.

One day, as I was walking down the cobblestone streets of the city, an Otomi indigenous woman handed me a flyer, her colorful skirts fluttering and her long braids tied together with a bright ribbon. Receiving flyers on the streets was common, but not on a quiet holiday afternoon *like this; she and I were the only ones on the street. The flyer was for an intensive workshop about flower elixirs. I was instantly intrigued, so I turned back to ask the woman about it, but she had vanished! I took this strange encounter as a sign and registered for the class.*

The teacher of the flower elixir intensive was a naturopathic doctor and biologist who had flown in from Madrid, Spain: Pedro Lopez Clemente. He taught in Spanish; luckily, after having lived in Spain in college I was fluent. Over that year he offered a variety of intensive seminars about flower elixirs, each one more profound and interesting than the last. Whenever Pedro was in town, I voraciously took notes on everything he said. When he went back to Spain, I studied with his foremost student who lived in Querétaro, and was mentored by another colleague of theirs. I studied over 100 elixirs that Pedro himself had collected from flowers in the Mediterranean and South America.

I loved the way Pedro taught, conveying not only the individual benefits of each flower elixir but also a big picture perspective. He said that we were at an interesting point in history, because the degrees of separation were diminishing. He was convinced that if only 3 percent of the world's population were taking flower elixirs, it would create enough benefit in the world to change the outcome of the future in a positive way.

Pedro warned us against remaining students forever, saying we'd get seduced by studying the orchids from the Amazon forest and the x-y-z flowers from other exotic places. The best method, he counseled, was to take what we knew and put it into practice. He felt that profoundly

understanding more than 100 flowers—and how they could help human beings—was enough.

I opened a practice in Querétaro offering Flower Elixir Therapy; however, not long after, I woke up one day feeling inexplicably like I was in the wrong place. The feeling was so acute that I decided to move back to the U.S., this time to Phoenix, Arizona. Within several weeks, I had my first clients in Phoenix. Later I realized that coming back when I did put me in the right place at the right time to meet my next spiritual teacher, which greatly enhanced my practice.

Over time, I built up a busy practice of one-on-one consultations. Once a month I met with my clients to talk about what was working—and not working—in their lives, and to explore what they really wanted in life. I would ask them what their ideal life would look like and customize a blend of flower elixirs for them each month.

What Flower Elixirs Are

Flowers are like the antennae of Mother Earth. Reaching their roots deep down into the ground, they are inseparable from the Earth's ecosystem of 4.8 billion years of wisdom and experience. The blossoms capture and emit large quantities of light from the sun. Of all the different parts of a plant, the blossoms have the strongest bioenergetic value, because flowers are the reproductive system of the plant and contain the most life force. This is why elixirs are made from the flowers and not the roots, leaves, or stems of a plant.

Flower elixirs are liquid infusions of fresh flowers. They consist of water that contains the bioenergetic imprint of the flowers. Alcohol is added to the water, acting as a natural preservative to help retain the flowers' bioelectrical signature. Flower elixirs travel through the acupuncture meridians, like an acupuncture treatment without the needles.

Historically, these types of flower remedies are called flower essences. They do not have a scent. To avoid confusion with aromatherapy and essential oils, we have always referred to them as flower elixirs. The word also connotes the traditional way they are taken, which is internally.

The Historical Use of Flower Elixirs

Flowers have been used for their healing benefits for thousands of years, in a variety of cultures from Australian Aborigines to ancient Egyptians. Some even say they were in prolific use in ancient civilizations such as Lemuria and Atlantis.

For more than a thousand years, yogis and yoginis in the Himalayas have used small round handmade pills that contain the vital essences of flowers, gemstone minerals, and water to support their meditation practice. Called *chulen*, a Tibetan word that means "taking the essence," they help sustain the meditators during long fasting retreats in which they eat only one to three *chulen* pills per day. Taking the essence of flowers or gemstones is part of longevity practices that are said to have the side benefit of preventing gray hair and wrinkles, while profoundly deepening meditation.[2]

In Western cultures, the earliest recorded use of the bioenergetic qualities of flowers for healing was in the 12th century, by Abbess Hildegard von Bingen. Hildegard was known as both a visionary mystic and one of the foremost scientists of her time. Later, Paracelsus, a doctor and botanist of the 16th century, was credited with observing that some illnesses have psychological roots. Each of them directed their patients to locate specific flowers from which to collect and drink the dew. As dew forms on the blossoms, the water is charged with the healing qualities, or the bioenergetic imprint, of the flower. This flower dew is considered to be the original flower elixirs of the Western world.

In modern times the name of Dr. Bach is closely tied to these remedies. Dr. Edward Bach was a British physician who became disillusioned with the medical system. He wanted to get to the root cause of physical imbalances, and he felt that Western allopathic medicine was focused only on treating symptoms. He became a homeopathic doctor and soon after he discovered yet another form of healing.

In the 1930s, Dr. Bach lived in the English countryside with fields of flowers all around him. He began to work with the dewdrops on flowers, just as Hildegard and Paracelsus had prescribed them to patients centuries before. Dr. Bach realized his patients needed more than just dewdrops, so he developed a solar-infusion method to increase production. He collected the flowers' mother essence by soaking the flowers in water in the sunlight; this water was further diluted in order to treat himself and his patients. During his lifetime he collected a total of 38 remedies, classified their healing properties, and documented the effects on his patients. Dr. Bach's work led to the resurgence of the use of flower elixirs in the Western world.

Currently, flower elixirs are prescribed by doctors in Europe. They are also available in almost every large pharmacy in Australia and are well known in Central and South America. Although widely accepted throughout the world, flower elixirs have gone largely undiscovered in the U.S. until now. They are carried in many health food stores, but people are uninformed as to how to use them to benefit from their true power. The time is ripe for flower elixirs to be adopted more widely.

How Flower Elixirs Are Made

In some ways, flower elixirs are made like sun tea. In the case of tea, the heat from the sun pulls the flavor and beneficial constituents of the herbs into the water. With flower elixirs, it's the *light* from the sun (or sometimes the moon) that catalyzes the flower to impart its life force into the water.

Through scientific studies like those of Dr. Rustum Roy, we know that water can act as a recording device; clustered structures in the water hold information. Just as a CD can have music or images layered and stored on it, so water can also have data imprinted into it. When flower elixirs are made, water records and retains the life force or bioelectrical energy of the flower—just like we saw in the photos of Dr. Emoto's water crystals.

Flower elixirs are made following lunar cycles. Fresh flowers are collected on either the full or new moon when the gravitational pull is strongest. The plant's life force is concentrated in the blossoms at that time.

We know the moon's powerful effect on the ocean tides. Similarly, if you ask farmers or gardeners, they'll tell you from experience that during new and full moons, plants have a surge of blossoms. Or, if you ask traditional winery owners in Italy, they'll tell you that they pick grapes and rack wine according to lunar cycles. This is likely due to the moon's effect on water, not just in oceans but in our own bodies and the bodies of plants. The lunar cycles cause the plants to pull up more water from the Earth into the vines, creating plumper and juicier grapes.

In the same way, flower elixirs are typically made when the life force of the plant is at its height, and the flowers have just reached full bloom and peak vibrancy. Flowers are collected into a clear glass bowl with pure water and allowed to infuse in the sunlight or moonlight, depending on whether the plants are day- or night-blooming.

The pivotal catalyst in this process is the state of mind of the collector. As we learned from the work of Cleve Backster in Chapter 2, plants are keenly sensitive to people's mental states. Years of spiritual practice may be needed to create the clear inner state that allows the collector to make powerful remedies. Master herbalist Stephen Harrod Buhner underscores this point: "All ancient and indigenous peoples said that they learned the uses of plants as medicines from the plants themselves. For, they insisted, the plants can speak to human beings if only human beings will listen and respond to them in the proper state of mind."[3]

After the "mother essence" is collected with the fresh, live flowers, it is bottled up with alcohol to preserve and maintain the flowers' life force in the solution. The mother essence is then further diluted several times for the practitioner's stock bottle, and again for the final flower elixir that is ingested. The dilutions are similar to the homeopathic process without the succuss-ing (vigorous shaking) process. The final remedy that is taken orally is so diluted that there is no botanical material left in the liquid, only the life force or vibrational imprint of the plant in the water and alcohol. For this reason, even people with severe allergies can take flower elixirs, as the solution contains no allergens, chemical constit-uents, or plant parts.

My Life in Flowers: Collecting My Own Flower Elixirs

After seven years of using Pedro's remedies in my practice, the timing was right, and I decided to start making my own flower elixirs. It began with a collection trip to British Columbia, Canada, in the alpine forests outside of Whistler.

It was early morning on a full moon eclipse in the spring. The birds were singing and everything was lush and green. I did tai chi and meditation near a river, and as I sat quietly, I reached down into the depths of myself and made a sincere prayer to find the flowers that humanity needed most. I asked to be guided to exactly the flow-ers that would benefit hundreds of thousands of people in the future.

When I set out to find the special flow-ers, I came to a fork in the road. I stood there, unsure which way to go. After a moment, a black bear ambled out of the forest and stood on the pathway. He stopped, turned his head, and looked me right in the eye, then continued on his way into the forest. I took it to mean that

he had beckoned me, and chose the path he had indicated.

My mind slipped into a quiet, meditative state as I continued walking through the forest, the light peeking through leaves and casting a kaleidoscope of shadows under my feet. I came to a place where the trail widened and flowers bloomed all along the sides of it. A butterfly appeared and fluttered around my head three times, then veered away and alighted on a pink flower. It fluttered its wings several times, and then landed on a red flower.

I would learn later that the first flower, a tower of pink jewels, was Pink Spirea. As I looked deep into the bunches of tiny pink blossoms that day, my heart suddenly felt sad and lonely, then just as quickly flashed to playfulness and laughter. The second flower looked like a butterfly itself, or a heart. It was Wild Fireweed, and as I looked deep into that flower I felt a twinge of pain and heartache, followed by lightness and a flood of ease and relief. I made mother essences of these two flowers, which are now widely used today.

I continued walking down the trail and sud-denly, right in front of my feet, a snake slithered out of the bushes, shimmying off into a huge patch of white flowers. The flowers turned out to be Yarrow, one of the best flowers for revitalizing the body's natural energy stores, especially after spending hours on cell phones, computers, and airplanes, or being exposed to any other kind of radiation.

The forest was overflowing with such amazing wildflowers that the day evolved into a flower elixir–collecting marathon. I forgot

about food and didn't miss it, I was so energized and in such a magical state of mind. I took copious notes on how I felt, what I heard, and what the flowers indicated they were for. I collected 15 flower elixirs that day. They would prove to be some of the most valuable remedies for my clients and community.

Finally, I was surprised to find myself at the edge of a quietly rushing river, shimmering with sparkles from the sunlight reflecting off the water. I did a short water ceremony before taking some back to infuse and potentiate all of the flower elixirs made that day. I later found out the name of the river: Golden Dreams. After bottling up all the mother essences made that day, I left them out under the night sky, the full

moon flooding them with light and filling up the bottles with moon juice.

Back in Phoenix, I used the mother essences from Whistler, Canada, to create the dilutions necessary for practitioner bottles to use with clients. For the next eight years, I used those flower elixirs while continuing to seek out other flowers in other parts of the world. Over time, as I came to understand the range of different effects that each of the flowers had on my clients' lives, I transitioned into only using the elixirs that I had hand-collected.

Currently our library of elixirs has over 150 flower and gem elixirs collected from all over the world. It includes Cactus flowers from the deserts of the Southwest, Lotus flowers from

Korea, the Bodhi Tree elixir from India, Primrose flowers from Mexico, and the Royal Poinciana tree flower from Bermuda.

Backyard Treasures

Though discovering flowers all over the world is exciting, some of the best remedies are found right in our backyards. Either we've planted them in our gardens, which means we already have an affinity with them, or unexpected flowers have popped up wholly on their own through the magic of Mother Nature, presenting us with what we need.

One spring day I walked into my backyard and spied an exotic-looking flower blooming all by itself. I live in Phoenix, Arizona, and while a wide variety of flowers grows here in the desert, I had never seen anything like this flower before. It looked like several parasols stacked on top of one another, in hues of lavender and pink with polka dots all over the petals. It appeared out of nowhere, like an alien dropped down from another planet.

After some research I found out that this flower was a spotted variety of Bee Balm. The common Bee Balm, which is red in color, doesn't typically grow in Arizona, much less its exquisite polka-dotted twin sister! I quickly set up to make a flower elixir of it, because I knew it could be useful in my practice. Bee Balm has turned out to be one of the most important remedies I use with my clients for healing past or current trauma. I have never seen another Bee Balm flower since!

Flowers sprout up in our backyards at the most auspicious times, to support us, heal us, encourage, and inspire us. Pay attention to what pops up unexpectedly in your backyard, garden, or anywhere you spend time, as they are blooming for you!

Explore: Flower Meditation

Everyone seems to believe that human thoughts and emotions are the products of the human mind, but I think otherwise . . . When people see a green tree, they all think that green trees are beautiful. Trees leave a sense of peace. When the wind ripples the surface of the water, the spirit becomes restless. Go to the mountains, and a sense of the mountains arises. Travel to a lake, and one feels the spirit of the water. These emotions all arise from nature.

MASANOBU FUKUOKA[4]

Reflect on your greatest challenge right now. What questions or heartache do you have? Write down a few keywords here.

_____

_____

_____

_____

_____

_____

Now go to your backyard. If you don't have a backyard, then go for a walk in a park or botanical garden. Have your challenge, heartache, or question in mind, and set out to find a flower* that will help you clarify your situation. Follow your instinct and try not to censor yourself. Don't worry about missing it—you can't avoid it! Don't worry about it being too simple—Mother Nature is simple. When you get the sense that you've identified a flower that can help you, take a seat. Get comfortable, sitting on the ground (if you can't sit on the ground, then sit in a chair with both feet touching the ground).

Close your eyes and focus on your breathing. As your thoughts bring you into the past or the future, keep paying attention to each inhale and exhale. Notice how your body feels. Try to relax any tension and then relax even more. When you notice your breathing getting slower and your mind a little more still, open your eyes and rest your gaze on the flower.

Make the intention to tune in to the flower and learn whatever it wants to teach you. On each inhale, visualize that you are breathing some of its life force into your body. As its life force fills you up, notice how it makes you feel. Continue this way for as long as you like. You may get insights in that very moment, or you may simply have a nice time outside, and then later in the day the message will become clear.

Download a guided audio version of this meditation here: www.lotuswei.com/flowermeditation.

---

* If you don't have any flowers in your backyard, you can also work with a tree.

CHAPTER 4

REAL PEOPLE, REAL STORIES: THE 15 MOST COMMON EXPERIENCES REPORTED BY PEOPLE USING FLOWER ELIXIRS

> *We can't solve problems by using the same kind of thinking we used when we created them.*
>
> ALBERT EINSTEIN

My Life in Flowers: Where It All Started

During my first 10 years in Phoenix, I provided one-on-one consultations full-time, seeing clients at my office at "The Farm," a luscious, green property with a large vegetable and flower farm, old-growth pecan trees, and several farm-to-table restaurants. I painted my office walls bright yellow and green and brought in some antique Chinese furniture and fresh flowers in vases. Clients would curl up across from me in a soft papasan chair with windows overlooking oleanders and apricot trees. It was soothingly quiet, except for the charm of occasional clucking chickens roaming the property.

People of all ages and walks of life found me: entrepreneurs, construction workers, CEOs, mothers with babies, children, teachers, artists, nurses, midwives, and retirees. I worked with people of every color who spoke either English or Spanish.

Doing consultations for over a decade was one of the best ways to learn about human nature and the powerful effects of flower elixirs. I found that there were two main reasons that clients came to see me. Often they had some major challenge in their life that was causing them pain and frustration: a divorce, an affair, the loss of a loved one, or an unfulfilling career. Some were plagued by feeling not good enough. Some were jealous or angry.

Alternatively, clients came to me because their lives were fabulous—but they wanted more. Their careers, businesses, relationships, and everything else were going well, but they felt there was something more to life they wanted to explore. They did not want to feel that they were missing something. They wanted to actualize and fulfill more of themselves and feel that their life was profound and meaningful.

After a decade of consultations, I began making products so that I could reach more people. The business grew so quickly that I could no longer provide one-on-one consultations. Fast-forward five years into the business, I longed for a deeper personal relationship with our customers, so I developed a series of six-month transformation programs.

From 20,000-plus hours of working with people, I learned two main things. First, every human being has some kind of suffering. It doesn't matter how much money you have, how attractive you are, where you come from. Everybody suffers. We all have heartache and something that keeps us awake at night. It comes and it goes, but we all experience pain and we all carry some kind of baggage from past experiences. None of us is exempt from this kind of stress. Second, I learned that flower elixirs work for everyone. Some patterns and situations take longer than others to unravel, but no matter what, flower elixirs accelerate personal growth for each of us when we use them regularly.

After listening to thousands of people talk about what happens to them when they take flower elixirs, I find that there are 15 common experiences.

What Flower Elixirs Do for Us

1. Flower elixirs reawaken joy.

People who take flower elixirs consistently seem to emanate good energy wherever they go. That good energy is tangible and noticed by people around them. They often report that the flower elixirs bring joy back into the picture when life seems to have chased it away.

After Abigail had her baby, she hit an all-time low. She was in love with her daughter, but felt totally lost and couldn't find her way out. This period of aimlessness, depression, and confusion lasted almost three years. She couldn't find anything that helped.

A week after starting flower elixirs, she felt a huge weight lift from her shoulders, and within weeks she felt like herself—her real self—a happier self. "It feels like the flower elixirs are altering me on a really fundamental level," she said, "taking away a fog and bringing me back to my core. Instead of dreading all the questions and 'what-ifs' I've had, they're now exciting."

2. Flower elixirs help us sleep better.

Because they dissolve static, tension, and stress, flower elixirs slow down our monkey minds, making it easier to wind down and to sleep more soundly.

Simon was the bellhop at the hotel I was staying at in New York City. We struck up a conversation as we rode up the elevator together, and he mentioned that he had a terrible time sleeping; in fact, he was only sleeping one to two hours each night.

I gave him a bottle of flower elixirs for sleep that contained Passionflower and Bird of Paradise essences. The next day, I saw him in the lobby and he said that he had slept for four hours. I didn't see him for several days, and then at the end of my stay we ran into each other again in the lobby. This time, Simon was amazed to report that he had been sleeping eight full hours every night and didn't know what to do with all his energy! He said that before, every time he drove over the bridge into Manhattan to work, he was worried he would get into an accident because he was constantly falling asleep at

the wheel. I asked him how long he had been sleeping only a couple of hours a night, and he said, "Ten years."

3. Flower elixirs enhance confidence and magnetism.

When we're confident and magnetic, people want to be around us. They feel inspired by us.

It was Benjamin's first appointment with me. He walked in confidently, a tall handsome man with coffee-colored skin, freckles, and a huge smile. During the intake interview, I asked him why he had come. He smiled and said life was amazing, but he believed that he had not yet reached his full potential and simply wanted "more."

*He was an entrepreneur seeking investment for a new development project in Costa Rica that would catapult his business to a whole new level. I noticed during the first appointment that he was clinging to his cell phone, and during our session he even answered a phone call. I was surprised that he would be willing to sacrifice time from our short appointment to answer a call. Often, that kind of attachment translates to "fear of loss," which typically does **not** make for a strong position in business. I made an elixir for him with flowers like Mandevilla to loosen attachments and African Daisy to loosen up his seriousness and invite more joy in. For his next appointment, I asked him to do something that was challenging for him—leave his cell phone in the car.*

At his second appointment, Benjamin came in wearing a Panama hat and a big smile. He had just gotten back from Costa Rica, and he told me that, for the first time, he had turned his cell phone off while he was there. He had decided to let go of the phone so he could be fully present and focus. When he landed back in the U.S., he turned on his cell phone and checked his messages. Among them were several from investors he had met with on his trip, saying they wanted to invest in his development project.

Benjamin credited the flower elixirs for his feeling so at ease and magnetic, which resulted in investors wanting to be a part of his project. He no longer experienced a fear of loss or of missing something. He was so confident and radiant that people trusted him and were drawn to working with him.

When flower elixirs are taken consistently beyond one month, the effects are much more lasting and profound. They begin to unravel our belief systems and shift habits and patterns we've carried with us for a long time.

4. Flower elixirs help us address our fears.

They offer courage, confidence, and ease in areas of our life where we have been afraid of something—from public speaking to flying on a plane.

Karen originally came to me because her husband had just died, and she was looking for something to help ease the grief. During the intake

appointment it came out in conversation that when her husband was alive they drove everywhere or vacationed in an RV, because she was terrified of getting on a plane. Since her husband's death, she yearned to see her family members on the East Coast, but refused to fly. I made her some flower elixirs and scheduled our next appointment.

After two months of taking the elixirs, Karen decided to visit her family. She used Lupine to help calm her nerves so she could fly. She admitted that she had to have a stiff drink on board that first flight as well; we laughed about it together, and acknowledged that this was a huge step for her.

Fast-forward several months, and she was flying regularly. It wasn't always easy, but she continued taking flower elixirs consistently, and even more frequently during the flights. She met new friends and took several vacations in Mexico. Within a year, she had so many frequent flyer miles accrued that she was getting free flights.

Karen originally took flower elixirs to allay the grief she felt at the loss of her husband. She not only got the relief she was looking for but also opened up a new life, transcending her worst fears and living the life she had always wanted.

5. Flower elixirs help us be more present.

We are bombarded with e-mails, texts, and social media. Our pace of life is speedy, creating mental static, dulling our awareness and causing us to lose focus. Within several weeks of taking flower elixirs, many people remark that they suddenly hear the birds singing and feel more connected to what's happening around them.

Barbara shares her experience:

"Flower elixirs help me to deal with emotions and physical ailments by keeping me in the present moment in a gentle way. I find that's the only way, because otherwise I'll just avoid discomfort. We all naturally avoid discomfort and distract ourselves by thinking about the past or future; anywhere but now! Flower elixirs help me just accept what is. I still have to do the work, but I feel like I'm not alone—I feel so supported.

I have never had such a support on an emotional level before—the flower elixirs push me, encouraging me to expand, but in a gentle, motherly way. They dare me at the same time they embrace me, and I'm centered peacefully in the middle of it.

In my profession I work a lot with trauma and people who carry traumatic experiences in their bodies. The flower elixirs also have a way of reaching people and healing them on that level. It's like an immediate, sharp clarity, at the same time it's the softest thing ever that touches your heart.

Flowers themselves have a magic quality, and there is an incredible lovely feminine energy in flower elixirs, like the love a mother has for her child. It stays with you.

I'm so happy right now. I'm happier than I've been in a long, long time. Things are really falling into place."

6. Flower elixirs magnify radiance and give us a joyful, luminous quality.

Our faces take on a new glow. There is a softening of any hard edges. Tension and stress melt away, and a youthful vibrancy arises from within. People often appear younger than before; other times they may look the same physically, but their energy comes across as radically different.

We encourage people to take before and after photos for that very reason. Changes can be seen in the face as early as one month after regular, consistent use of flower elixirs, with more dramatic effects after four to six months. Depending on each person's unique makeup, what changes in the face differs: some radiate more clarity and joy, others exude more peace and ease. People who are shy by nature often emanate increased confidence and strength, while most everyone looks softer, gentler, and more loving when taking flower elixirs regularly.

Here's a story from Rhea:

"I had never taken flower essences before. I heard about the six-month program from a friend. She told me that they make you more present, allow you to be, and let go of things. I was going through a time of transition in my life. I was moving out of a really cute little home and losing a really good friend.

Not that I was doing terrible—I work with crystals and meditate and try to keep a lighter blueprint. But after taking the flower elixirs for several months, I started to get a lot of compliments about my face when I was with people. Here I was turning 50 and I felt like I was getting younger and younger. People would say to me, 'What happened to your face?!' My eyes got clearer. My whole sense of well-being transcended to a new level.

People would comment on how I was being around them as well. The elixirs keep pushing me to be me. I can feel them in my body. Whenever I go against the grain and am not being myself, I can feel it. They keep me on track to be who I really want to be, and what I want to express and share.

I love that they're from the Earth. Everything is here for us—right in front of us."

7. Flower elixirs accelerate personal growth and evolution.

Over time, flower elixirs slowly and gently show us anything in our lives that's not harmonious, so we can look at it and consciously change it. All of us have habitual patterns, often so habitual that we are not aware of them at all. Flower elixirs gently bring them to our awareness.

Nina grew up in an abusive family and found herself repeating the pattern in a physically and emotionally abusive marriage. She was afraid to leave her husband because she hadn't had a job

for years and didn't have anywhere to go with her two children. At the same time, she knew she had to get out.

She came for an appointment with me, started taking flower elixirs consistently, and brought her children for appointments, too.

This created a huge shift in her life. She started practicing meditation to calm her nerves. She investigated legal support and created her exit plan. After eight months, she left her husband and never looked back.

8. Flower elixirs awaken insights and help us see ourselves in a new way.

Sometimes flower elixirs bring up aspects of ourselves that we have been avoiding. With the support of the elixirs, this happens in a way that first strengthens and stabilizes our emotions. By the time we are introduced to aspects of ourselves that we don't like, we find it easier to be gentle with ourselves, and can simply refine or change our behavior without dwelling on judgment.

Elizabeth shares her story:

"My entire life I was high strung and moody, but it got to a point where I was freaking out over anything and everything. I would get really upset. I had a hard time sleeping. I could never turn off my brain. I took an anti-anxiety medication every day to turn my brain off.

I had panic attacks at the grocery store. I didn't spend time around people, because I was emotionally on the edge and they didn't want to get sucked into it. I was a mess. I would start crying all the time. My emotions were so much larger than me.

I started taking flower elixirs because I felt so stuck and trapped. I wanted to make something different happen. Immediately things started happening. When I took the Cereus essence I got a new creative flair and starting making things. I suddenly had lots of new ideas for things I could make and sell. I hit it off with a woman who sells beautiful fabrics. A couple months later, while both she and I were taking Lilac flower elixir, she decided to leave all of her fabric with me when she moved. The fact that somebody would give me $30,000 worth of inventory was incredible.

I've taken flower elixirs regularly for almost a year now and I'm not like how I was before. I sleep better. I don't need to take anti-anxiety medications anymore. I notice that the flower elixirs separate me from my feelings. It's not like I'm a zombie or that I don't have emotions—they just don't take me over anymore.

I wasn't the first person to notice the changes in me, because after six months of taking flower elixirs regularly, I found out that I had breast cancer, and my relatives and friends started asking me, 'What are you doing? You're handling this so well.'"

Flower elixirs allowed me to stay me, without feeling like I was a monster. When you have breast cancer, you have all these tubes and stuff coming out of you. But I didn't go around feeling that I was hideous, I just saw it as a transition.

I've tried a lot of different things: self-help books, affirmations, exercise, acupuncture, antidepressants, yoga. I've spent a ton of money on therapists. I've tried everything. Flower elixirs work for me. They work better than a therapist.

One of the biggest things that doesn't happen anymore is that my whole life I've had huge esteem problems. It's easy for me to get down on myself. Now I'm getting older—I see changes on my face. I could get focused on feeling ugly or not qualified to do anything, or feeling that no one wants to hire me . . . loser-y feelings. But I don't really focus on that anymore. I don't have that negative self-chatter anymore.

The circumstances of my life have not changed, but I feel different. I don't dwell on the negative. I am more accepting of things. I know that everything is temporary.

Flower elixirs have also helped me to see that change is not the end of the world. I've never been good at that, but they're helping me see the good in change.

9. Flower elixirs wake up our inner observer.

Just as when we practice being the observer in meditation or mind training, flower elixirs give us the psychic space to discern more clearly what's real and what's simply habitual. Also, when we feel a new spaciousness between us and our self-limiting thoughts and emotions, we don't get as caught up in them. Instead of acting on them, we see them for what they are and just let them pass.

Angela shares:

"I learned about the flower elixirs about six weeks before my mom died. When my mom

transitioned, the rest of my family was melting down . . . and I was fine. I'm not saying it was easy, but it took the sharpness away from her death. I was the one person in the family who was able to see the beauty in it. It really softened the experience. As soon as my mom died, I went to have a cry and order flower elixirs.

After several months of regular use, I noticed a curious phenomena. All the nasty shit that I would say to myself . . . everything went completely silent. I could tell you to the minute it disappeared. And I didn't even know that it was there before. Suddenly there was this big open space. Here I was, this meditation and yoga teacher, and I had even more spaciousness. And then in the spaciousness I would start noticing sweet commentary in my mind like, 'Damn, my skin looks good today.' In my mind I was saying kind things to myself.

Before, the negative self-talk was always a part of my mindstream. Now it's so rare, that when it does happen it's really screaming obvious and it hurts. Right away I notice it and ask myself, 'Where is this coming from? I'm not going to talk shit to myself for the rest of the day.' It's like a spiritual smackdown.

I could even make excuses about it before. Even with my to-do list I was being hard on myself: 'I need to do a face mask, because I'm getting older.' Now I think to myself: 'I need to do a face mask, because it feels good.' The flower elixirs soften the edges in my head. All of my emotions are soft, and it's easier to sit with everything."

10. Flower elixirs help us feel more like "us."

Flower elixirs cleanse our energetic fields of energies that are not our own. Whether the energetic residues come from being around other people, from past sexual partners, or from toxic places where we spend a lot of time (work, for example), flower elixirs strip away everything that is not us, to bring out our true nature.

Flower elixirs even benefit us when our moods are affected by weather changes. Laura shares:

"When I started taking flower elixirs, I didn't have any major problems or issues to overcome—I was just curious. I felt like there was always room for improvement. I knew I would experience something, but didn't think it would be this profound.

I live in Maryland, and during the winters I would suffer from Seasonal Affect Disorder. After so many cold, gray days, I'd wake up in the morning and not feel like myself. I had no energy. Usually I'm outgoing and talkative, but during the winter, I wanted to stay home and keep to myself. To my surprise, after using flower elixirs, I realized I can be my normal self in the wintertime, which is huge. It's something that I've always struggled with, and I realized that nothing else in my life has changed, except using flower elixirs regularly.

Now instead of suffering from the bleakness of winter, rolling out of bed grumpy—I wake up excited to get up. I'm more attentive to my relationships—I go to the outings and parties we're invited to, whereas in previous winters, I just didn't have the energy to go out. I also found myself completing huge projects around my house that I had been putting off for years, such as cleaning out and organizing my garage.

I just feel so much more peaceful when I'm taking the flower elixirs. I feel like I'm living more in the moment of things and I feel more connected to everything around me, including nature. There's clarity and a feeling of completeness—I feel more myself."

11. Flower elixirs help us identify and address family and cultural patterns.

It's not only good looks that get passed down through our grandparents' genes; we also inherit their ways of thinking.[1] Our thoughts are typically not our own; they are a regurgitation of family thought patterns applied as a filter over each of our lives. It's like using a filter in Instagram or a photo app: no matter what the subject of the photo, the filter gives it a certain look, style, or vibe.

We have other filters that come from how we grew up and the experiences we had that affected us on a deep level and instructed us about life. Habitual patterns reside in our cellular memory, running in the background. Flower elixirs help us identify which of our thoughts and behaviors are "filters," and which are truly who we are at our core.

Emily shares:

"When I was a child I had an abusive experience with my grandfather. Until recently, I thought it was my fault, that there was something about me that caused it. I had lots of shame around it and because of this for the last 25 to 30 years I felt very alone, like I was on the outside of my family looking in. I maintained a pattern of silence and I experienced a deep sense of loss with my family. I had never spoken about that childhood experience until about 10 years ago—and I was not met with a lot of support from my family.

Flower elixirs have helped me work with all of these emotions, when before I used to suppress everything. With flower elixirs I feel like I'm working through things a lot faster. When strong emotions arise, it now only lasts a couple of days; I come back to myself a lot faster than before. I'm able to maintain a sense of presence and observation rather than getting pulled in.

After using flower elixirs for several months, I felt capable of forgiveness, for both myself and my family. Now when I am with them, I don't feel so separate or like the black sheep anymore. I definitely feel more of a connection—and I think they feel it too. I don't feel so alone.

In the last few months I noticed another pattern I hadn't been aware of: taking on a responsibility for the family. My silence was a way of keeping the family together. Previously I felt like I needed to protect my mother from what had happened to me with her father. It *was a huge turning point—to realize that I'm not responsible for her happiness.*

My pattern has been to take on other people's stuff. That is changing as well. In another case, a family member spoke to me about things that were bothering them. They had the expectation that I should do something about it, and I realized—this is not mine to fix. I was able to speak to them about it, 'I understand that this is making you unhappy, but this is not my responsibility.' I have more of an awareness or observation of the pattern vs. being fully in it. This has been a really big shift for me.

All of these insights have positively affected my relationships with my husband and daughter. Now I can ask for help and communicate better about working together and get everyone doing their part—rather than feeling like everything relies on me."

12. Flower elixirs dissolve self-limiting beliefs.

Most people have one or more self-limiting beliefs. *I'm not good enough. I don't deserve it. I can't do it. I don't have what it takes.*

These beliefs are usually buried in the subconscious. Most of us don't even know they exist or notice the sneaky ways in which they manifest. They may affect our everyday behavior, but because they were instilled in us at such a young age, identifying them can be like trying to see our own eyelashes. Over time, flower elixirs make us more and more aware of when self-limiting beliefs are in play, and they offer

us the enhanced mental stability and clarity to see and uproot them. Our thoughts and emotions are passing like the clouds, and our true nature is like the sky. Rather than get stuck in the clouds, flower elixirs help us to understand more deeply the potential of the sky.

Rachael shares:

"When I was a child my parents had a horrible divorce. For this reason, I never wanted to go through a divorce myself. I hung on a lot longer in my marriage and put up with a lot more than most people would have because of my past.

After over a year of taking flower elixirs, I'm in the beginning stages of separating from my husband. Flower elixirs have aided me in coming back to who I am in my truth, to stand in the authenticity of who I am.

For example, in conversations, my husband would say something that's totally off the wall and completely abusive. In the past, I would argue back and say something in defense. Now I think about my kids' best interest, my best interest, and the best outcome for everyone.

Before I would second-guess myself. I would get stuck in old beliefs or patterns. I could be easily manipulated. But now I can stand in my own truth. I can see through all of it. I really have clarity about what's going on.

It's not like there's a voice saying, do this or do that . . . it's more of a lightening of my own consciousness. I'm being lifted and elevated to a purer form of expression and understanding. I know it sounds strange, but I feel sparkly in my heart. If there's a rough scenario or a challenging situation I feel it shift very quickly. I feel the flower elixirs shift me to the highest place I can be, doing the highest good. It brings out my best self."

13. Flower elixirs magnify our strengths and unveil hidden talents.

Each of us possesses a wealth of potential that we've not yet begun to tap into. Using flower elixirs helps us upgrade our "software" by becoming aware of our patterns, so we can actively rewire our own minds over time. Though we may not even know what is possible right now, this growing awareness promotes a rapid expansion of our personal potential.

With consistent use of flower elixirs, people find themselves making changes in their lives that they wouldn't have expected, such as quitting their jobs, starting new businesses, moving, or leaving relationships that are not working. People usually move through these transitions with great ease and are later surprised at how seemingly effortless it was to make radical pivots in their lives.

Beth shares:

"Flower elixirs have enhanced the work I've already done on myself without all the trying and effort. I'm much more in tune with myself. They remove fear and doubts, and allow the divine part of myself to be seen. I can hear my inner whisperings clearly. Five years ago, I wouldn't have been talking about things like

this, but flower elixirs have helped me embrace my strengths and gifts so I know what they are.

For starters, multitasking no longer has any appeal to me. I don't even try it anymore. I've been reading about meditation and mindfulness practices for a decade, but this allows me to finally accept the lesson that I've been wanting to embody: no more multitasking, just be present.

Flower elixirs have also helped me see that we are more than our labels. I understand that more deeply now that I'm more than a wife, a mother, or an engineer, my job title. I embrace the fact that I have more to offer, and I don't need to create a new label for it.

And people are more drawn to me now that I use flower elixirs. People will stop me in the store and say, 'You're buying bok choy? I want bok choy!' I can't tell you how many times people approach me on the street—it's happening more and more since taking flower elixirs. I get crazy comments all the time, like last week's yoga class. Someone came up and grabbed me and hugged me and said, 'I'm so glad you were here with us today!'

After about a year of taking flower elixirs I decided I wanted to focus on my creative expression. In my job as an engineer, I can creatively solve problems and lead projects, but I wanted more opportunities to be creative. The flower elixirs helped me see that I've been creative my entire life. I had simply labeled every creative thing I'd done as a 'duty.' For example, every year I send out birthday cards to nieces and nephews, about 30 cards each year. About five years ago, I started making my own cards.

People loved them, but because I felt it was obligation or a duty, I never labeled that as creative.

I suddenly realized I have been creative my whole life! I sew and make my own clothes. And 12 years ago we went gluten-free and since then I make everything gluten-free. When we moved into our house eight years ago, I painted the house. I painted the stairs purple with stencils. It was really creative, and people always remarked about how beautiful it was, but in my mind I reduced it to the fact that I had made a mistake while painting, so I used stenciling to cover it up.

So I'm sitting in my office at work. I look around me and I see the beautiful fabric hanging, photos hung up on the walls, orchids, crystals, and essential oils. I work in an engineer's office, yet I've created this beautiful environment, and here I was telling myself I wasn't creative.

I had a revelation: flower elixirs help you see who you really are."

14. Flower elixirs affect the people around us.

We're influenced energetically by those we spend the most time with. My flower essence teacher used to describe it this way: We exchange "packets" of information when we're around other human beings. If we share a kiss with someone, we exchange a higher degree of information through bodily fluids. And if we have sex with someone, we exchange the highest degree of information, even to our ways of thinking and perceiving the world. Furthermore, when we sleep in the same bed with someone regularly, we become more like that person.

If we live in the same house, or spend lots of time with certain people, we become more like them. We rub off on each other both behaviorally and energetically.

By using flower elixirs, we not only positively affect our own lives but also the lives of the people around us. For example, a long-term client's husband wasn't interested in taking flower elixirs; as a clinically trained therapist, he thought the whole idea was too "woo-woo." But his wife continued to get a new formula every month, and over time, people began to notice changes in his behavior and appearance, too.

Another client of mine, Kathy, started taking flower elixirs for self-love. After about a week she called me in shock and delight. "My husband bought me a dozen roses! He hasn't done that in over ten years!" Flower elixirs that inspire self-love often create a boomerang effect so that love gets reflected back to you through the people around you.

Ultimately the more we love and accept ourselves the more we can love and accept others. People feel the warmth that we emanate, and they want a part of that. Most people are secretly very hard on themselves, so when we are gentler and more loving, others sense that and lean in.

15. Flower elixirs attract better people into our lives.

After several months most everyone comes to this conclusion. We attract people with our same vibe, and if we're consistently refining our energies and ourselves, it only makes sense that the type of people who resonate with us—and are magnetized to us—will also be more and more refined.

People report this phenomenon with co-workers, friends, romantic partners, family members, and even strangers. On top of this, there appears to be a heightened sense of synchronicity, in that we often find ourselves in the right place at the right time, so that opportunities are drawn to us, reflecting our readiness to expand.

Ana shares:

"Ever since I was little, I had anxiety, and the Night-Blooming Cereus elixir helped me understand it. After that I continued to take flower elixirs regularly and felt the sunshine come over me. I started journaling a lot during that time. I wrote love letters to myself about what I wanted, and what I wanted to attract. I was also very clear about what I was willing to accept about myself. I would write letters to myself: 'I love you for this and I accept this about you . . .'

That month was when I first met and started dating my boyfriend. Now my friends tease me saying, 'That's the flower elixir that you attracted your boyfriend with, right?' Soon after, my boyfriend told me that exact same thing that I had written in my journal—about what he loved and accepted about me. It was as if I radiated it out and it bounced back to me from the outer world. Eighteen months later, we are still together.

Since taking the flower elixirs I've experienced other 'flower miracles.' Twice I've had people I didn't know give me flowers at the store out of kindness. Then, when I started taking Peony elixir, I decided to move and was looking at my abundance and money situation. Soon after, I had a date planned with my boyfriend and he brought me a bouquet of Peonies—without knowing what elixir I was taking!

I used to just put things on a vision board, but it was with flower elixirs that things actually began to happen. I wanted to be closer to nature. Now I'm living in Santa Barbara and it's beautiful—I'm in nature and it's close to the beach! My financial situation is where I want it to be. I'm decorating my new house and it's so bright and flowery! My life has changed so much. With flower elixirs I feel like I am able to manifest exactly the kind of life I want—but even better."

Explore: Your Own Private Consultation

One of the most valuable services I provided for my clients during consultations was to act as a witness and a sounding board. I took notes on everything they said and observed their facial expressions and body language. I reflected back to them what I saw and kept records of their progress and transformation. When they came in for their subsequent appointments, often they would forget how they had initially felt. When they would read my notes of what they'd said verbatim, they were often shocked.

Eventually, I started taking before and after photos and shooting video footage of my clients. Even if clients recorded only a few sentences about why they'd come and what they wanted to get out of flower elixirs, it served as a record of how they felt at that time. Months later, they could review the videos and photos and see how their faces, voices, body language, stories, and lives had changed.

This exercise invites you to create your own private consultation at home. Simply answer the questions below, and for extra credit, take a "before" selfie and shoot a short video of yourself on your cell phone. Trust me, within several months you'll really want to see your "before" photo and video. You don't have to show anyone else if you don't want to; this is for you, to see where you've come from, because you'll soon forget how you feel right now. The short video is invaluable, because you really get a clear picture of your energetic signature right now.

You're the best person to consult with, because you know yourself better than anyone on the planet. You hold the keys to your future in your hand. There is no one better equipped to point you in the right direction and illuminate your next steps.

And why settle for less? Life is short. The nature of flower elixirs is that they accelerate personal growth, so steer this ship exactly where you want it to go. How would you like your life to unfold and bloom over the next few years?

In the first section, you look honestly at your life and pinpoint any sticky areas that might be holding you back; this can also give you clarity about which flower elixirs you want to start with. The second section is for visualizing what is possible, and the third section is for writing down exactly how you'd like your ideal life to be.

Why is this important? When I had clients, most people breezed through their Ideal Life goals within 4 to 6 months! And if you don't write them down, not only will you not know where you're headed, you'll forget where you were. It's important to get a snapshot of how you feel and what you want right now, so that later you can see clearly how you have grown. And of course, you can do this process as often as you want as you evolve over time.

Your Life Now

Let's take a look at where you are right now. Jot down what comes to mind in response to the following questions:

What's working in your life?

_____

_____

_____

What's not working?

_____

_____

_____

List any physical discomforts.

_____

_____

_____

List any emotional/mental discomforts.

_____

_____

_____

Jot down any habits or patterns you'd like to shift.

_____

_____

_____

What are you most grateful for right now?

_____

_____

_____

Your Ideal Life Brainstorm

A. Reflect & Imagine

After having read through the experiences that other people have had, take a moment to envision what's possible for your life. Now imagine that anything—ANYTHING—is possible. Free your mind and envision what your ideal life is like.

- Imagine you experience more joy and confidence. How would that feel?
- Visualize yourself as magnetizing bigger and better opportunities, and more interesting and refined people. Which patterns and beliefs would dissolve?
- If you could be in the present moment more often, what would that look like?
- Imagine the people around you transforming with you. How might they do that?
- If you could accelerate your personal growth, what would be available to you?

B. Write It Down

Now is your chance to dream big. The following questions are describing your ideal life; ANYTHING is possible!

In no particular order, write down the first 30 words that pop into your mind regarding your ideal life:

1. _____

2. _____

3. _____

4. _____

5. _____

6. _____

7. _____

8. _____

9. _____

10. _____

11. _____

12. _____

13. _____

14. _____

15. _____

16. _____

17. _____

18. _____

19. _____

20. _____

21. _____

22. _____

23. _____

24. _____

25. _____

26. _____

27. _____

28. _____

29. _____

30. _____

Jot down 6 to 10 words that describe how you feel in your ideal life.

1. _____

2. _____

3. _____

4. _____

5. _____

6. _____

7. _____

8. _____

9. _____

10. _____

In your ideal life, what are you doing that you LOVE?

_____

_____

Write down the most important aspects of your ideal life, taking into account the following areas. Be as specific and concrete as you can.

Health

_____

_____

Career

_____

_____

Money

_____

_____

Relationships

_____

_____

Family

_____

_____

Spirituality

_____

_____

Creativity

_____

_____

Fun/Hobbies

_____

_____

CHAPTER 5

THREE PHASES OF TRANSFORMATION

> *If you want to change the world, first try to improve and change within yourself.*
>
> DALAI LAMA XIV[1]

My Life in Flowers: Jen's Story of a Full-Bloom Transformation

Ultimately, flower elixirs don't do *all* the work for us, but they do show us the way, making it obvious which behaviors to adjust. With regular, consistent flower elixir use, three stages of transformation occur. During the first month *The Honeymoon* is predominant. After the honeymoon period, there is an enhanced strength and stability that arises, at which point the *Peeling Off the Layers* phase becomes more evident.

When I consulted with clients one-on-one, I noticed that after four to six months the changes they were experiencing internally would be reflected back to them externally, such as changing jobs, falling in love, leaving a relationship, or attracting exciting new opportunities. This marks the beginning of the final phase, *Weeding the Garden,* which can unfold continuously over months, years, and decades of regular flower elixir use.

To illustrate how the phases of transformation are expressed in someone's life, I'd like to introduce you to one of my clients, Jennifer Paul, who has been taking flower elixirs consistently for over a decade. Her story is typical of a full-bloom transformation.

Phase One:
The Honeymoon

When Jen came to my office for the first time, she was overwhelmed and frustrated by her job. She battled depression, was 40 pounds overweight, and regularly experienced fatigue. Her skin was pale and puffy. Her marriage was rocky; she and her husband had frequent bouts of blaming each other, which left her feeling alienated and unloved.

Mostly, Jen felt disempowered and hopeless. In her words, she wanted to be less of an "addict"; she believed that her own personal freedom depended on her body being free of toxins. While she had been sober for eight years, she'd been on antidepressants for a decade and was unhappy to be relying on pharmaceuticals, especially when the medical system told her she would not have success without being medicated. She felt heavy, frustrated, and angry.

While it wasn't unusual for people to arrive at my office with a laundry list of stressors, what was remarkable about Jen was her commitment to the process. I made her a formula of flower elixirs as was customary and she committed to monthly sessions, getting a new elixir blend each month. When Jen discovered how powerful

flower elixirs were, it was a turning point for her; she began to feel hope that she could be both healthy and happy.

Almost immediately after Jen started taking flower elixirs she felt better. She no longer felt doomed, a feeling she had had from a very young age. As she felt better and better, she was flooded with hope. She felt lighter and more joyful, and had a strong desire to start singing.

During the first month of taking flower elixirs (daily, at least five times each day), most people experience a honeymoon period. A whole layer of stress, irritation, and worry dissolves, while a new experience of everyday joie de vivre emerges.

During this time, people say: "I hear the birds singing around me; I didn't hear them before!" or "I just feel like I'm in the right place at the right time," and "I feel so much more peaceful and emotionally balanced." Irritation, worry, nervousness, and stress seem to magically and effortlessly disappear and you feel more YOU. You feel *so* you, you might not even attribute it to the flower elixirs.

Why? Flower elixirs harmonize the everyday static of life from electronics, Wi-Fi signals, lack of nature time, stress, and other energy-scattering influences that we can't see. They're like liquid chi—an infusion of positive energy—that travels through the acupuncture meridians. As a result, most people feel a difference in their state of mind in as little as three to five days. The most dramatic results are experienced within the first month, because we feel so tangibly different to our usual state of being.

Some of the most notable results during the first month's honeymoon are: deeper sleep, letting go of things that bother you, and no more bickering with you-know-who. Out of the blue the people around you are friendlier, spontaneously offering compliments. You feel happier and more aware and people notice it and comment on it.

The best part is that this feeling becomes the new norm. The initial honeymoon feeling doesn't disappear—it's simply that if you continue taking flower elixirs, this becomes your new baseline and your normal way of feeling. You forget that you used to experience a rougher edge to life, a shorter fuse, or a more fragile nervous system.

If you stopped taking the flower elixirs after one month, you'd likely feel that edge creep back and tension and stress arise again. This is normal in our modern lifestyle due to the stressful nature of our everyday lives, lack of time in nature, and excessive use of technology.

However, if you keep taking flower elixirs regularly for several months, you feel stronger. Mentally and emotionally you feel calm, stable, and more equipped to reflect on your behavior patterns with greater attention.

Phase Two: Peeling Off the Layers

Gradually, everything that didn't match up with Jen's ideal life began to change. She decided that she wanted to get off her medications, and asked her psychiatrist to lower the dosages slowly to wean her off them. She faced her internal challenges head-on—observing and working with old emotional patterns. She changed her eating habits and lost weight. Her face began to have a rosy glow.

Taking flower elixirs is about waking up your best self: your most loving, peaceful, fearless, happy, impactful, innovative genius self. Flower elixirs help you become more aware and use that awareness to be a better person each day. Any part of you that's not full of ease becomes more apparent.

With enhanced emotional stability and neutrality, you slowly start seeing things about yourself that you haven't noticed before. You can gently unpack habits, patterns and behaviors one by one. Anything that's not harmonious, you'll notice. Any area where you aren't operating from your highest self will become obvious.

As your awareness increases, if there are any insecurities, irritations, frustrations, or worries under the surface or "running in the background," you will see them clearly. As the flower elixirs awaken a neutral, nonemotional stance, it's as if you are watching a movie with an awareness of the screen itself, instead of getting immersed in the acting of the characters. Thus it's easier not to get sucked into old patterns, and course-correct or respond in a different way if desired.

People who use flower elixirs regularly describe it this way: "It's as if there is more space between me and my emotions." At this stage, when you're experiencing stress, it's easier to just observe it (saying to yourself, "Oh, isn't that interesting?"), instead of reacting with full-on emotionality.

This ability to see all patterns with neutrality allows you to get to the root causes of anything in your life that's not harmonious. Here's an example. You start taking flower elixirs, and within several months you notice one Sunday evening that you're feeling grumpy. This may have been happening over and over . . . but until now you hadn't realized that it happens every Sunday. You stop to ponder it and discover that you're dreading going to work. You reflect a little further and notice the ball of tension forming in your belly when you think about your experience at work. It's almost as if you had been on autopilot and suddenly got a little more clarity. With this realization, you start looking for a job—and find yourself in a new job within a month.

Getting to the root cause means:

- Discerning what in your life brings you discomfort or pain.

- Seeing the areas in your life where you're not being your best self.

- Having the clarity and strength to transform it.

As a result of your acting differently, people around you start to mirror that back and alter their behavior around you.

I remember leading a workshop in Maryland where one woman said that her boss was impossible to communicate with; everyone on her team had a hard time relating to him, which obviously strained the work environment. After several months of taking flower elixirs like Hong Kong Orchid for love and Red Hibiscus for peace, she noticed her boss being warmer and kinder to her. Over time she developed a good working relationship with him while her colleagues looked on in disbelief.

When your presence is soft, sparkly, peaceful, and loving (you at your highest, best self), everyone is attracted to that. People like you and want to be around you.

We all constantly rub off on each other. We affect each other in every moment. We either cheer each other up and inspire each other to be our best selves, or we resonate at the lowest common denominator and bring out the worst in each other. If you shine your most sparkly self and spread good energy simply by being who you are, people around you start responding to you differently.

Phase Three: Weeding Your Garden

After two years of consistent flower elixir use, Jen accomplished what she had originally thought was an impossible dream: she moved to a smaller community several hours away from Phoenix in the beautiful woodlands of northern Arizona. Despite naysayers concerned with the downturn in the economy, within two months Jen found the perfect house and teaching job.

After five years of consistent flower elixirs, Jen looked ten years younger, and as each year passed she grew more beautiful. Her teaching career became more satisfying as she increased her training and skills. Her relationship with her husband transformed into one of compassion, understanding, kindness, and friendship like never before. They gained a mutual appreciation of their differences.

Jen and her husband, Ron, in 2005.

Years later, having consistently taken flower elixirs, Jen and Ron.

Now Jen sings in a choir and in a band with her husband. Their relationship has never been better, and they travel occasionally to perform in concerts. Musically and creatively they're on fire, which has had the unexpected benefit of improving their sex life.

After ten years of flower elixirs, Jen left teaching to follow her dream of helping the dying and their families. She also provides shiatsu treatments and retreats.

For a decade, Jen took flower elixirs consistently, getting a new blend each month. In that span of time, she went from feeling powerless and out of control to unveiling her true potential. Now she is in a position to help others.

In phase three, you weed out anything in your life that's not good for you, starting with people and environments: *Tell me who your friends are and I'll tell you who you'll be.* When you take flower elixirs on a regular basis, the situations and the people who are not making you a better person become more and more apparent; in fact, they stick out like a sore thumb.

Anyone or anything that doesn't bring out the best in you no longer seems to fit into your life. You start feeling less tolerant of anything that negatively affects you. For example, it could be an old friend from high school who hasn't changed since senior year, a neighbor who drinks too much, or someone who gossips. It can be a place, an environment, a type of food, or a habit

that makes you feel yucky afterward. In any case, you get really clear on when it's time to let go.

The weeding process occurs not only with people and environments, but also with habitual patterns. For example, I used to think I was the most peaceful person ever. Yet, years ago, flower elixirs brought me to the sudden revelation that I can be very impatient.

My flower elixir teacher Pedro used to say that being impatient is "not being at peace with the way things are" and this creates obstacles. I certainly don't want to create obstacles, so now I am acutely aware of when impatience arises, observe it, and dissolve it by quietly watching it. Flower elixirs help you to be more mindful and aware of your own habits, so that you can take charge of them, instead of letting them take charge of you.

Another effect of regular use of flower elixirs is a more acute realization of impermanence—that life is extremely precious. The result? Letting go of disharmony becomes more effortless. It's easier to let go of the stuff that doesn't serve you, and it catalyzes clarity about how you want your life to be.

As a result, you free up space in your life. Weeding out people, patterns, and bad habits opens up space for a higher caliber of people, places, experiences, and habits to come into your daily life.

Some examples: You notice yourself seeking out new friends who are on the same wavelength as you. You seek out people who aspire to be their greatest selves, people who want to live up to their potential. New opportunities that are more positive and supportive of your highest goals suddenly fall in your lap.

You embark on adventures, take classes, change jobs, move to another city, or make other large leaps of faith toward a higher and clearer expression of YOU. The reason this happens is because flower elixirs help you refine your thoughts and emotional patterns. You cut through self-limiting beliefs and embrace what's possible.

Accelerating your evolution on the inside triggers the world around you to evolve more rapidly. Your external world reflects back to you the internal evolution that's taking place. Like always attracts like, and the more harmonious, clear and expansive your energy is, the faster you magnetize opportunities beyond your wildest dreams. Here are some examples: You feel more loving, which attracts a new love—or more kindness from your kids. You feel more confident, and

suddenly someone offers you a dream job. You feel more courageous, and out of the blue, you're invited to speak to a large audience.

I know this can happen for everyone, because I worked one-on-one with hundreds of clients full-time for 12 years. During the first appointment we would talk about what was working and not working in their lives. AND, we'd talk about their six-month goals, even goals they thought weren't possible.

After about four months of taking flower elixirs, clients would notice that their external worlds were reflecting back to them the changes that they were experiencing on the inside, through new opportunities, new jobs, new relationships.

This type of harmonization of the inner/outer realities, as well as the rapid acceleration of personal growth, occurs for as long as you are taking the flower elixirs. Over time, flower elixirs magnify your strengths and bring out your special qualities. They bring out the shining, happy you, which attracts goodness from every direction. You look more beautiful and radiant, because happiness and clarity make you gorgeous. As a result, your effect on other people becomes more powerfully positive, because we do not exist within a vacuum. As human beings we are powerful: how we show up in the world has a constant effect on others.

When you're happy, you make other people happy. Scientists have proven that if your friend's friend's friend (whom you don't even know) becomes wildly happy, it has a more beneficial effect on you than if someone put $5,000 in your pocket.[2] Likewise, if you become wildly happy, it positively affects people that you haven't even met yet. Think about that!

Here's a quick summary:

If you take flower elixirs regularly you can experience . . .

Phase One (the first month)

You feel happier and stronger and freer from everyday stress and chaos. You feel more YOU. That feeling becomes your new "normal."

Phase Two (the second month and beyond)

You identify anything that's not ideal in your life and gently get to the root cause of it. You experience more space between you and your thoughts and emotions (neutrality). People around you start acting differently, in a positive way.

Phase Three (after about four months of regular use)

You continue to peel off layers of limiting patterns, people, and habits.

You make room for a bigger and better version of your life.

The world shows you just how magnetic you've become, reflecting back to you new opportunities. Your personal growth inspires others to grow.

Imagine yourself as your *best* self: your biggest, most peaceful, loving, courageous, powerful self. Flower elixirs accelerate personal growth and offer a fast track to reaching your full potential.

Have you taken flower elixirs before? If you haven't, and you've come this far in the book, it's a good sign that you're ready to try them.

If you have taken flower elixirs before, let's discover an entirely new flower experience!

Explore: Flower Elixir Bathing Ritual

Bathing in flower elixirs is one of the fastest ways to get their benefits, as your whole body is submerged in their sparkly energies. A fabulous way to start a new flower elixir, this ritual gives you a jump start, providing access to all of your meridians and energy points simultaneously. It's as if your body, mind, and psyche hit the refresh button. It's also a valuable time of introspection: as you relax in the bath you give your mind enough spaciousness that insights can arise as the elixirs take effect.

Select the flower that you want to work with for the next few weeks. Take a moment to create an intention for what you'd like to create in working with the flower elixir you chose. Gently wipe down the tub with baking soda and lemon juice to cleanse it energetically, preparing it for the flower elixirs. Fill the tub with warm water and add nine drops of the flower elixir you're currently intrigued by. Submerge your entire body in the water, cleansing energetic toxins and getting infused with the flower's qualities. Soak in the bath for 15 to 20 minutes; relax and breathe, meditate, or reflect on your intention for the flower elixir. Notice any insights that arise.

Flower elixirs can be added to baths any time of the day; however, doing this ritual in the mornings before noon, while the sun is rising, will give the elixirs a slightly amplified quality. If desired, flower elixir baths may be taken daily.

CHAPTER 6

YOUR TOP 10 QUESTIONS ABOUT FLOWER ELIXIRS

> *If we analyze or dissect a flower, looking for the flower among its parts, we shall not find it . . . And yet, we cannot deny the existence of flowers and of their sweet scent.*
>
> DALAI LAMA XIV[1]

My Life in Flowers: Florecidas in Mexico

On the southern coast of the state of Oaxaca, Mexico, I experienced a full moon Temascal ceremony. It's similar to a sweat lodge, except that it takes place inside a mud structure. The ceremony began with offerings of corn and herbs to the four directions, along with prayers invoking positive spirits and forces of nature. Each of us in our small group was cleansed with sacred burning herbs from the region, the spicy smoke curling around the curves of our bodies. Then we removed our clothes and entered, one by one,

into the mud hut. The burning coals were stoked, and it was hot—very hot. We stayed for what seemed like ages, beads of sweat rolling down our skin, using long bundles of fresh herbs to whack our arms and legs and stimulate circulation.

When we emerged, a woman was standing in front of a huge well with hundreds of flowers strewn on top of the water. She motioned to me to stand in front of the well while she dumped an entire bucket of flower water on my head. As the cool water flooded over my hot skin, every cell in my body responded and I felt as if years had been lifted away. I didn't feel like speaking, and my senses were acutely aware of every sound, *sight, and smell. The night was dark and the Earth seemed to vibrate around me.*

While Asians captured the essences of flowers into small pills and Europeans drank the morning dew from flowers, the Mayans in Central America had for centuries made their own type of flower essences for use in special ceremonies. Referred to as *florecidas*, these waters were considered sacred.[2]

Performed as a cleansing ritual, *florecidas* required soaking flowers or herbs in water in the sunlight for several hours, after which the water was poured over the head and body and then allowed to air dry.

In the Temascal, I sweated out all the toxins in my body and used aromatic bundles of herbs to boost the cleansing process. This prepared me for the more subtle energetic purification of the flower essences.

Flower elixirs benefit anyone and everyone regardless of the state of the physical body; however, cleansing the body of toxins makes the tangible effects of the flower elixirs more apparent and obvious as they occur.

1. How Do I Prepare My Body for Flower Elixirs?

In modern life our bodies accumulate a lot of toxins, from pesticides in our food and heavy metals in our environment to the chemicals in artificial fragrances and personal care products. Cleansing the body and reducing its "toxic load" help make the body and mind a clean slate from which to notice the precise effects of flower elixirs.

Methods of cleansing the body include spending time in the sauna, taking cleansing baths*, exercising, or drinking lemon water. By eliminating toxins, we enhance our mental awareness and clarity, getting the most out of flower elixir use.

Another way to gently cleanse the body in preparation for flower elixirs is to eliminate substances that can induce a kind of mental cloudiness; for example, regularly consuming processed white sugar and high fructose corn syrup can create a dullness in our awareness. This may prevent us from recognizing the insights that arise as a result of taking flower elixirs. Processed white sugar can be replaced with maple syrup, coconut sugar, dates, honey, or natural sources of cane sugar such as evaporated cane juice to maintain a heightened clarity in awareness.

Other substances that can create an even more marked cloudiness in awareness are cigarettes, marijuana, and other types of drugs. Substances that do not affect flower elixir use are coffee and mint (including mint toothpaste).

While the effects of flower elixirs can usually be felt within several days, regular consumption of white sugar, cigarettes, marijuana, or other drugs can delay the experience of tangible benefits by about a month. The delay, however, does not mean that the flower elixirs are not working; in fact, sometimes family members will notice a change before the person taking them does. It simply means that there is a delay in the awareness of the results, or in having a direct experience of a shift in state of mind.

---

*   Cleansing Bath: Dissolve 2 cups of epsom salts + 2 cups of hydrogen peroxide in a hot bath. After 20 minutes get out and wrap up in a sheet or blanket and sweat for 15 more minutes. For more details, see the Pomegranate flower.

In the case of psychotropic medications such as antidepressants, anti-anxiety drugs, or other types of medications for mental and emotional stress, there can also be a delay in the perception of benefits by about a month. However, there are no contraindications for combining flower elixirs and medications, especially as the only side effects from flower elixirs are joy, peace, and clarity.

2. How Do I Choose the Right Flower Elixirs for Me?

Among the Iroquois, it has been said that if a person becomes ill and needs a plant for healing the plant will stand up and begin calling, helping the person who is ill to find it.

STEPHEN HARROD BUHNER [3]

There are many methods to figure out which flower elixirs to choose. The good news is that all of the methods teach us that we can trust our intuition. A part of us knows exactly what we need, even though we may not know it intellectually.

My favorite way to find out, quickly and effortlessly, is to see which flowers you're most attracted to visually. It can be the color or the shape; it doesn't matter why. Just notice which ones you like. If you were in a flower shop, which flowers would you pick out? If you were on a vacation, which flowers would you move closer to and take photos of? In short, what are you drawn to? These are the flowers that will benefit you most in that moment.

This is the wonderful thing about Mother Nature's remedies: they call to us. We are drawn to them. We engage in a relationship of adoration and intrigue—and that's when the magic begins.

Sometimes there are flowers that we are averse to. Often, this means that the flower offers us a valuable lesson. In this situation, the flower represents a quality that we are not eager to see or address. If we notice a flower that we feel a serious aversion to, we can take note of that and when we're ready for it, work with that flower too, as it can provide valuable clarity about something we've previously wanted to avoid.

3. Is It More Effective to Take Single Flower Elixirs or Combinations?

Single and combination flower elixirs are equally effective, but they work in slightly different ways. Combination flower elixirs target an issue from many directions, as they work synergistically. They tend to create more noticeable effects immediately, often within minutes or days. I have also noticed that combination formulas rarely result in healing crises, which seem to be more common with single elixirs (see more about this in #6 on page 84).

On the other hand, because each flower has its own specialty, single flower elixirs target very specific patterns. They work deeply and subtly, so while it may take longer to discern the effects, those effects can be profound.

If you want to pinpoint the results from a flower elixir, you may want to take only one single flower elixir or one combination elixir at a time, because it's easier to track the results specific to that flower or combination of flowers. However, you can take more than one flower elixir at a time and more than one combination elixir at a time.

4. How Do I Take Flower Elixirs?

Flower elixirs are traditionally taken internally, by placing the drops in your mouth. Before you open the bottle, gently smack the bottom of the bottle on the palm of your hand three times to wake up the flower elixirs. For best results, take them a minimum of five times each day.

There are several ways to take them internally:

1. Take five drops sublingually or dropped into your mouth.

2. Add the five drops to a glass of water or other beverage.

3. Add a dropperful of flower elixirs to your water bottle and repeat each time the water bottle is refilled. This is helpful if it's hard to remember to take them five times a day.

Often when I give presentations, someone will shout out, "I need a gallon of that!" We all laugh together, but the interesting thing is that if you drank a gallon of flower elixirs not much would happen. It's kind of like exercise: for noticeable results, it's better to do it frequently and regularly than to do it for a few days once each year. Similarly, rather than drink an entire gallon of them at one time, you'll find flower elixirs much more effective and transformative by taking a few drops every hour for an entire day.

Flower elixirs will penetrate the energetics of the body most rapidly when taken without food. However, as long as use within meals are not considered a replacement for taking them five times each day, flower elixirs can be used in food preparation to enhance food and the way people feel during a meal. For example, adding flower elixirs to salad dressings or beverages (anything that does not get boiled) is particularly interesting, fun, and beneficial when having guests over.

Though flower elixirs are traditionally taken internally, they can also be infused into mists, oils, and other topical mediums. After many years of research and personal experience, I have noticed that the external use of flower elixirs is just as effective as taking them internally, as long as they're used with the same level of frequency: the same remedy, a minimum of five times each day.

Whenever someone asks me what form of flower elixirs is most effective, I always respond this way: the one you'll actually use five or more times each day is the one that will be most effective. Some people really like to take things orally; others prefer to put something on their skin or to mist around themselves and their space. All of the methods will be equally effective, as long as they are used with the same level of frequency.

When I first made flower elixir products, I set up at farmers' markets and I loved watching people come up to our booth. We were downtown and we would get a fair number of transients—folks from halfway houses or people who hadn't yet been able to kick a drug addiction. They, too, stopped by our booth to check out our flower cards and elixirs. I loved when they approached our booth because the effects were so vivid. Our usual protocol was to have them choose their favorite flower(s) from several flower photographs. We'd tell them what their selection meant, and ask them to close their eyes while we gently misted them, letting the refreshing flower essences rain down on them.

When they opened their eyes, their faces changed. Their expressions shifted and softened. With some people, their eyes changed; it was almost as if they had been wearing foggy contact lenses that suddenly disappeared into crystal-clear lucidness. Sometimes a few tears would spring to their eyes—not out of emotion—it was something else, a rapid clearing away of emotional or energetic residue. These visible reactions to the flower elixirs can happen anywhere, with anyone, whether the flower elixirs are taken internally or on the skin; however, with some people it is more obvious than others.

5. How Do I Know the Flower Elixirs Are Working?

Most people start to feel something, even if it's just a shift in their state of mind, within two or three days. Of course, it's different for each person, and each flower impacts us differently with its unique qualities. For most people, however, it feels like lightheartedness or clarity of mind. Most people sleep more deeply, and some say they feel more in tune, as if they're in the right place at the right time all the time. For others, insights arise, in the form of effortless aha moments.

For example, as I mentioned earlier, once after taking a particular flower elixir for a few days I got a clear sense of how impatient I could be. I was taken aback as this was new information for me; I thought I was really calm and relaxed. What surprised me the most was that my impatience was so obvious after that! With this new awareness, I could now do something about it.

Sometimes the insights from taking flower elixirs arise quickly like that, as if from nowhere, like flipping on a light switch. When that happens, we can rejoice that we see an aspect of ourselves that we hadn't seen before, and we now have the power to change it. Other times the changes are slow and gradual. Your family and friends may see the shifts in your behavior before you do.

And sometimes, albeit rarely, the effects are imperceptible to the person taking the elixirs. In my 20,000-plus hours of making flower elixirs for clients, the only client I ever had claim that he felt "nothing" from the flower elixirs was a man in his 70s. He came in for his second monthly appointment, saying he had taken the flower elixirs but didn't notice anything different. I started asking him about his life over the last few weeks and his response included statements like this: "Well, I went golfing for the first time in ten years! And I cleaned out the garage and I hadn't done that in seven years . . ." In this case, it wasn't that the flower elixirs weren't working, it was simply that he wasn't attributing the recent extraordinary events of his life to the effects of the flower elixirs.

Jotting down notes in our phones or quick journaling practices can be extremely helpful for capturing insights from flower elixirs. Oftentimes we are so caught up in our everyday lives that we don't realize what effects the flower elixirs are having on us. Or we may notice something but not be able to pinpoint exactly what it is. By jotting down a few words each day or each week about what's happening in our lives, we can shed light on meaningful transformations that are occurring in our behaviors and thought patterns. By being more self-aware, we can consciously be a part of the process, thus speeding up our personal growth.

6. What if I Feel the Opposite of What I'm Supposed to Feel?

When a flower elixir targets a pattern that is deep-seated, invisible to us, or ripe for change, it is possible that for a brief period we feel the exact opposite of what we think we should feel. The flower elixir may be showing us what has been preventing us from developing the quality that it imparts by amplifying our awareness

of what's in the way; there's no opportunity to ignore it any longer. It's unavoidable that we become aware of it, which makes it easier to change our behavior or thought patterns to be more beneficial.

Let's say you start taking Pink Magnolia flower elixir, which magnifies our ability to be kinder to ourselves by taking more breaks and time for self-care. Pink Magnolia is indicated when we find ourselves giving all of our energy to others, whether it's loved ones, children, friends, or colleagues. We say yes to everything and take care of everyone else—to the detriment of ourselves. If this is a long-term and deep-seated pattern, we initially may extend ourselves *even more* to others and run ourselves ragged. This makes our behavior so obvious to us that we exhaust the habit and thereafter find it easier to maintain a healthy balance that includes taking care of ourselves.

This is what is known as a "healing crisis," which only happens rarely. It sounds worse than it actually is: a heightened emotional state for about 24 hours, as the remedy unravels a particular pattern. The emotions come up to come out, as if we were reliving a suppressed emotion in accelerated speed as it rises up to a conscious level to be released. It usually consists of one day that feels more emotionally sensitive; we have a good cry or reflect on something from the past. Then the next day we feel better than ever, as if something has been cleared out. Also, when it occurs, it's not excruciating—it's more like a good, needed rain in the desert. After a nice rain, everything flourishes. As we take flower elixirs more consistently it becomes even

more rare. It typically happens within the first few months of regular flower elixir use, if at all.

7. Do I Need to Believe in the Flower Elixirs for Them to Work?

In my years of making flower elixirs for clients, I had many clients who were skeptical. We would talk and get to know each other in the initial intake consultation. Many of them would say at the door on their way out, somewhat reluctantly, "I really like you, Katie, but I just don't believe this is going to work." I would laugh and tell them not to worry, just take the flower elixirs five times each day and see what happened. Without fail, they would come back in one month for their next appointment, astonished at how effectively the flower elixirs worked.

I've seen countless cases of skeptical people give flower elixirs a chance, and what I've noticed is that the most skeptical folks become the biggest supporters, once they realize for themselves that it's real and it works.

I welcome healthy skepticism and, in fact, I encourage it. I always recommend that people try things for themselves, because the only way to truly know if something works is through personal experience. Likewise, I only recommend methods that I myself have tried over a long period of time and know that they work from my personal experience.

Some people ask if flower elixirs could be just a placebo. One of things that convinced me personally that they're not is that I've seen so many noticeable and quick results with babies, children, pets, and even plants—none of whom have a concept of placebo effect. Developing careful self-awareness helps us identify the effects of flower elixirs and view the changes in our lives objectively.

8. How Long Do I Use Flower Elixirs?

Flower elixirs are usually taken for at least a full cycle of 21 days or 3 to 4 weeks. Just as 21 days is the optimum time period to change a habit, similarly with flower elixirs it takes about 3 to 4 weeks to experience a shift in awareness with a particular habit, or to see how the quality of the flower expresses itself in your psyche.

However, there are times when the full 21 days are not needed. Occasionally within several days the body is ready for a different elixir. When there is a neutral feeling about the flower—no attraction and no aversion, then it's likely that the flower is not needed anymore. Or if you feel very drawn to another flower, you can combine the two (or more) elixirs during that time period.

Sometimes flower elixirs are needed for longer periods of time. For example, after a car accident or surgery, flower elixirs are recommended for one to two months to release the effects of the cellular memory of the trauma and harmonize the body's energy fields. For behavioral habits or mental and emotional patterns that developed during childhood, longer periods of time working with a particular flower elixir may be required to unravel the deeper levels of those patterns.

One of my clients committed to taking the same flower elixirs for six months because she felt they were uprooting old patterns that were preventing her from giving and accepting more love. She said that her habits and patterns around love had imprinted themselves so early in her life—and repeated themselves so much over the course of her life—that she wanted to dedicate at least six months to working on that particular issue.

If we think about how long a particular habit or pattern has been engrained in our way of being, it gives us some insight into how long it may take to uproot that pattern. A habit we've developed over the course of our lives will take longer to unravel than one that has developed more recently. However, regardless of the time the pattern has been in existence, flower elixirs help us gain more awareness of it right away, so we can start consciously working with it.

Flower elixirs are like energetic vitamins: they balance out the fatiguing effects of modern-day electronics and daily stresses, and are a valuable support for wellness and vitality. If we don't have enough time to spend in nature—to recharge us and calm our nervous systems—this is one way to bring nature and the joy of flowers into the cities and into our daily lives.

It's like whatever else we do for self-care: Would we stop working out, doing yoga, practicing meditation, eating healthy food, getting massages, or ‹ insert favorite method of self-care here › when they improve the quality of our lives and our well-being? Flower elixirs are not addictive, but people do like feeling that they are at their best all the time. Once people use flower elixirs regularly, they notice how much it takes the rough edge off of life and how much more stable their minds are. After experiencing higher levels of happiness and creativity, people usually want to keep that going, just like they do when they see the results of working out, meditation, and healthy eating.

Beyond just feeling happy and healthy, people who want to accelerate personal growth, who are looking to gain insights into their behaviors or patterns and want to understand themselves better or improve their relationships—these people are even more motivated to continue using flower elixirs regularly. Those who value attaining their full potential usually feel a sense of urgency, that life is short, and they typically continue using flower elixirs to sharpen their focus and efforts in that direction.

9. What if I'm Sensitive to Flowers or Alcohol?

Flower elixirs are usually made with alcohol as a preservative to maintain the energetic strength of the remedy. When we take five drops of flower elixirs preserved with alcohol, the general herbalist's rule is that this amount of alcohol is equivalent to what the body produces from the natural fruit sugars in a quarter of a banana. The effects of such a minute amount of alcohol, therefore, are negligible.

However, if alcohol is not permitted in one's lifestyle, or in the case of allergies to alcohol, here is a way to dilute the remedy.

Put three drops of the remedy into a quart of water. Then take five drops of that water, at least five times each day. This quart of water with flower elixirs will last for one week stored in the refrigerator. At the end of the week pour the remaining water into the tub and take a bath. Or you can pour the water onto a houseplant, or in a pet's water bowl, spreading the benefits around the house.

Like homeopathic remedies, flower elixirs are diluted several times after the original collection of the "mother essence." For this reason even people with severe allergies can use flower elixirs safely; after the dilutions, there are no plant parts present or detectable in the remedies.

Also, just as homeopathic remedies are prepared from poisonous plants like belladonna and arsenic, flower elixirs can be made from poisonous flowers. Since there's no actual flower material in flower elixirs—only the energetic imprint—we can safely tap into the healing properties of poisonous flowers that often have very beneficial qualities.

10. How Can I Use Flower Elixirs to Boost Social or Work Situations?

Once when I was in Korea for business, I went to a lunch meeting with six men in black suits and ties. As was customary, we all took off our shoes and sat on the heated floor at the restaurant. The men had just come from their offices and looked very serious; the atmosphere was slightly tense.

I reached into my purse and pulled out a bottle of flower elixirs for laughter and joy, and they watched with curiosity as I added some to each of the pots of hot green tea sitting on the table. Five minutes later, the men who had looked so serious and straight-faced were joking like school boys and laughing like crazy.

Whenever I'm in a situation where it's slightly awkward—maybe it's a group of people who don't know each other, or a business meeting—flower elixirs always save the day. They strip away a layer of tension, pretense, and anxiety about what others think and just allow everyone to relax and enjoy each other. When it's the first time someone has ever used flower elixirs, the liberation of tension can feel quite euphoric, leading to giddiness and laughter.

I always carry a bottle of flower elixirs in my purse, so when I go out with friends or business colleagues, I have some flower power to help us all relax, laugh, and enjoy life.

Explore: Fresh Flower Cleansing Ritual

You don't need to travel to Central or South America to experience a *florecida*, or fresh flower cleanse. You can create a similar flower-powered experience at home.

First, decide what your intention is for the flower cleanse. Do you want to gain clarity on an issue? Magnify a particular quality in yourself? By being clear about what you want, you'll be more open to recognizing the flowers that will provide what you are seeking.

Next, venture out into your backyard, garden, forest, or other natural environment where flowers grow. Locate flowers that you feel particularly drawn to or intrigued by, as this will indicate that they are specifically of benefit for you at this time. They must be growing in the ground, and in full bloom.

Important: Make sure that you have first researched whether or not the flower is toxic. Do not use flowers that are toxic or poisonous (see the list of "Poisonous Flowers" in the Appendix for some common examples). Also, if you obtain the flowers from a garden, make sure that pesticides or other toxic chemicals are not being used on the plants.

When you've identified the flower you want to use, close your eyes and connect with the essence of the plant. Ask permission to cut a few blossoms for your bath and request the plant to help you with whatever your intention is. Without touching the flowers with your fingers, cut* them with scissors so that they fall into a clear glass bowl full of pure water. Cut enough flowers to cover the surface of the water, and place the bowl in the morning sunlight. If they are night-blooming flowers, soak them in the light of the full moon.

Allow the flowers to infuse in the water for about 3 hours. Strain out the flowers. Pause to remind yourself of your intention, and then take the water and dump it over the top of your head, allowing the water to infuse you with its qualities.

In warm weather, if you wear a swimming suit, you can do this ritual outdoors. In the winter months, you can do this in the bathtub.

---

*   If the flowers have long enough stems, they don't need to be cut. They can just be bent over into the bowl.

CHAPTER 7

FLOWER ELIXIRS FOR BIRTH, DEATH & EVERYTHING IN BETWEEN

Flowers live, they are perfect and they affect us . . .
they make us know why we are alive and human.

ELIZABETH ALEXANDER[1]

Life is full of surprises: unexpected miracles, breathtaking experiences, and deep devotional love. Not to mention stormy emotions, wacky situations, and heart-wrenching pain. In either case flower elixirs can be our go-to liquid clarity that sits on our desks or fits in our purses, giving us a boost in our everyday lives. Flower elixirs enhance the good times and soften the intensity of the difficult times.

This chapter is separated into two sections. The first part describes how flower elixirs can enhance women's wellness, pregnancy, childbirth, and motherhood. The second part describes how to use flower elixirs for pets, romantic relationships, travel, smoking cessation, meditation/yoga practices, hospital stays, and hospice/end of life transitions. You can use this section of the book as a reference, coming back to it again and again as you approach these different areas in your life.

FLOWER MAGIC
FOR WOMEN & CHILDREN

Flower Elixirs for Pregnancy & Birthing

Flower elixirs are a powerful force for good during pregnancy, because they reduce both mama's stress and baby's stress. Studies show that maternal stress has measurable effects on the fetus, and some experts believe that how babies experience the womb affects their development later in life.[2] When mothers experience less stress and more love and peacefulness during pregnancy, their babies experience those same positive states of mind.

Flower elixirs may be taken at any stage of pregnancy, and there are no limits or precautions because they are so diluted. There are no plant parts in the liquid infusion, so the precautions that are taken with herbs and essential oils during pregnancy do not apply. Flower elixirs that enhance love are vastly beneficial during pregnancy, so that expectant mothers feel softer, gentler, and kinder toward themselves. Hong Kong Orchid helps mothers fully accept and love themselves regardless of how their body is changing and growing. Pink Magnolia helps mothers take more self-care breaks and be less apt to push themselves too far. Bodhi Tree elixir magnifies a nurturing and patient love and devotion toward oneself and others.

During birth, flower elixirs can be a huge support for first-time mothers who are not sure what to expect, or for mothers who have previously had uncomfortable or traumatic birth experiences. Flower elixirs can eliminate fears about giving birth, calm and soothe the nerves, and in general help both mama and baby have less stress during labor. Regular use of flower elixirs like Lupine, Silk Floss, and Red Hibiscus that increase calm, courage, and confidence are recommended about one month before the due date and can even be taken in the delivery room.

Here's a lovely story from one of my clients who used flower elixirs throughout her fourth pregnancy:

"Although I had had my previous three children at a hospital, I decided I really wanted to have my fourth child at home. My family was not very supportive of it; they were afraid and their response was, 'Well, we'll pray for you.' On top of their concerns, during my last trimester I heard three birth stories from women who had children born still. Even with confidence in our midwife, I had a lot of fear going into my homebirth journey, so I used the flower elixirs for love that Katie recommended. She also recommended some for my husband who was going to be my birth coach. I ended up being in labor for two days. I misted myself with flower elixirs during my entire labor to help me calm down and accept the birth journey,

whatever it was meant to be. I noticed that I felt a profound serenity and a comforting sense that I was safe. My mantra was, 'I will give my baby the birth that she needs.' When I wanted to sleep after being in labor for the first day, I misted myself with calming, relaxing flower elixirs and listened to a meditation. I slept so peacefully it was unbelievable! Our fourth labor was such a different experience than with the ones we experienced with our first three children. Even after being in labor for two days I experienced peace and calm. That sense of anxiety and rushing to get this labor over with was completely lacking. It was so comforting to labor in peace and trust that we were giving our baby the birth that she needed. We went on to have a beautiful homebirth right in the spot we consecrated with flower elixirs. I know the flower elixirs worked—I don't think we would have stayed home laboring for a total of 45 hours if I hadn't let go of the fear and anxiety that had crept into my pregnancy. Now with this baby, more than any of our other children, people say, 'Wow, she's so happy.' She definitely affects people more than my first three babies. I believe it's because she received all the good energy from the flower elixirs when I was pregnant."

During her pregnancy, this client used flower elixirs of Hong Kong Orchid, Pink Magnolia, and Pink Lotus and switched to using flower elixirs of Lupine, Silk Floss, Passionflower, Bird of Paradise, and Red Hibiscus during her 45-hour labor.

Flower Elixirs for Postpartum

After the baby is born, new mothers can take flower elixirs to address postpartum blues and help adjust to the changes of being a mother. If mom is taking flower elixirs, baby gets the emotional benefits through nursing and cuddling.

My recommended flower elixirs for postpartum adjustment are African Daisy and Pink Spirea, because they awaken joy, laughter, and letting our inner child play. I also recommend Passionflower, Dandelion, and Bird of Paradise for new moms experiencing sleep deprivation. These elixirs can help them quickly fall into a state of deep sleep and rest when there's an opportunity. The baby, in turn, also feels more deeply relaxed and sleeps for longer periods of time.

If new mothers need to go back to work, but would rather spend all day baby gazing, flower elixirs for motivation, like Red Bird of Paradise and Bamboo, assist in a smoother transition.

Flower Elixirs for Babies

For the first year or so, the baby will get the benefits of whatever flower elixirs the mother is taking through nursing. Once they are weaned, babies and toddlers can take most flower elixirs right in the mouth. (If honey is added to the flower elixirs, it is wise to wait until after the age of one.)

Flower elixirs can also be added to baby's bathwater; if the season and garden support it, a fresh flower elixir may be made for this purpose.

FRESH HOLLYHOCK BABY BATH

Adding flower elixirs to a baby's bath is a gentle and delightful way to infuse the bathwater with flower power and give baby a boost of good energy from Mother Nature. It will not have any scent, because flower elixirs are the bioenergetic imprint of the flower in water. Essential oils can be too strong for baby's delicate skin. As a flower elixir, Hollyhock flower enhances love and a warm-and-fuzzy feeling. As a tea infusion, the Hollyhock nourishes the skin.

If you have hollyhock flowers growing in your garden, you'll want to select several blossoms that are in full bloom. Before you collect the flowers, reflect on the wishes that you have for your baby, and request the plant to nourish your baby with whatever is most needed right now.

Remove as many blossoms as necessary to fill the surface of a clear glass bowl of water. Soak the hollyhock blossoms in pure water in the morning sunlight, placing the bowl on the ground. Leave the bowl in the sunlight for about 3 hours.

After 3 hours, carefully remove the blossoms from the water with wooden chopsticks or strain out, pouring the Hollyhock elixir–infused water into the baby's clean bath water. Bathing a baby in this Hollyhock water will revitalize and soothe the baby.

You can also use a flower elixir mist, and lightly mist in the space around your baby (being careful to avoid their eyes). During teething pains, colic, and before nap time or nighttime sleep cycles, using a gentle flower elixir mist is the easiest way to administer flower elixirs to babies. Calming flower elixirs like Lupine flower are the best for teething and colic, while Passionflower is the best for regulating sleep cycles.

I remember one day when we were set up at the downtown Phoenix farmers' market. A woman was carrying a baby whose serious expression seemed a touch cranky or sad. He looked like a little old man. I offered to mist the baby lightly with flower elixirs for laughter. The mother welcomed it, so I held the bottle about three feet over the baby's head and misted so that it came down on his face. Immediately his expression changed. He giggled and looked around, happy and engaged. It was like sunshine came over his face and transformed him. The parents looked on in amazement. The flower elixirs in that mist included African Daisy and Pink Spirea.

Babies are surprisingly receptive to flower elixirs; often you'll notice an immediate positive reaction in their body language, mood, and behavior. After the age of one, little ones can take flower elixirs that contain honey, which masks the sharp taste of the alcohol, and has numerous health benefits in itself. Toddlers and children like the sweet taste of honey drops, so they're more inclined to experience the flower elixirs as a positive ritual. Making the experience a ritual can become a bonding experience for parents and children. It can involve being present

with one's feelings, noting when a shift needs to occur, using the flower elixirs together, and sharing a nice moment.

Flower Elixirs for Children

Just like babies, children are open and sensitive. Their acute moment-to-moment awareness helps them quickly absorb and process energies from nature, including flower elixirs. Children usually show signs of the effects of flower elixirs quickly; moods can shift within moments, and major internal shifts can be noted within as little as a week.

Some mothers set aside a little time in the morning to take flower elixirs or mists with their children and make wishes or intentions for the day. In other families, it is the children who will approach their parents and suggest that they all use flower elixirs if they are feeling stressed. Teaching them at a young age to have tools and skills for dealing with stress, and to create special rituals for themselves, gives them a good start. Flower elixirs are a safe, gentle tool that they can use for the rest of their lives.

One of my clients came to her appointment distraught, because her young daughter had learned the word *hate* somewhere and was using it a lot. She kept having temper tantrums and saying, "I hate you, I hate you," to everyone around her, even her teachers. She was full of anger and resentment toward her sister, her parents, and everyone at school. I gave the mother flower elixirs for love, self-love, compassion, and kindness, including flowers of Fireweed, Rose, and

Nectarine Blossom. Even I was surprised when she reported within a week that her daughter was no longer using the word *hate* and her tantrums had subsided. She was affectionate again and had brought her teacher a gift.

Flower elixirs that enhance focus, clarity, and follow-through, like Red Bird of Paradise and Euphrasia, are helpful for children when they procrastinate doing homework, cleaning their rooms, or doing chores. Calming and confidence-boosting flower elixirs like Royal Poinciana, Silk Floss, and Black Bat flowers are beneficial when children start school or experience stress at school. At home, if there is sibling jealousy or bickering, flower elixirs for love and compassion, like Fireweed and Nectarine, can be added to water or other beverages for the entire family.

The easiest way to give children flower elixirs is the traditional way of taking them in drops from the dropper bottle. If the bottle is out in the open in a communal space such as a kitchen countertop, then they can reach for it and take the elixir as needed. Since there is no possible way for overdose to occur, children can have an unlimited amount.

In order to get the five doses in each day, if the child brings a water bottle to school, a whole dropperful can be added to the water bottle. Another way to introduce flower elixirs in school is to gift the teacher with flower elixir mists that can be used during class to calm the children and make the environment less chaotic. The teacher also gets the benefits.

When it's time for bed, a sleep ritual parents can offer is to give their child a short foot rub with an oil infused with flower elixirs for sleep. The feet are one of the most receptive areas of the body, and because of the reflexology points, a foot massage is like getting a full body massage. Whether flower elixirs are massaged into the feet, misted on the pillow, taken internally, or applied to pulse points, their regular use is a wonderful practice or habit to instill in children as they are winding down for bedtime. Some of the best flower elixirs for sleep include Passionflower, Dandelion, and Bird of Paradise.

One of the most important ways to encourage children to use flower elixirs is for the parents to model self-care by using them themselves. If the entire family is using flower elixirs, then children get used to seeing this as a valuable tool for emotional and mental support in their lives, which benefits the entire family and introduces them to a method of self-care that they can use for the rest of their lives.

Flower Elixirs for Adolescents

Flower elixirs can be a huge support during one of the most confusing and tumultuous times of our lives. At the precise moment when our hormones are raging and we're experiencing a slew of intense emotions that we don't even understand—flowers can come to the rescue.

In my practice I worked with many adolescents and usually the flower elixirs consisted of flowers for self-acceptance, confidence, and courage. For example, during adolescence, Hong Kong Orchid dissolves fears of being seen and heard and magnifies our ability to be the fullest expression of who we are. Silk Floss helps us feel comfortable in our own skin. Black Bat Flower dissolves worry of what others think and helps us be our own best advocate. Royal Poinciana helps us be fearless, direct,

and at ease in asking for what we want. Imagine having a boost like that during adolescence! Then, imagine *every* adolescent having access to these types of empowering flower elixirs!

As our culture doesn't teach children—or adults for that matter—any methods for how to work with intense emotions, a simple natural remedy like a flower elixir is highly beneficial. It gives teens natural support and a reminder of the magical world they live in—the world they thought they had lost by becoming a teenager. Furthermore, taking an elixir is fun and doesn't require counseling appointments, medication, or talk therapy. It helps teens feel more connected to what's truly important to them in an autonomous and independent way. It's a way they can help themselves remember to trust their own intuition and better judgment during a time when it's constantly tested—and avoid getting swept up in social and peer pressures.

Flower Elixirs for Women's Wellness

In this section we'll focus on two areas of women's health: the menstrual cycle and menopause. With the menstrual cycle often comes PMS, cramps, and irritation. Using a flower elixir like Pomegranate flower can balance out women's reproductive systems. When women use flower elixirs regularly each day, they notice that cramps go away or greatly diminish and cycles become like clockwork. For women who are tracking or predicting their cycles on paper or with an app, Pomegranate flower elixir helps the cycles become regular to the day, making it easier to track peak ovulation times, when trying to become pregnant or avoiding

fertile times to refrain from getting pregnant. It also greatly reduces other PMS symptoms, such as mood swings, irritability, and tender breasts.

Though I usually recommend flower elixirs to be taken at least five times each day for maximum benefit, I have noticed that in terms of benefits of women's health and cycles, using this elixir once each day or applying an oil infused with Pomegranate elixir to the belly daily is usually sufficient to have significant results. Note: It is not a remedy for acute situations, for example, if you are experiencing cramps and use Pomegranate for the first time, the pain-relieving results will only be slight; however, if you use the elixir regularly for one month, by your next cycle, you'll notice tremendous improvement and, in most cases, total elimination of PMS symptoms and cramps. For women with endometriosis, cysts, or more complicated reproductive issues, using Pomegranate at least five times each day is recommended, not as a cure, but as an elixir that empowers the reproductive system to sustain its own natural balance and self-healing capabilities.

For some women entering menopause, Pomegranate flower elixir can actually bring the menstrual cycle back. Some women like that and others would rather not have their periods anymore. During menopause, the most common symptoms include waking up in the middle of the night and not being able to get back to sleep, along with hot flashes. Flower elixirs for sleep, such as Passionflower and Bird of Paradise can be helpful for menopausal sleepless nights. It may not stop you from waking up, but by using the flower elixir upon waking, if you put your head back on the pillow, you'll fall right back to sleep, rather than stay wide awake for several hours.

Flower elixirs such as Rose can bring in a sweetness and feeling cared for while hot flashes take over the body in all their fiery glory. Hong Kong Orchid and Silk Floss help us more smoothly adapt to our changing bodies and accept ourselves with the loss of collagen in our skin or gray hair. Mandevilla helps us adjust to transitions and experience more patience, while Hollyhock soothes irritability and softens our character.

SPECIAL APPLICATIONS

Flower Elixirs for Pets

One of the ways we know that the effects of flower elixirs are not a placebo effect is that animals show marked differences in their behavior while under their influence. Flower elixirs can be used for any emotional discomfort in pets—past trauma, separation anxiety, sibling jealousy, hyperactivity, sadness, or listlessness—offering effective support for shifting their emotional states.

My dog, Joy, used to get sad every time I left on a trip. I travel quite a bit, and it was making me sad to see her get so mopey. For several years, each time I left my roommates would give her flower elixirs like Nasturtium and Pink Spirea to cheer her up while I was away. Now each time I take out my suitcase, she quietly watches me, but after I leave she doesn't get mopey anymore.

There are a variety of ways that flower elixirs can be administered to pets. You can put seven drops in their water bowl each time you fill it up with fresh water, or you can add it to their food or drop it onto a treat. Some dogs and cats like the taste of flower elixirs, so you can put the drops in your hand and they will happily lap them up. Other pets smell the alcohol and get turned off; for them, you can put flower elixirs in your hand and then pet them with that hand. Some dogs like being misted with flower elixirs, especially in the hot summer. Flower elixirs can also be added to your pet's bath routine. After washing and rinsing them, have a quart of water handy to which you have added three drops of each flower elixir and pour it over them like a rinse without washing it off. Towel off as usual.

One of my clients, Aubrey, had a cat that was really jealous of her new husband. The cat was so "pissed off" about taking second seat to the husband that he repeatedly peed on the bed and the couch to mark his territory. Aubrey gave him the blend of flower elixirs I made for him, which included Fireweed for dissolving anger and encouraging forgiveness. After a week he stopped peeing and never did it again. Many years have passed with no mishaps.

Flower Elixirs for Relationships

We all need a little love from time to time, but many of us have the habit of looking for love from the outside—from other people—when where we most desperately need it is from within. Mother Nature comes through in the most magical way with flowers that enhance self-love, making us fall in love with ourselves so completely that we don't need to look for love from the outside. When we cherish ourselves, we're peaceful, content, and comfortable in our own skin. We feel beautiful and worthy in our own way.

The flowers that bring out those qualities in us have us feeling so comfortable with who we are that it enhances our magnetism and charisma. Without seeking it, we naturally attract love, and this love is more stable, because it is based not on lack but expansion. Our capacity to love others is proportionate to how much we love ourselves. Instead of looking for someone else to fill us with love from the outside (which is not possible anyway), we can use flower elixirs to help us fill ourselves up from the inside, so we have more to give. That way two whole people can come together and be even bigger and better than when they were alone.

By using flower elixirs regularly, we not only get comfortable with who we are but we also become aware of habits or patterns that don't serve us, so we are more likely to make better relationship decisions. Flower elixirs enhance our most endearing human qualities, our softness, vulnerability, and authenticity, which make for strong building blocks in any type of relationship.

In my practice I have seen a lot of people find and develop really positive love relationships after having taken flower elixirs regularly for some time. The elixirs tend to soften our rough edges, allow us to let go of the past, dissolve resentment, and cut through insecurities. For example, flowers like Wild Fireweed enhance forgiveness and heal old wounds of the heart, while Pink Magnolia helps us be kinder to ourselves and take more breaks for self-care. Hong Kong Orchid enhances our ability to be accepting of ourselves

and comfortable with who we are, along with a healthy dose of sensuality.

One female client reported that, when using flower elixirs regularly for self-acceptance and love, she was frequently approached by men for casual conversation, and the men who approached her seemed balanced and stable. She was surprised that when she shifted her internal world there was an immediate reflection of that back to her, via these new interactions in the outer world.

When relationships get messy, flower elixirs can also be an effective method for enhancing our positive qualities. They help us develop patience, clear communication, listening, compassion, and kindness. They unravel self-limiting patterns, so that each partner in the relationship can better understand how to grow personally and with the other partner.

Some flowers, like Papaya flower, help people understand quickly whether or not there is compatibility in a partnership. If two people are not compatible, the flower elixir makes it clear, so that ending the relationship can be done in an amicable and peaceful way. Likewise, when two people are compatible, Papaya flower helps the couple experience a new depth in their relationship and in their understanding of each other.

Flower elixirs that awaken and strengthen love in us can be taken for all kinds of relationships, with our parents, in-laws, children, stepchildren, siblings, and colleagues. Flowers of Rose, Hollyhock, Bodhi Tree, Jasmine, and Nectarine are particularly helpful for enhancing various forms and expressions of love.

Flower Elixirs for Travel

During travel there are a variety of challenges, especially when we travel by air. We're subjected to the radiation that exists in the upper atmosphere, which can be fatiguing. We can easily get dehydrated. Being in different time zones throws off our sleep and eating schedules. We're surrounded by people, which can make us feel energetically drained. Then there are stressors like waiting in long lines, worrying about making a flight on time, and dealing with security.

Flower elixirs like Yarrow revitalize the body after airplane travel. Flower elixirs for patience and kindness, like Nectarine, Hollyhock, and Bodhi Tree, are helpful for allaying the impatience and irritation that can arise during travel, and flower elixirs for sleep and vitality can negate or reduce the effects of jet lag and travel fatigue.

On one trip to India for a spa and hospitality conference, it took me over 30 hours to get to Delhi. When I did arrive, it was 6:30 A.M., which meant that the best thing to do was stay awake all day, so I could reset my sleep schedule. For the weeks leading up to my trip, I had taken several flower elixirs for travel, including Yarrow. I also put them in every glass and bottle of water I drank on the plane and took them often as drops in the mouth. For the first week I was in India, I took them every few hours. I was amazed at how manageable the jet lag was after traveling so far and being awake for so long. In the afternoons when I felt a little sleepy I would take the flower elixirs, and they gave me so much vitality I never had to take a nap.

I shared this story with my friend Michon who was planning a trip to Singapore and the Philippines. She, her husband, and her mother followed the same protocol and couldn't believe how little jetlag they experienced. They stayed in Asia for about a month and when they flew back home, they didn't follow the protocol. Michon said without the flower elixirs it took her several weeks to recover from jetlag after arriving home.

Flower Elixirs for Meditation & Yoga

I love teaching meditation classes, and at the beginning of class I mist the room with flower elixirs—and the students too, if they're open to it (they almost always are). They come in full of the stress and busyness of their day, and then are expected to sit quietly and observe their minds and bodies. Using relaxing and calming flower elixirs helps us slow down a little, calms the nervous system, quiets the mind, and sharpens our awareness.

As an awareness tool, meditation is the perfect companion for flower elixirs. Both practices gently highlight our blind spots, one by one. As flower elixirs work their magic, meditation and self-awareness practices become a valuable tool for accelerating insights and consciously shifting our behavior.

Among flower elixirs for meditation, Spider Lily brings in a sense of lightness, Banana blossom offers a sense of mental spaciousness, Date flower can provoke euphoria, and Bodhi Tree helps practitioners come from a place of love.

Yoga instructors often use flower elixirs during their classes to induce self-love, joy, and meditative states during practice. They can even be infused into water bottles. Elixirs for love can be misted in the room during heart-opening poses. At the end of a yoga class, flower elixir—infused oils can be dispensed into the students' hands so they can massage their own necks or feet before they lie down for savasana, a restful pose.

Flower Elixirs for Smoking Cessation

Flower elixirs can help people maneuver more easily through letting go of addictions, including smoking.

When I first started my business, I used to get a lot of printing done at a local printer. Most times it was Eric who helped me out. Eric had tubes in his ears and was technically deaf, but he was fluent in sign language and could read lips like a pro. I loved Eric. He was a young gentle guy who was sort of unimpressed with everyone around him. He went out for beers with his friends on the weekend and he smoked a pack of cigarettes every day. One day Eric mentioned that he was trying to quit smoking. I came back with a flower elixir mist and told him, "Any time you feel like having a smoke, go outside, mist this around you and take a few deep breaths." The next time I saw him, Eric told me that he had successfully quit and was now several months into being smoke-free.

Flower elixirs can even address addictions when there's no conscious desire to quit.

My car mechanic was inspired to take flower remedies because he was feeling a bit down. After a month he decided that he wanted to quit smoking. This wasn't a part of the original plan—it just occurred to him after a month of taking the flower elixirs.

Each time he had the urge to smoke he used a flower elixir mist to calm down, take a deep breath, and get through that moment. Within a month he had lost the craving and had quit smoking completely. His wife said she had never seen him happier.

Smoking marijuana has a whole other level of ramifications associated with the addiction. Marijuana, especially when used regularly over a long period of time, buries and represses emotions. Upon cessation, emotions like anxiety, panic, and depression can arise, due not only to the natural cleansing process of the body, but also as a result of the repressed and compacted emotions arising from the psyche. Flower elixirs can provide emotional stability during this stage of emotional intensity, as well as strengthen mental stability, discipline, and personal resolve to stay clean.

When Shannon first came to see me, she had been smoking marijuana off and on for 10 years. She smoked daily in the evenings after work or before bed, and felt she was unable to sleep without it. Though it wasn't her reason for coming in for an appointment, after several months of consistent flower elixir use Shannon suddenly felt that while smoking she was a muted version of herself—that it hindered her growth. She immediately quit, and once she became more settled into who she was, sleep came easier. At the time of writing this book, she has been marijuana-free for over seven years, and she says she feels stronger for having healthier ways to deal with stress and find peace. She is happy not to have a crutch any longer, and to be free of guilt.

Several flower elixirs that are helpful for smoking cessation are: Lilac, for releasing unhealthy attachments and embracing change, and Pink Primrose and Giant Spider Lily for getting beyond the irritable or panicky stages of withdrawal with more ease. Passionflower relieves anxiety and helps us sleep better at night, while Bodhi Tree elixir is indicated if there is a sense of not feeling safe while sober. Red Hibiscus and Lupine offer hope, a fresh perspective, and a sense of peaceful support during the withdrawal

and detachment process. Brugmansia allows us to take more (smoke-free) self-care breaks, without feeling lazy or self-indulgent.

Flower Elixirs for Hospital Stays

One late night I got a call that my 99-year-old grandmother had had a stroke. Vera had driven a car well into her 90s, driving to assisted living centers to help out other elderly folks. She was strong and always of service, but now half of her body was paralyzed and she could no longer speak. The next day I flew to Minneapolis to see her. My aunt and I stayed at the hospital with her for a week, until we brought her home.

Since she could no longer move the left side of her body, the nurses had to come each day to give her a sponge bath. They were using a mineral oil–based lotion made from petroleum, so I offered some lotion that I had. It was my grandmother's favorite lotion, one that I had made with a flower elixir that I had collected of the powerful Night-Blooming Cereus Cactus flower that inspires fearlessness, courage, and taking a huge leap toward your full potential. At first the nurses were a little reluctant to break protocol, but when they smelled the lotion their faces lit up. The simple act of using that lotion seemed to turn what had been a banal chore into a luxurious ritual. They remarked how much they loved the scent and the way the lotion made them feel. It was interesting to see how such a subtle shift changed the nurses' experience from drudgery to enjoyment and pleasure, which of course was

was unconscious, almost comatose. His wife said he had been like this for days. Obviously death was near. He was lying on a hospital bed, his skin pale and his mouth open and dry. He had lost the ability to swallow or control the muscles in his throat, so he could no longer eat or drink.

The room was quiet, as were we. We had wanted to give him flower elixirs, but we couldn't put anything in his mouth. Then I had a thought. I misted my hands with flower elixirs and caressed his bald head, moving my hands down from his crown to his face. His body shuddered, as if throwing off a wet coat or something no longer needed, and he yawned and opened his eyes. This was the first time he had woken up in days! It was stunning to see how even someone who was unconscious—and who had been for days—could have such a visceral reaction to the application of flower elixirs. Lisa got a chance to have a meaningful connection with him and exchange some last words before he drifted back to sleep. He died a few days later.

If flower elixirs are helpful during life, they are even more helpful during dying, when so much is unknown and we are facing leaving our loved ones behind. During hospice or end of life transitions, flower elixirs are beneficial for the dying and also for the caregivers and family members.

Darla used flower elixir mists as her father was dying; she continually misted him and the room with flower elixirs for love and peace. The hospice staff kept remarking that something felt different in their room (without knowing about the flower elixirs). The family of a dying person experiences not only grief but also exhaustion, from staying all hours and caring for their loved

transmitted to my grandmother. That one simple change dramatically improved the care that my grandmother received there.

Hospitals are typically not restful or healing places. Bright fluorescent lights, few windows, highly processed food, and interrupted sleep take their toll, and this is felt by the patients as well as the family (and probably the staff as well). Using flower elixirs throughout hospital stays, for both the patient and the family or caregivers, is a powerful way to bring the joyful feeling of nature into the hospital room and infuse a hospital stay with more calm, comfort, and humor.

Flower Elixirs for Hospice

My best friend Lisa's uncle had had MS for a long time and I had seen him occasionally driving in his scooter, feisty as ever. Now, in hospice, he one. Darla said that having flower elixirs was a tremendous emotional support for her and her family during that time.

Flower elixirs can address and ease the complex emotions we go through during the dying process, for the person in transition and the family members at the bedside. Some of the best flowers for this time are White Magnolia, Pink Lotus, Bee Balm, Bodhi Tree, and Mandevilla flower.

Explore: Flower Elixir Ritual for a Loved One

Want to share the gift of flower elixirs with a loved one in a soothing ritual? Here is a simple, yet loving act that can be shared in a variety of different situations: Perhaps your child has a fever. You partner just got home from a stressful day at work. Your best friend is in labor. An elderly family member is in the hospital. You get the picture. Here's what you do:

Obtain a clean piece of natural fabric such as 100 percent linen, cotton, or silk. Dip the piece of fabric into a bowl of water that you've squeezed some lemon or lime juice into, along with five drops of your flower elixir of choice. It's as easy as that!

Then there are many creative ways to use this flower elixir—infused piece of cloth to create a nice experience for a loved one:

- Put the cloth on their forehead.
- Give them a sponge bath (if it's summer or in a heated room).
- Create a relaxing moment in a yoga or meditation class.
- Wrap a warm wet towel around each of their feet in cold winter months.
- Offer an icy towel in hot, sticky summer months for wiping their face and neck.

Optional method: Replace the piece of fabric with a pouch containing quartz crystals or quartz powder, which magnifies the energetics of the flowers. First, cleanse the quartz by placing it in a bowl of sea salt overnight. Once cleansed, place the crystals inside a pouch of natural fabric, such as linen, cotton, or silk. Follow the instructions from above.

CHAPTER 8

THE BIG PICTURE: CREATING A FLOWEREVOLUTION

> *What can we gain by sailing to the moon if we are not able to cross the abyss that separates us from ourselves?*
>
> THOMAS MERTON

My Life in Flowers: Night-Blooming Catalyst

After a decade of witnessing mind-blowing transformations occur in my clients' lives, I realized I needed to get these flower treasures out to a broader audience. I would speak at events and when I asked, "Who has heard of flower elixirs?" no hands went up. Meanwhile, back at the office behind closed doors, I was seeing people peel off the layers of what wasn't them and emerge into fully blossomed selves that were happy, magnetic, and powerful.

I counted up how many clients I could see in a day, a week, a month, a year, and finally, in a lifetime. I would be able to work with a maximum of 78,000 clients if I was fortunate enough to live a long life—and without any vacations! A few tens of thousands of transformations just wasn't enough. I wanted everyone on the planet to have *access to the kind of transformation I was seeing. I started making wishes and looked for a way to reach more people. I wanted to make a worldwide impact, and I wasn't sure how.*

One day my friend Lisa, who runs a business making organic chocolate, met the executive chef of an up-and-coming resort in Scottsdale, who wanted a custom chocolate. She invited me to the meeting as the formulator of the herbs, spices, and flower elixirs for her chocolate. During the meeting we learned that they were also opening a spa and they wanted a signature scent for the spa, along with a suite of bespoke products. Spontaneously the thought, "I could do that!" leaped into my mind, even though I had never done anything like it before and was competing against a large chemical fragrance company for the business.

For the next few months I spent day and night formulating different blends of essential oils for the signature scent and mixing body scrubs, lotions, and oils for the spa, along with teas, elixirs, and drinks for the restaurant. Each week we had two or three meetings with the staff, in which I would lay out the latest array of goodies I had made for them to test. One lucky full moon in May, I brought in a new sample and it was unanimous. Everyone loved it! After three months of work, the uncertainty was gone and we were hired to roll out the signature scent and spa products, and the organic chocolate, for the flagship spa of the largest hotel group in the world.

As we left that meeting and walked to the car, I stopped dead in my tracks with awe. In front of the yet unopened resort was a cactus with a huge bud on it. Though I'd never seen this cactus before, I felt sure it would bloom that night. I took it as an auspicious sign, so I did what anyone

would do—I snuck onto the empty property at 10:30 P.M.

The flower was in full bloom, illuminated by the light of the full moon. I had never seen such an enormous flower in the desert. It was luminous, the petals like soft white feathers in the moonlight. In the middle was a perfect mandala of bright green and yellow stamens. I was overwhelmed by its splendor.

At this point, the security guard had begun to circle me in his golf cart, wondering what I was doing there so late. Determined to make a flower elixir from this extraordinary beauty, I cut the flower and took it home. That night I made a full moon flower elixir, and decided to infuse it into all the products I would make for the resort and spa.

Later I found out that the flower was a species of Night-Blooming Cereus (Echinopsis candicans) that blooms for one night, dying by the morning time. This particular plant only produced flowers during the full moon or new moon in May. This night-blooming beauty catalyzes us to take a huge leap toward reaching our full potential. It unravels and dissolves any fears that would limit or prevent us from taking that leap.

That serendipitous meeting with the Night-Blooming Cereus changed my life and my business. It worked its magic on me, rewiring me so I could step into this challenging new business role—from flower elixir therapist to entrepreneur. I went from only seeing clients behind closed doors to formulating dozens of lotions, soaps, scrubs, and spa products, figuring out how to produce them by the thousands, and training a team of over 50 people.

In addition to formulating the signature products, I was called on to make some custom gifts for the President of the United States when he came to stay at the resort just after it opened! Mother Nature answered my deepest wish, showing me a way to magnify the impact of flower elixirs by making them known and accessible to more people. She has answered it again by giving me the opportunity to write this book.

Changing Your Personal Trajectory Will Change the World

Each and every one of us is on a trajectory right now. We live with an infinite array of possibilities at our fingertips, based on the choices we make: one big Choose Your Own Adventure story. Yet, it can be overwhelming. There are many temptations to become lazy and complacent, or to give up on our dreams or on ourselves.

In my search to find the most useful, expedient, and joyful way to support everyone in reaching their full potential, it became clear that there was no method so effective, fast-acting, and transformative as flower elixirs.

Consider this: We live in a vast world with tens of thousands of species of flowers. Every one of these flowers supports our well-being with specific transformative powers. They are waiting to be called upon and here to be of service.

The world is ripe for flower power. As the concentration of the most vital and awakening qualities of the botanical realm, flower elixirs are the perfect fit for our complex, busy, and nature-deprived modern lives. It takes a mere

30 seconds each day to weave flower elixirs into our personal daily rituals; it doesn't require a gym membership, hours of talk therapy, or years of journaling and self-inquiry. And yet it accelerates personal growth and yields profound self-discovery.

And here's what's equally exciting: if we take flower elixirs, it affects other people positively as well. People around us feel the difference. Our current state of mind is affecting others; why not offer them our best selves? Flowers exist to help us wake up our own goodness and strength. Using flower elixirs catalyzes positivity within us that ripples out to the rest of the world.

New Trajectory, New World: Jennifer Paul Again

When I reflect on my clients who were the most diligent—who for years, no matter what, made space for flower elixirs in their days—I see how completely the trajectory of their lives changed. Consider Jen Paul. Imagine that she had never found flower elixirs. Imagine that she had ignored that little spark inside her that believed she was capable of thriving in every area of her life. Imagine that she had given up. Where would she be today? And where would all the people be whose lives she has impacted by living her biggest, best self?

But Jen didn't give up. She kept going. Month after month, she kept taking flower elixirs, more than 120 bottles to be precise. Over 15,000 times in the last decade she stopped momentarily to put five drops in her mouth, a total of 75,000 drops. Drop by drop, with this simple action, she affirmed quietly to herself her deep desire to blossom and flourish in life. Before she even knew how, she asked to express a fuller, richer, ever more exquisite version of herself and to pour that self into the world with her body, speech, and mind.

During the last decade, as she and her husband broke through preexisting relationship obstacles and patterns, it was inevitable that he would experience an evolution in his love for her, and that it would affect what they mutually infuse into their music. Along with concerts and performances, they now hold a regular community music gathering, inspiring others to sing and share the joy of music with them.

In recent years Jen has learned how to reach out to her father and honor his advice, something she had found herself resisting her entire life. As she shifts that pattern, her father is spontaneously healing from years of compounded suffering over not being acknowledged in that way. Over time the clarity and love growing between them will positively affect the entire family.

When I met Jen, her son was a little boy; he's now a handsome and talented young man. For the past 10 years he has watched his mother go after her dreams in every aspect of her life, and realize most of them. What better way could she have inspired him to also believe that he can go after whatever he wants in life?

I remember years ago Jen saying out of the blue, "I really want to sing." And she remembers me encouraging her to just keep singing. Now on her website she has testimonials from people whose lives she has touched. My favorite is this one from a woman who invited her to come and sing to her mother at the end of her life: "My mother was blessed to have you at her bedside during her final transition week. I could feel her relaxation and pleasure as she listened to your beautiful songs and felt your healing touch. She used no morphine at any point in her transition. She had no pain and only minimal anxiety in part because you were present in helping her transition. I remain grateful for your gentle voice; your healing songs still sit in my heart." Jen's singing touched the dying woman, and it touched and comforted her grieving daughter too.

Jen brought her best self to each of these five people, and to many others who were changed by the blossoming of her essence and its full expression in the world. Her love, care, and singing ripple out beyond her.

Creating a Ripple Effect

Imagine that the goodness of those five people, nourished and inspired by Jen to fully express itself, ripples out to the five people that they most impact in their lives.

In fact, it's not just five, but *countless* people that we are continuously affecting with our thoughts, words, and actions. Think for a moment: Whose kindness and love has most affected you in your life? Whose lives do you most impact, and how?

This ripple effect is happening right now in the lives of everyone around us. Each of us is part of a massive tsunami of the legacies we leave in our wake all the time. What waves and ripples are you creating? What are you leaving in your wake today, this month, this year?

If you knew of a way you could exponentially multiply your positive impact, wouldn't you want to take it?

Instigating a Flowerevolution

My dream is to create a Flowerevolution, a worldwide ripple effect of positivity, a flower-fueled revolution that occurs spontaneously through our inner evolution.

This revolution is like turning over a new leaf—an upheaval of everything that no longer serves us, making room for the purest of little green sprouts and flower buds to come toward the light and bloom! It's about attaining our full potential by seeing beyond what we think is possible. Changing the world starts from within. With a little effort and intention, each of us can be a vastly powerful agent of change—*right now*.

Imagine that flower elixirs were woven into the everyday fabric of life all over the world. In the same way that we all now have a cell phone, we would also have a flower elixir handy. Flower elixirs would be widely available and understood as an effective method for de-stressing, and for accelerating our own personal evolution. Imagine what the world would be like if every person's best self were liberated and brought out into this world! Even if only a certain percentage of people experienced this, the ripple effect would touch the world a thousand times over.

Currently, flower elixirs are as little known as essential oils and aromatherapy were in the 1960s and '70s. Nowadays everyone has heard of essential oils, has experienced real lavender oil, and understands the benefits of aromatherapy. While today only a small number of cutting-edge people are using flower elixirs with great results, it should not take decades for flower elixirs to become more widely known; they will gain widespread recognition much faster now because of the Internet and social media. Before long, elixirs from flowers all over the planet could be available in spas, wellness centers, doctors' offices, airports, and apothecaries around the world.

Flowers, their elixirs and effects, are beyond mathematics; they cannot be calculated. They are our teachers, our guides, and our supporters. They remind us of our interconnectedness with one another, the Earth, and everything around us. We are not alone. We don't have to do this unaided; flowers are ready to help us. They embody purity, love, and joy, and awaken all that and more within us. With their help, there is no plateau: we continue to unfold like the petals of a flower as we bloom into our full potential.

PART II

THE SECRET TEACHINGS OF FLOWERS

*To reclaim ourselves we must tap once again that ancient participation
in the deep life of the Earth of which we are a part. We must know that world
as surely as we think we know the one in which we have lived so long.
To know it we must use some faculty other than mind.*

JOHN SEED

Let's find out what message the flowers have for you today!
Go to pages 120-123, where you will see all of the flower photographs. Choose the flower
you're most attracted to and turn to the page indicated.
Here's what you'll find on the individual flower's page, and how to read it:

FLOWER NAME

LATIN BOTANICAL NAME

ACTIVATE

Learn what quality the flower activates in you, in one word.

MESSAGE

Take to heart this distillation of the message of the flower.

MY LIFE IN FLOWERS

Read a short anecdote about how I discovered the flower and what I love about it.

WHY IT'S SPECIAL

Identify what makes that flower or tree so extraordinary.

ICONS

Discover the key attributes of the flower, whether it's highly
fragrant, edible, easy to grow, used as an herbal remedy
or floral dye for fabric, or if it's poisonous or toxic.

 HIGHLY FRAGRANT
 EDIBLE
 HERBAL REMEDY
 EASY-TO-GROW
 FRUIT BLOSSOM (FLOWERS TURN INTO FRUITS)

  FLORAL DYE
 EXTREMELY POISONOUS
 POISONOUS
 TOXIC OR SKIN IRRITANT

WHAT IT REVEALS

Discover why you're attracted to this particular flower over all the others.
You'll always be visually attracted to what you need most.

Note: You may relate to only some of this information. Each flower has many different benefits, and sometimes we resonate with part, but not necessarily all, of what the flower embodies. Other times, the entire section resonates, and we feel "seen through" in the most magical way. Learn from the parts that resonate with you, and discover your current state of mind or current challenge.

ASK YOURSELF

Reflect on the questions. See what answers arise and glean insights.

WHAT THE ELIXIR CATALYZES

Find out exactly what you would feel if you spent time around the flower daily
(plant it in your garden), or if you took its elixir regularly for several weeks.

EXTRA CREDIT

Evoke the flower's quality within you with these simple action steps.
You can choose to do one or all of them.

IN ESSENCE

Get to the core essence or benefits of each flower.

If you're a flower lover, you may want to read all the sections. If you just want to gain some quick insights, you can skip to the *What It Reveals* section. Read it, reflect on the questions from the *Ask Yourself* section, and choose one item from *Extra Credit*.

There are many ways to tap into the power of these flowers to magnify specific qualities in you. Here are a few ideas for working with each flower:

- Plant them in your garden.
- Photograph them and put them on your walls or in your space.
- If they're available in cut flowers or in a pot, put some on your desk.
- Spend time around them in parks and botanical gardens.
- Draw or paint them.
- Use their flower elixirs internally, topically, or in the bath or shower in your daily life.

Which flower(s)
are you most
attracted to?

Turn to that page
to discover
something about yourself!

215   349   297

273   129   137

125   133   235

159   251   319

191

141

315

257

177

149

225

145

153

301

221

241

165

201

197

181

279

341

311

211

335

187

307

245

325

207

357

353

285

269

229

345

331

263

291

171

AFRICAN DAISY

Osteospermum

Activate: Playfulness

Message: Be silly.

One year African Daisies appeared magically in our front yard. We didn't plant them; perhaps the previous owner had planted seeds many years before and the plants went dormant from not getting enough water. As we watered the trees, the Daisies seized the moment, sprouting in their vibrant colors.

The Daisies were a light purple with a bit of pink, the center of the flower the most intriguing of all: rich indigo hues and fluorescent orange pollen. I suddenly began to see them all over the world during my travels, in shades of magenta, pink, purple, yellow, and white.

Why It's Special

African Daisy is a hardy flower native to South Africa, commonly found in garden landscaping and cheerful flower pots. They love warm sunny areas and rich soil, but they can also survive in poor soil conditions. If the African Daisy's soil becomes too dry or experiences drought, they drop their flowers and go to "sleep" or hibernate until better hydrated. Some varieties of African Daisy are "whirled," appearing like a child's pinwheel.

What It Reveals

If you're attracted to the African Daisy, you may have recently felt like you have a lot of responsibilities on your shoulders, and that you do not have time for fun. Just as the African Daisy guards its seeds when it doesn't have the right conditions, in the same way there may be aspects of you that have gone dormant and are waiting for when the conditions are right.

You may feel too stressed for fun, or that there is too much at stake to be playful. This may be due to past grief, or simply a habit you have. Alternatively, pride may prevent you from experiencing the joy of playfulness, for fear of looking silly, being frivolous, or wasting time.

Ask Yourself

In what areas of my life might I be overly serious?

When do I cut myself off from joy or playfulness?

What brings me joy?

When do I allow myself to play?

What the Elixir Catalyzes

The African Daisy flower elixir dissolves excessive seriousness when we find ourselves too busy or stressed for humor and play. It promotes joy and helps us understand that play is not frivolous but full of curiosity and wonder, which enlivens us and gives a fresh quality to everything we do.

It also helps us understand that joy is an important marker for creating the life we want to live. As a method for clarifying our life's path and purpose, if we move closer to what brings us joy, it often leads us to our special abilities, talents, or potential.

Also, when we're able to laugh at ourselves, it takes the pressure off. We don't have to be perfect and superhuman. We can act with humility and humor, instead of being serious and aloof. Laughing and finding joy in everyday life encourages us to connect more deeply with people around us.

Extra Credit

- Go to an amusement park and ride on the roller coaster or twisting teacups until you start to laugh uncontrollably.
- Head to an ice cream shop and get five scoops of fun flavors on a cone. Share with a friend.
- Wear a funny wig and watch how it cheers people up.
- Get in touch with your inner child. Close your eyes and visualize yourself as a small child. Ask the child what it wants to do and see what answer you get. Then do that and have fun! Being joyful relaxes you and benefits every area of your life.
- Watch a funny movie and laugh until all your muscles relax.

In Essence

Dissolves	*Magnifies*
Excessive seriousness	Joy, playfulness, and silliness
Pride	Recognition of your talents and life's path
Confusion about life purpose	

ARCTIC LUPINE

Lupinus arcticus

Activate: Deep peace

Message: You are supported.

The first time I really appreciated Arctic Lupine flowers was on a flower elixir collection trip in British Columbia, Canada. Lupines grew everywhere in the wild, and their leaves were just as beautiful as their flowers. I felt such a deep peacefulness in their presence.

Later, traveling through Washington State, I noticed that the areas of the freeway that became the most congested were where the Lupine flowers grew most abundantly. It was as if Mother Nature provided beauty as a relief, to balance out the human stress of being stuck in traffic.

In the southwestern U.S., a desert variety of Lupine covers the mountainsides in indigo during the spring—it's stunningly beautiful!

Why It's Special

There are over 200 species of Lupine in North and South America, also called Bluebonnets in some areas of the country. Part of the Legume family, its beans are a nutritious replacement for soybeans, and have historically been eaten by cultures all over the world.

Lupines are one of the hardiest plants around, and they are team players—they support other plants and the environment. Like pioneer plants, they survive and nourish barren lands, increasing nutrients and nitrogen in the soil in order to support more life. For example, Lupine was introduced on the volcanic island of Iceland, where 75 percent of the land was barren, to enrich the soil and prevent erosion.

Arctic Lupine grows all along the western edge of North America from Oregon to Alaska. Each stem has about 30 flowers with bright green starlike leaves.

Historically, in some regions the nocturnal snowshoe hare would munch on the leaves of the Lupine. In response, to deter them, the plant developed a neurotoxin that increases in levels at night when the rabbits come out for midnight snacks.[1]

What It Reveals

If you're attracted to the Arctic Lupine flower, you've got a lot going on! You're juggling too much at once, or you may be in transition with lots of change occurring in your life. You probably feel like you could use more support!

You may feel stretched too thin and overwhelmed, or you may be experiencing low-level worries or anxiety. The times in our lives when we're especially drawn to this flower include moving, changing jobs, having a baby, caring for small children, or dealing with the pressure of stressful deadlines.

Ask Yourself

What big changes are occurring in my life right now?

What am I responsible for?

How often do I try to go it alone without asking for help?

Do I have enough support? What is my support system like?

What can I delegate or hand off to a helper?

What activities or work can I offload right now to streamline my life?

What the Elixir Catalyzes

Arctic Lupine flower enhances an experience of deep inner peace and calm. It gives us the sense that we have a team of support around us, strengthening us to move gracefully though life's challenges.

Arctic Lupine is especially helpful when we feel heavy, in over our heads, or bombarded. It brings in a comforting sense of safety and protection, which helps us feel secure enough to expand into who we truly are.

Desert Lupine—another kind of Lupine flower that grows in the Southwest—has a similar effect to Arctic Lupine, but is more targeted toward fear or being frozen with panic.

Extra Credit

- Create and refine systems and routines that support you.

- Whatever aspects of your life can be automated, set that up to save time.

- Get a house cleaner, car washer, laundry service, meal deliveries—whatever it takes to feel supported, even if it's temporary while you move through your transition.

- Reach out to the people around you and ask for help, and don't hesitate to ask for help again.

- Make sure you're getting regular healthy meals to support your energy. Take vitamins, superfoods, or adaptogenic herbs to keep up your stamina.

In Essence

Dissolves	*Magnifies*
Worry, anxiety, overwhelm	Calm, comfort, peacefulness
Heavy heart	Sense of safety and protection
Feeling stretched too thin	Effortless strength to move through life's challenges

BAMBOO

Bambuseae

Activate: Unwavering determination

Message: Make the impossible possible.

There's something special about a bamboo forest. I love the kung fu movies when the characters hop from limb to limb and swish through the leaves. In the main room of our office we put floor-to-ceiling photographic wallpaper of bamboo, so it appears we're in our own peaceful bamboo forest.

Why It's Special

Bamboo is actually a grass, though the idea of its being a "tree" somehow fits its height better. Bamboo is one of the fastest-growing plants in the world. Some types of bamboo grow up to three feet per day!

Bamboo is impressive not only for its speedy growth but also for its strength. With a compressive strength greater than concrete, wood, or brick, and a tensile strength matching that of steel, it's no wonder that it's used in construction in Asia. Interestingly, even though bamboo is as strong as steel, it's also flexible and supple.

What It Reveals

If you are drawn to Bamboo, you may be planning a big project or about to engage in something that challenges you. You may want to take what you're doing to the next level, and need an extra shot of determination.

You may have big ideas, yet have lingering reservations about going all out, or occasional doubts that you have what it takes. Hesitation and holding back may be preventing you from really tapping into your full potential and going after your biggest, wildest dreams.

Ask Yourself

In what areas of my life am I not sure if I have what it takes?

In what situations could I use a little more determination?

When do I catch myself getting wrapped up in thinking other people are more qualified or more talented?

Are my perceived limitations physical, emotional, or mental?

What the Elixir Catalyzes

As an elixir, Bamboo is unparalleled for making the impossible possible. It gives us the ability to accomplish something against all odds. Bamboo dissolves the thought pattern, "I can't do it." It acts as a boost of stamina, determination, and follow-through. It offers unfaltering strength, persistence, and tenacity, with a perfect balance of flexibility and gracefulness.

Bamboo also enhances focus, clarity, and awareness of how our everyday actions relate to our greater goals. It deepens our understanding of our actions as a part of the bigger picture, and makes us unwavering in doing whatever it takes to accomplish our aims.

Bamboo eliminates fears and nonconstructive enmeshment with others. It dissolves the habit of looking at others' accomplishments and feeling small. It keeps us from looking at other people instead of looking straight ahead at what needs to be done.

Bamboo may also be used during growth spurts, for athletic injuries, or to strengthen the bones, tendons, ligaments, and tissues.

Bamboo can be a helpful elixir for anyone desiring more energy, stamina, and power.

Extra Credit

- Take out a piece of paper and write down the dreams you feel are so big that you rarely (or never) share them with others. Think of what you'd love to do that's outside of your comfort zone. Write it all down in bullet points and keep them in a place where you can come back to that piece of paper over and over again. You may not know the how, but you don't have to. Just start looking at them as real possibilities. If there are actions you can take, now is the time to begin.

- Make a list of all the obstacles you've overcome in the past.

- Look how far you've already come; look how much you've already accomplished and let that fuel you forward.

- Ask for help. Make a list of people, like coaches, mentors, guides, or friends who can offer support, direction, resources, or referrals.

- Notice what aspects of your project you can delegate.

In Essence

Dissolves

"I can't do it"

Impotence, fears, feeling small

Lack of follow-through, stamina, or determination

Magnifies

"I can do it"

Unfaltering strength, persistence, tenacity

Focus, clarity, relationship of daily actions to larger goals

BANANA BLOSSOM

Musa acuminata

> **Activate:** Spacious mind
>
> **Message:** Slow down a little.

Though I had seen many banana trees when I lived in Mexico and traipsed through the jungles from Chiapas to Tulum, I didn't make a flower elixir of the Banana blossom until I lived in the Arizona desert a decade later. I met a botanical genius who had created his own little sustainable oasis in the desert, with palm-thatched huts, hot rock saunas, and self-cleansing lily ponds. His every thumb and finger was green, and he could get anything to grow in the desert, even flowers that should only grow in the tropics or herbs that should only grow in the moist, black soil of Oregon.

I spent a day on his land, which was a paradise by any standard, much less in the dry Arizona desert. It included a bamboo forest, a banana tree forest, enormous avocado and loquat trees, tiny unraveling ferns, and other secret treasures, like white and yellow bog irises, exotic-looking cashmere plants, and explosions of elderflowers. I chewed on sour grass and ate hollyhock petals and sweet mulberries. I got intoxicated with aromas of fruity roses and tulsi holy basil. His living garden was lush and full of revitalizing plant medicines and nourishing food.

One of the plants that I felt most embodied the lusciousness of this utopian wonderland was the banana tree. Coincidence or synchronicity would have it that I arrived at this magical place on the full moon—when flowers are right at their peak—so I climbed up on a ladder and made a flower elixir of the blossoms exploding out of the top of a huge banana tree.

Why It's Special

The life cycle of a banana plant is a short three years. It shoots out from a potatolike root with "eyes" and grows tall. From the top of the plant a gorgeous pink and purple bud hangs down, called an inflorescence. Little white and yellow flowers hide under each section of the purple inflorescence, and these are what ultimately turn into bananas. After the bananas come and go, the tree dies. Many more banana trees grow up from its roots.

Banana plants are a pioneer species, meaning that they take keenly to growing on land through which a fire has just passed; they are one of the first species to grow in such areas. They are also known as a keystone species, which means that they open the door for more wildlife to come into specific environments, because they regenerate so rapidly and provide a food source for so many different animals.[1]

What It Reveals

If you're attracted to the Banana blossom, you may have recently been feeling pressured for time or worried that you won't make a deadline or accomplish something within a specific time limit.

You likely feel like you're always on the go—rushed or worried about making deadlines. The scurry of today's lifestyle rarely inspires the great ahas of the century, and it can sometimes squeeze you so tight that the channel to your best potential is squelched and temporarily shut down.

Simultaneously, you may crave taking a vacation on a tropical island somewhere. You may feel like slowing down your life's pace and dedicating time to yourself to decompress.

You may also be experiencing fears around time frames regarding long-term or life goals such as finding love, getting pregnant, establishing a career, or growing a business.

Ask Yourself

When, or in regard to what, do I feel rushed or under pressure?

In what areas of my life do I worry that I won't have enough time?

During what activities does time disappear for me?

In what environments do I feel like I have all the time in the world?

What the Elixir Catalyzes

The Banana flower elixir dissolves fears of not being able to do something within a specific time limit. This can apply to work projects with deadlines, for example, when we worry about not being able to complete the project in a given time line. Banana elixir helps us trust ourselves and our ability to get things done on time.

Banana blossom gives us confidence in our ability to achieve our utmost priorities, simultaneously helping us feel more at ease, stable, peaceful, and honest with ourselves and others about our progress. It frees our mind of the fears around time, so that time doesn't rule us. Instead, we rule time.

Oftentimes we get our best ideas when we're able to step away from the pressures of e-mails and phone calls and other people's emergencies. When we allow our minds to relax, stretch, and perceive the world with more awareness, we can more fearlessly and effortlessly accomplish our aims in a way that's beyond what we think is possible. In science they call this the state of "flow," and it happens when you're able to let go and your time is relatively unstructured—even if it's only for a short period.

Banana blossom enhances the experience of being totally in the groove, when time seems to stretch itself and a huge amount of work, creativity, or innovation is churned out in a very short time. When we slow down a little—enough to let the pressure subside—and we can be ourselves and in tune, euphoria and effortlessness arise.

Extra Credit

- Set your goals lower than you think . . . so they allow time for play, miracles, and unexpected diversions to light you on fire and bend time.

- Give yourself more downtime; allow your creative juices to recharge.

- Delete the sentence "I don't have time" from your vocabulary and do your top priority projects first, always.

- Eliminate multitasking. Work for 25 to 30 minutes on one task without distraction.

- Read the book *Essentialism: The Disciplined Pursuit of Less*, by Greg McKeown, for wonderful tips on how to prioritize your life around what's truly most important to you, and how to say no in order to uphold that.

In Essence

Dissolves	*Magnifies*
Hurrying	Spacious, expansive mind
Feeling anxious	Bringing projects to fruition with ease
Worry about not having enough time	Slowing down to rest and feel nurtured

BANANA YUCCA

Yucca baccata

Activate: Hidden potential

Message: Uncover your secret talents.

The Banana Yucca plant grows all over the American Southwest. It blends in with the desert landscape most of the year and isn't particularly captivating—until it blooms. Then a stalk shoots up from the middle of the plant with dozens of exquisite creamy white flowers hanging down like bells.

Even though it's a pretty common plant in the desert, I had never seen Banana Yucca in bloom until I spied the unexpected white blossoms in my backyard. I got down on my hands and knees to look up into the flowers and discovered another world. The floral bells are milky and cream-colored, with a stamen in the center that forms a star.

Why It's Special

Banana Yucca flowers bloom during spring and early summer in the southwestern U.S. and northern Mexico. The plant only grows to about four feet tall, and the fruits are banana-shaped and sweet-tasting.

The Yucca plant is often confused with the agave plant. Whereas Yuccas can be identified by the stringy fibers that emerge from their leaves, and the abundance of soft, bell-shaped flowers that hang down in clusters, the agave is fleshier. When it blooms, a huge stalk emerges from the center like a torpedo, growing to over ten feet tall, with hundreds of tiny flowers on it. Of these two similar plants, the Yucca is more of a feminine plant, while the agave is more masculine.

The many stringy fibers in the leaves of Yucca plants were used by Native Americans to make rope, baskets, sandals, and cloth. Its roots were used to make body soap, shampoo, and laundry soap, because its juice is slippery, foamy, and rich with saponins, which are a natural detergent.

What It Reveals

If you're attracted to the Banana Yucca flower, you may have secret talents or abilities that you are not even aware of. You may have a big vision, but not understand fully how it will all play out. Being drawn to this flower signifies that you are capable of great things and that you are ready to come out of your shell. You may have been experiencing subtle stirrings or urges to break out—to experiment with who and how you are in the world.

As Yucca enhances the feminine qualities in each of us (women and men alike), if you are drawn to Banana Yucca, it is time for you to collaborate with women to make your biggest vision a reality. You may surprise yourself with what you can accomplish when you set your mind to it and engage the minds of collaborative women who want to see you succeed. Alternatively, if you're not working with women, you may want to develop more of the following qualities within yourself: collaboration, empowerment, networking, leadership, and intuition.

Ask Yourself

What am I working on? What would I like to be working on?

What are my secret aspirations, the ways I want to make a positive impact in the world?

Is there something I have wanted to bring to the world, but have felt shy or nervous about?

Are there any women or groups of women that I could partner with to expand the potential of what I do?

What the Elixir Catalyzes

Banana Yucca flower brings hidden talents to the surface. It awakens a deep sense of purpose and a desire to make our mark in the world. It dissolves insecurities around our capabilities and enhances our ability to make unexpected leaps and bounds in our progress toward reaching our goals.

Banana Yucca fosters the accomplishment of our aims though collaboration with women. It favors achievement through cooperation, communication, intuition, and holistic thinking.

Under the influence of the Banana Yucca flower elixir, you may surprise yourself with what you're capable of, generating inspiring big picture thinking and integrated, comprehensive plans.

Extra Credit

- Allow your secret aspirations to arise, and start attaching visual images and words to them. Create a mind map, a vision board on Pinterest, or a visual collage by cutting out images from magazines and pasting them on a large poster board or card stock. Visual imagery can be more energetically expansive than lists of goals. It lights up your right brain and your intuitive side in ways that you wouldn't imagine, and draws out what's hidden in your subconscious. Spark the magic that occurs when you start putting imagery to your vision.

- Consider getting together with a group of women (or mostly women) to help you achieve your vision through collaboration, cooperation, communication, and magnetism.

- Make a list of what you're good at, no matter how big or small. Notice any themes or trends.

- Do more of what brings you joy. Discover hidden talents by doing more of what inspires you.

- Reflect on what you've been good at in the past, and what has brought you the most fulfillment.

In Essence

Dissolves

Shyness about purpose in life

Insecurity about capabilities

Feeling solitary or out there on your own

Magnifies

Hidden talents, power, and sense of purpose

Unexpected leaps and bounds in progress

Collaboration and leadership

BEE BALM

Monarda punctata

Activate: Hope

Message: Be still.

One summer day, a random flower I had never seen before bloomed auspiciously in my backyard. There was only one of them. No one had planted the flower; it seemed to pop up of its own accord. The flower petals were purple and white, with beautiful polka dots on them.

I was intrigued by the flower because it looked like a pagoda, or a series of parasols, one on top of the other. In Eastern traditions, the parasol is a sign of protection from harmful forces and illness. It also represents the spaciousness and expansiveness of the sky.

Why It's Special

Bee Balm belongs to the mint family. Also known as Horsemint, it is a flowering scented herb that is native to the United States. The leaves and flowers of Bee Balm are used in a tea commonly known as Oswego tea, drunk by several Native American tribes. From the Lakota to the Ojibwa to the Navajo, many tribes used this plant for fevers, colds, coughs, nausea, digestion, and acne.[1]

What It Reveals

If you are attracted to the Bee Balm flower, you may recently have had a traumatic experience. If not, there may be trauma from the past that still affects you on some level, even if you're not conscious of it.

Alternatively, you may be experiencing anguish or sadness. You may also find yourself getting distracted, unable to focus on one thing, or feeling frantic or tense.

If none of the above sounds appropriate, then it could simply mean that your daily stresses are starting to take a toll on you. It's important for you to take more time off, so you don't burn out.

Ask Yourself

Have I experienced any trauma?

Have I been in any accidents or natural disasters?

Has my heart been broken?

Am I in a major transition in my life?

If yes to any of the above, how did my experience affect my perspective about life?

What kind of nourishing experience could I create that would dissolve distraction, tension, or anguish in my life now?

What the Elixir Catalyzes

Bee Balm soothes the intense stress and anxiety that occurs as a result of traumatic experiences. These experiences alter the natural balance of the body and mind, so that it may be hard to sit still or focus. We can become easily distracted or stare off into space. We may find it too painful to be in the here and now, as we can become filled with despair. As a result, we can also become irritable or easily annoyed, or feel like no one understands what we're going through.

If not related to a traumatic event, this flower elixir helps us adjust to any kind of change or transition that disturbs the natural balance in our lives. We may feel like we're in over our heads, or doing an impossible balancing act, causing us to spin into distress. Bee Balm soothes the nervous system, allowing us to focus and be more lighthearted. It inspires hope and compassion after stressful events.

Extra Credit

- Take some time alone or with a close friend and do whatever it takes to nurture yourself.

- Eat nourishing foods and make sleep a priority.

- Take a time-out from life in order to heal yourself from the inside out.

- You may find that traumatic experiences shift your perspective about life. Embrace these new perspectives, if they are positive, and allow them to shape and mold you into your wisest self.

- Be kind and gentle with yourself.

In Essence

Dissolves

Distraction, tension

Anguish, despair, sadness

Trauma, post-traumatic stress

Magnifies

Soothing calm during times of transition, trauma, and heartache

One-pointed focus

Lightheartedness, hope, compassion

BIRD OF PARADISE

Strelitzia reginae

Activate: Connection

Message: Quiet your mind.

Bird of Paradise flowers tolerate the salty ocean breezes and grow virtually everywhere in Los Angeles; in fact, Angelenos rarely need that flower elixir because there are so many Bird of Paradise flowers in their environment. In Phoenix, Arizona, where I live, and in other deserts in the world, however, there is an abundance of Earth and air elements—but little water and wood. As a result, oftentimes in dry or desert environments people have busy minds and tend to be more intellectual than heart-centered. Bird of Paradise is helpful because it quiets the mind, helps people slow down a little, and sleep more soundly. It grounds people and helps them operate more from their hearts.

The combination of the five elements in any geographical area affects its inhabitants and what elixirs they need as a whole. Each individual has unique needs, but the elements skew which flowers people are most drawn to.

Why It's Special

The Bird of Paradise flower resembles an actual bird of the same name. The flower is native to South Africa, where it's called the Crane Lily. It has three to five orange petals with two to three rich blue petals, and is pollinated by a beautiful jewel-toned bird called the sunbird, which is related to the hummingbird.

Bird of Paradise is the perfect flower for people with allergies, because it produces no airborne pollen. The only time the pollen is released is when the sunbird perches on the flower to drink the nectar, and its weight opens up the petals. As it hops around on the flower, it gets pollen all over its feet and then moves to the next flower, pollinating it.

What It Reveals

If you are attracted to the Bird of Paradise, you likely tend toward analytical thinking. When a problem arises, rather than rely on intuition, you'd rather solve it intellectually. You are likely articulate with your speech and come up with lots of ideas, but sometimes those ideas never stop, exhausting you. You may experience monkey mind or loops of thoughts that make you less effective or cause you to stay awake at night.

Sometimes being too much in your head can make you feel disconnected from those around you, or others may express that they feel distant from you. This may be because your overabundance of thoughts keeps you too much in your own world.

Ask Yourself

Do I have a habit of being too much in my head?

Do I tend to overanalyze?

Have I had difficulties sleeping recently?

When do I have mental monkeys?

Have I felt disconnected from others lately?

What the Elixir Catalyzes

Bird of Paradise elixir quiets the mental monkeys and helps us have a more meditative state of mind by bringing energy from the head down into the heart. It helps us let go of overanalyzing situations and being skeptical of things we don't understand. It helps us better connect to people around us and operate more from quiet observation and intuition.

Instead of processing intellectually, we become more open to creative solutions and right brain thinking. We operate from observation or experience rather than from what we think. As a result, we feel more connected to everything around us.

Extra Credit

- Slow down a little. Listen, really listen.
- Only speak when you're looking directly in someone's eyes.
- Resist the temptation to mentally "figure things out"; relax your mind and let insights arise naturally.
- Follow your gut once in a while.
- Spend time around children, elderly people, or pets—anyone you have a soft spot for.

In Essence

Dissolves

Overanalyzing, thinking too much, monkey mind

Being skeptical of things that cannot be explained logically

Overly intellectual or superficial relationships with people

Magnifies

Quiet, meditative mind

Moving from head to heart

Feeling deeply connected to others

BLACK BAT FLOWER

Tacca chantrieri

Activate: Fierce compassion

Message: Advocate for yourself & others.

I saw the Black Bat Flower for the first time in the Naples Botanical Garden in Naples, Florida. A flower that typically only grows in Southeast Asia, the Black Bat Flower is one of the craziest, most interesting flowers I've ever seen.

While looking deep into the flower, I felt many strange sensations. The scent is really interesting too—I remember taking a deep inhale of the flower and then writing down notes to describe it. After the first whiff I literally wrote down "scary . . . with a softness behind it." The second time I smelled it, it was all sweetness and purity. Black Bat helps us face a lot of facets of ourselves that can be scary, which is part of the reason why it can at times feel disconcerting to gaze into the flower.

Interestingly, as I was making this flower elixir, an enormous black snake emerged from the foliage into the center of the garden pathway. It came slithering out and then was still, as if sensing me. It sat there for a while, and then went back into the leaves.

Why It's Special

The color and shape of Black Bat Flower are intriguing, with two large black bat wing petals reaching out to the sides and an array of long, skinny "whiskers" cascading down, which account for its common name in some parts of Asia as Tiger Whiskers. When the flower is in full bloom, the little pieces that bloom remind me of an eel with its mouth open and the teeth bared. Black Bat Flower is the only flower I've ever seen that simultaneously reminds me of three different animals.

The Black Bat Flower originates in tropical areas like Burma, China, and Thailand and is a very rare flower, listed on the endangered species list. It's a very difficult plant to grow, because it likes consistently moist soil along with a slight breeze, so it doesn't like greenhouses.

A plant lover who spent thousands of dollars cultivating Black Bat Flowers and trying to keep them alive said that Bat Flowers do not adapt to how you want them to grow. They are not particularly demanding once they're given everything they need to succeed—humidity and protection from strong winds—but you have to give Bat Flowers what they require.[1]

What It Reveals

If you're attracted to the Black Bat Flower, you may be adapting too much—going with the flow too often—when what's necessary is for you to speak your mind and state your case clearly. Or there may be an animal, a child, or elder who could use your support. Or perhaps there is someone at work or home who needs you to stick your neck out for them. Advocating for yourself or others may be in order.

Black Bat Flower also can indicate the need to reflect on what is a source of anger or fear for you. If you see repeating patterns—and can isolate situations that trigger anger or fear—you can gain insights and respond wisely.

Black Bat shows us how to use the energy of anger for beneficial means. Anger may not be a pleasant emotion, but it can teach us when other people have crossed the line or been inappropriate with us or with people we care about. It's okay to bare your teeth when necessary.

Just as the Black Bat Flower requires specific growing conditions, we require certain conditions for thriving. When we don't speak up, we may feel resentful or disappointed about missing an opportunity to improve a situation or clarify a relationship pattern.

Ask Yourself

In what areas of my life am I wavering or hesitating?

Is there someone in my life who requires my advocacy? Who might need me to stick up for them?

What are the conditions I require in order to thrive?

When am I not clear about what I want?

If I could transform anger or fear into courage in a specific area, what action would I take?

What the Elixir Catalyzes

Black Bat Flower transforms our anger into courage and strength that has a positive impact on everything around us. It dissolves the violent qualities of anger and helps us identify the sweetness and purity behind it, resulting in fierce compassion and protection of what we love. This flower appears to have teeth and helps us bare our teeth to show our strength and use our growl in a positive way—to protect and honor ourselves and others. For example, it's a good flower elixir for new mothers, to assist in developing protective strength and eliminating fear and insecurities about being a mother.

Black Bat Flower gives us a burst of confidence and the power to propel ourselves forward. It helps us project ourselves and our voice, awakens our fearlessness and readiness to be our own best advocate and protector, and gives us the strength to stand up for ourselves and others. Anger can be used to get things done, make a stand, and be a force for good in the world.

Black Bat also transforms fear and insecurity into strength. It dissolves dread, fear, worry, and emotional debris. It can even cut through panic and intense fears like paranoia, phobias, fear of being seen, watched, or exposed, fear of going crazy, and fear of spiders and snakes. It also dissolves fear of public speaking and speaking up.

This flower is also indicated when experiencing the "dark night of the soul" or our deepest fears and obsessions. It is a helpful elixir during transitions such as hospice, especially if the person is experiencing a great deal of fear, panic, or anxiety.

Extra Credit

- Ask yourself: What would I do if I were absolutely fearless? Write down your answers. Repeat once a week for one month and watch what happens.
- Reflect on what makes you angry and how that translates to advocacy, or how you can use that energy for good.
- Do something you're afraid of.
- Stick up for or advocate for someone this week.
- Practice asking for what you need to thrive.

In Essence

Dissolves

Rational and irrational fears, paranoia, phobias

Impurities and insecurities, physical and mental toxins

Dread and worry

Magnifies

Strength, confidence, fearlessness

Ability and readiness to advocate for oneself or others, protection

Fierce compassion, protective anger, productive ferocity

BODHI TREE

Ficus religiosa

Activate: Boundless love

Message: True love is unconditional.

The first time I went to India I went immediately to Bodh Gaya, to the place where one of the most famous Bodhi Trees grows. As I arrived and walked around the huge courtyard, I began to cry. I suddenly felt so at home. I walked around the courtyard several times, observing all the strange sensations I was having.

I did not realize until later that this was the very place that the Indian prince, Siddhartha, vowed to sit under the Bodhi Tree until he became fully enlightened. The Bodhi Tree there now is said to be the nephew tree of the original Bodhi Tree that grew in that very place around 500 years B.C.

Each year thousands of monks, nuns, and people from all over the world come to visit this place. On any given day, you'll hear chanting and prayers, see incense billowing up to the sky, and most of all, see many people making wishes for world peace. It's one of the most magical and powerful places I've ever been to. Imagine feeling thousands of people's positive energy, prayers, and wishes for humanity. The good vibes in the air are palpable.

Why It's Special

The Bodhi Tree is a fig tree that is sacred to practitioners of Buddhism, Hinduism, and Jainism, since Bodhi means "awakening" or "enlightenment." The tree is native to India, Nepal, Burma, Sri Lanka, and southern China. The Bodhi Tree is a symbol for enlightened body, speech, and mind, and the leaves are shaped like a heart.

Not all of the *Ficus religiosa* trees are called "Bodhi" Trees. Bodhi is a special name reserved for those trees that belong to an unbroken lineage from the original *ficus* tree that sheltered the Indian prince who became known as the "Buddha," or awakened one. A branch of the original tree took root and grew in Sri Lanka in 288 B.C. and is now the oldest living tree in the world.[1]

Bodhi Trees are used in traditional Ayurvedic herbal medicine for many different physical imbalances: heart disorders such as a weak heart or heart palpitations; jaundice, diabetes, asthma, and epilepsy; and infectious, inflammatory, and sexual disorders. It is also considered an overall tonic for the body.

In addition to using the Bodhi Tree leaves as a tonic, there is a ritual for healing in which family members will water the Bodhi Tree each day for seven days in a row, making wishes for their sick relative to become well.

The leaves of this tree always move, even when there is no wind. Scientists say it is because of the long stalk and broad leaves, while spiritual followers believe that the tree is accompanied by Devas or beneficial spirits.[2]

What It Reveals

If you are attracted to the Bodhi Tree or its leaf, you may be wishing to express your love more deeply, or you may be yearning to fuel your spiritual connection. It may be time to carve out some extra time for meditation, prayer, or spiritual practice.

Whatever it is that connects you with the divine, whether it's a specific practice, creative expression, or spending time in nature, make time for more of that and be intentional about it. There may be gifts and treasures that are waiting to be discovered when you give that extra time to awakening your spiritual side.

Ask Yourself

How often do I feel a deep sense of unconditional love and what inspires that?

Are there any areas of my life where I don't feel safe or loved?

In what ways can I show others more patience, kindness, and tenderness?

What feels sacred to me? What inspires my spiritual connection? How can I trigger that on a daily basis?

What the Elixir Catalyzes

The Bodhi Tree elixir catalyzes an all-encompassing love that pacifies negative emotions. It helps us cut through fears and anxiety, as well as experience unwavering peacefulness, openheartedness, and tenderness. It magnifies patience and the ability to accept others as they are, forgiving and unconditionally loving them without wanting to change them.

Bodhi Tree calms aggression, anger, and violence and inspires kindness and gentleness. It awakens devotion and a deeper experience of spiritual connection. It helps us embrace life as it is, perceiving the sacredness woven into the fabric of everyday life.

Extra Credit

- Reflect on all the ways loved ones, family, friends, and total strangers have been kind to you in your lifetime.
- Make time each day for prayer, reflection, or gratitude practices.
- Create an altar or special space that inspires a sense of sacred or spiritual connection for you.
- Spend time under a tree or plant a tree.
- Give yourself permission to practice meditation 15 to 20 minutes each day for a week. Explore how it impacts your life.

In Essence

Dissolves	*Magnifies*
Feeling disconnected from your spiritual life	All-encompassing love and devotion
Feeling unsafe, fearing violence, or being violent	Patience and accepting others as they are
Negativity, aggression, obsession	Tenderness, openheartedness, softness, gentleness

How to Make Tree Leaf Skeletons

Making leaf skeletons is easy and fun—and creates a nice memento of any tree that you love. You can use them to decorate handmade greeting cards, wrapping paper, or bookmarks. Thicker or waxier leaves tend to work best, like Magnolia, Bodhi, Hong Kong Orchid, Maple, Mango, or Gardenia.

Place 1 cup of super washing soda (also called sodium carbonate) in a nonaluminum metal pot with 4 cups of water and a large handful of thick, waxy leaves. Important note: be sure to wear latex gloves, as the pH of the washing soda can irritate your skin, and take care not to splash it into your eyes.

Bring the mixture to a boil, then reduce to a simmer. Simmer for 90 to 120 minutes, then turn off the heat and remove the leaves with a spatula or slotted spoon. Transfer the leaves into a large bowl of cool water. You'll notice that the fleshy part of the leaves is no longer there, leaving only the skeleton. If there are still leafy parts hanging on to the skeleton, you can gently remove them with a toothbrush, holding one end of the leaf gently with your other hand or a pair of tweezers.

Dry each leaf between paper towels and place between books to keep them flat. You can paint the leaves or dye them different colors if you wish.

BRUGMANSIA

*Brugmansia **x** candida*

> **Activate:** Ease
>
> **Message:** Let go & let loose.

I was staying at my friend Kamal's place in Santa Monica, California. It was a cool night with the full moon glowing, and I walked outside into his garden. The first thing I saw was a tree with huge conical flowers hanging from the branches. I stood under the tree and looked up into the massive silvery blossoms. It was a "double" Brugmansia—inside each of the trumpet-shaped flowers were swirls of creamy white petals. The flower was otherworldly, and made me feel as if I had just entered some unknown paradise.

I found a low-hanging flower and gently placed my nose into the ruffly swirls, inhaling deeply. The fragrance was intoxicating and zingy, almost overwhelming in an electrifying way. It's a crisp but heady fragrance that makes you completely stop. You can't be thinking or talking about anything—all you can do is stop everything, stand still, close your eyes, and breathe deep. It's as if you're drinking light or inhaling moonlight; afterward you feel a little floaty.

I later realized that two close friends and one family member had that same tree right outside their front doors. I reflected about each of their personalities and what they had in common. All three of them work hard, are ultraresponsible, do what they say they're going to do, and are reluctant to put the responsibility of their projects into others' hands. You learn a lot about people by seeing what's in their garden and around their house, and you learn a lot about yourself by looking at your own garden. We're always attracted to those flowers whose healing benefits we most need, so we surround our homes and fill our gardens with flowers that not only heal us, but magnify our greatest qualities and potential.

Why It's Special

Also known as Angel's Trumpet, the luminescent Brugmansia flower is native to South America. More than endangered, this flower is listed as extinct in the wild and now grows only where cultivated.

The Brugmansia belongs to the poisonous nightshade family, along with potatoes, tomatoes, and belladonna, and all parts of the Brugmansia plant are poisonous. Some people call this flower Datura—it does, in fact, look similar—however, Datura's funnel-shaped flowers grow upward toward the moon, while Brugmansia's hang down from the tree like pendulums.

Brugmansia flowers can be found in white, apricot, yellow, red, and pink, in either single or double blooms. The fragrance is the strongest at night, and like many other night-blooming flowers, it is pollinated by moths.

Medicinally, it's used as a topical poultice for arthritis or infections, and as a general anti-inflammatory. The Kacha, or Urarina people in the Peruvian Amazon basin have used this plant in shamanic rituals. However, if you have no prior experience with this plant, do not experiment with it—it can be fatal. Just spending time around the Brugmansia in your garden or a friend's garden can enhance its qualities in you.

What It Reveals

If you're attracted to the Brugmansia flower, you likely work very hard. You don't like the thought of disappointing anyone. If you say you're going to do something, you follow through; you are responsible and reliable. You like helping people and you know how to get things done. You are flexible and patient with others.

When your sense of responsibility is taken to an extreme, however, it can lead you to overwork or worry about letting people down. You may feel anxious about taking a day off, calling in sick when you need it, or rescheduling plans. You enjoy life, but at times you may feel that your presence at work is vital, which can lead to sacrificing your self-care for work.

If, over a long period of time, you sacrifice your self-care, you run the risk of feeling hardened, resentful, bitter, or impatient. If you've had stressful situations occur in the recent past, you may find it difficult to show your soft and vulnerable side. The pattern of not asking for help can lead to overwhelm or injuries. In some situations, you may be forced to ask for help or to streamline your work load.

Ask Yourself

In what types of situations do I find myself being overly responsible, to my detriment?

Do I feel indispensable at work or worried about letting others down if I'm not present?

Is there a relationship between lack of "me time" and the impatience or stress that I experience?

When do I let life's challenges harden me instead of soften me?

When do I find it difficult to be vulnerable in front of others?

When in the past have I been the most successful at taking a challenging situation and transforming it into insights and personal strength?

What the Elixir Catalyzes

Brugmansia flower elixir is for those occasions when we find ourselves tending toward workaholism, or when we fear that if we're not involved in a certain project, something might go wrong. When we find we're letting challenging situations harden us, Brugmansia softens us into vulnerability and patience.

When we work long hours or bring work into our minds during our free time, it has the potential to disturb our sleep. Brugmansia dissolves anxiety and helps us let go and let loose, inspiring a deep experience of calm and, as a result, better sleep. It encourages us to problem-solve, find creative solutions, and delegate when necessary.

Extra Credit

- Ask for help.

- Put together a support system in areas where you tend to try to do everything on your own. If it's difficult to put together a support system, then it's even more important!

- Write down a list of the current challenges you are having, and what you are learning from them. Find their positive side.

- Take more self-care breaks. Identify what recharges you and schedule it into your day.

- Schedule in a short walk outdoors every day to unplug from work and appreciate nature.

- Get your hands in the dirt—put some flowers in pots, or plant some vegetables.

In Essence

Dissolves	*Magnifies*
Excessive seriousness and responsibility	Ability to ask for help and create a community of support
Feeling alone	Assimilation of change and growth
Allowing life's challenges to harden your heart	Ability to surrender to vulnerability
	Transforming reactivity into strength and power

CHOCOLATE DAISY

Berlandiera lyrata

Activate: Simplicity

Message: Cheer up.

Unlike the flowers that grow on cacao trees whose beans are used in making chocolate, this little Daisy does not lend itself to any chocolate production—except for its buttery, exotic chocolate scent.

My mother has a large patch of these sunny yellow daisies in her garden and the chocolaty aroma is divine. One summer I housesat for her while she was out of town and experimented with the Chocolate Daisies, making an enfleurage—an aromatic butter from soaking many days' worth of flowers in fat. Each morning I would pick the newly bloomed daisies and place them in coconut oil, after removing the old ones. After many days' worth of chocolate flowers, I was left with a rich, chocolaty serum that I gifted my mother upon her return.

Why It's Special

Chocolate Daisies are native to the southwestern U.S. and northern Mexico. They are an edible flower and if you pluck a stamen and put it in your mouth, you'll delight in the flavor of unsweetened chocolate.

The yellow daisies bloom during the night, releasing their chocolate aroma in the early morning. By late morning, the sunny-yellow petals fall off, leaving behind a beautiful green disc that contains the seeds.

Traditionally, Native Americans have used these flowers as an herbal remedy to soothe stomach upset, calm nervousness, and stimulate courage.[1]

What It Reveals

If you're attracted to the Chocolate Daisy, you may be yearning for simplicity. You likely have a current project that feels complicated or overwhelming, or you may have too many choices to make all at once. When things are overcomplicated, you end up feeling confused and tied in knots—unable to move or make clear decisions. When you do act, you may feel unsure or like you're wading in muddy waters.

When there are too many details, you may go round and round in your head, mentally chewing on the options and outcomes. When you overthink things, you tend to get more and more serious, which makes you mentally cramped and less open to unexpected creative solutions. If that's the case, it's time to simplify.

Ask Yourself

When I look at my office space and home space, where do I see clutter?

Where am I surrounded by items that don't reflect me?

What am I overthinking and overcomplicating? Do I have any
projects or relationships that are messy or complicated?

In what ways can I simplify my life?

What cheers me up?

What the Elixir Catalyzes

Chocolate Daisies untie mental knots and get us unstuck from the paralysis or confusion of overcomplication. They release tension from being entangled in messy situations or snagged in mental dilemmas.

Chocolate Daisies help us release doubts, apprehension, and hesitation, freeing up more space for joy and simplicity. Streamlining life keeps our focus on what's essential. Keeping things simple results in mental spaciousness that elicits spontaneity and joy.

Extra Credit

- Tidy up your space to help your mind feel clearer and sharper.
- Limit your daily to-dos to three main priorities.
- Make "Keep it simple" your new mantra.
- Catch yourself when you get stuck in the details.
- Limit your e-mails to five sentences or less.
- Read the book, *The Life-Changing Magic of Tidying Up,* by Marie Kondo.

In Essence

Dissolves

Feeling like things are muddled or messy

Tendency to overcomplicate things

Magnifies

Cheerfulness, lightheartedness

Simplicity, ease of doing things

Fun, laughter, energy

Scrumptious Chocolate Daisy Body Balm and Body Oil

Here is a recipe for a decadent Chocolate Daisy body balm and body oil to treat yourself with!

To make the body balm: Place a handful of Chocolate Daisy flowers facedown in solidified coconut oil. This will extract the chocolaty oils. Set aside for 24 hours.

Remove the flowers and replace with another handful of fresh flowers. Repeat numerous times until the flower balm has the desired intensity of scent.

To make the body oil: Heat coconut oil on low heat until it is liquefied. Fill a jar full of as many blossoms as you have. Pour the coconut oil over the flowers, submerging them with oil. Cover with cheesecloth and set aside for 24 hours.

Using a pair of chopsticks, remove the flowers and replace with new, fresh flowers. Repeat numerous times until the oil has the desired intensity of scent.

DANDELION

Taraxacum officinale

Activate: Relaxation

Message: Dissolve tension.

Dandelions grow all over the world and most people have positive childhood memories associated with them. Children everywhere delight in blowing the soft puffball of seeds into the wind while making wishes, "popping the heads off" the flowers with their thumbs, and rubbing them under their chins to see if their skin will turn yellow.

Dandelions are often called a "weed," which is typically a plant whose redeeming qualities are not yet understood. For example, in the U.S. it's common for people to put copious amounts of pesticides on their lawns to kill Dandelion flowers. Yet most "weeds"—and the dandelion is no exception—are valuable sources of food and medicine.

Why It's Special

Dandelion means "lion's tooth," and if you turn a Dandelion sideways and study it, you'll find that the jagged edges of the leaves look like lion's teeth. Historically in Europe, Dandelions were used extensively as a food source. All parts of the Dandelion plant are edible: the flowers, leaves, and roots. Dandelion flowers are also used to make a delicious wine. Leaves are used for making salads and green juices, and they are rich in vitamins and minerals.

In traditional Chinese medicine, it is said that having all five tastes in one's diet results in a long life. However, in modern cooking, the one flavor we taste very little of is the bitter flavor. This is a perfect example of Mother Nature providing an abundance of exactly what we need, as Dandelions—a great source of bitter—grow enthusiastically in many different environments around the world.

Dandelion tea made from boiling the roots in water or infusing the leaves is a rejuvenating nutritive tonic. It has a stimulating and beneficial effect on the liver, strengthens the kidneys, and clears the skin.[1]

What It Reveals

If you're visually attracted to the Dandelion flower you may be experiencing neck and shoulder tension or knots in your upper body. Alternatively, your body may be asking you to become more aware of how you store stress in your muscles, so that you can release it consciously and avoid more severe physical issues in the future. Tense muscles can lead to body alignment issues and poor posture.

Ask Yourself

When I'm stressed, where do I store tension in my body?

How many hours each day am I sitting at a desk or computer?

What physical areas of my body fall out of balance with stress?

What extra steps can I take to protect myself?

How often do I wear high heels?

What the Elixir Catalyzes

Dandelion flower elixir helps us identify how we store stress and tension in the body and allows us to release it. It's a powerful elixir for clearing static and accumulated stress from our muscles.

Especially effective for quickly releasing neck and shoulder tension, Dandelion elixir is one of the most valuable flower elixirs for massage therapists and bodyworkers. Used in mists and massage oils, it helps their clients relax more deeply. Massage therapists don't have to work so hard at massaging out the knots, as they quickly begin to dissolve on their own.

Extra Credit

- Get a massage.
- Take lessons in the Alexander technique and practice being "Neck free."
- Explore healing arts like Feldenkrais, Thai massage, and Myofascial Release techniques.
- Make yourself a cup of dandelion root tea. Add cinnamon and ginger to add sweet and spicy to the bitter.
- If you work at a computer every day, invest in a standing desk or an exercise ball to sit on for better posture. At the end of each day, lie on the ball, stretching your chest wide open.
- Make it a priority to do some stretching every few hours during the day to get your blood flowing and loosen up your muscles.
- Wear flat-soled shoes as much as possible to prevent muscular tension.

In Essence

Dissolves

Tension in the neck and shoulders

Emotional causes of physical tension

Mental tension

Magnifies

Awareness of causes of tension in the body

Joyful persistence

Mental freedom

DATE PALM FLOWER

Phoenix dactylifera

> **Activate:** Freedom from extremes
> **Message:** Shift the paradigm.

The first time I saw a Date Palm tree flowering, I remember thinking that the pollen could be collected for a face powder. The massive cluster of thousands of flowers was so thick with silky pollen, I felt a visceral sense of how rich and abundant we are on Mother Earth.

When I collected the Date Palm flower elixir, I tried to follow my usual protocol but it just wasn't working. I kept hitting walls and getting stuck. It was as if the plant was forcing me to break the mold and find a new way. So I sat still, opened myself up, let go of my usual ways of doing things, and just watched my breathing for a while. I let everything slip away and, in that moment, the floodgates opened. I got unstuck and felt expansive and creative. It was clear that this was one of the major aspects of the Date Palm flower—opening to a completely new, effortless, and unhurried way of doing things.

Why It's Special

Date Palms are over 50 million years old, so old that no one knows for sure when they originated. Date Palm trees now grow all over the world, up to 75 feet tall.[1]

Date Palm trees are dioecious, which means that some trees are female and some are male. The male tree has enormous clusters of flowers that do not produce fruit but are loaded with pollen. The wind blows the pollen from the male trees onto the female trees, resulting in pollination. When the female flowers are pollinated, they turn into the delectable sweet fruits we know as dates. If it weren't for the wind and its beautiful pollen-filled breezes, we would not have luscious dates to snack on.

What It Reveals

If you are drawn to the Date flower, you may be going to an extreme in your way of thinking in a particular area of your life, taking an approach that's either too rigid or too loose. Indications of being too rigid are: worrying too much about what others think, feeling overly responsible, feeling contracted or tense or holding back. Indications of the other extreme of "too loose" are: a lack of discipline and boundaries, such as enmeshment with others to the point of nonproductivity, or losing yourself by ignoring your own needs. This extreme can also manifest as living in the clouds or lacking a clear plan or structure.

These two extremes can play out in a variety of situations, such as work, love relationships, food/lifestyle habits, and belief systems. An example of too rigid would be a Western medical doctor who refuses to open his mind to any other healing modalities. On the other hand, too loose would be a person who constantly searches for higher states of being through drugs or esoteric practices, to the point of neglecting daily responsibilities.

In our own lives the extremes may not be as obvious as in the above examples, but we can observe when we are inflexible about something in a disproportionate way. For example, stressing about the way the dishes are organized in the dishwasher and believing there is only one "right" way to do it reflects a tendency toward too "tight." On the other hand, too "loose" can manifest itself when we have a habit of saying to ourselves, "That's good enough."

There is no perfect balance; we may find ourselves on opposite ends of the spectrum in different areas of our lives. The key is to be aware of when we tend toward an extreme. We can look at how we approach what's important to us in our lives and determine when and how we tend to go overboard in one direction. Whether it's concerning our love lives, relationship to food, daily habits, or simply how we approach a project, Date flower helps us find a middle ground.

Ask Yourself

In what areas of my life am I too rigid, too tight, or too hard on myself?

In what areas of my life am I unaware, undisciplined, sloppy, or careless?

What inspires me to do things differently or think outside the box?

In what ways could I tweak the way I do things so I move closer to a middle ground?

What the Elixir Catalyzes

Just as the Date Palm requires both male and female trees to procreate, its flower teaches us to find the balance between two poles. The fruits of our labor arise when there is a meeting in the middle. The Date Palm flower helps us find a middle ground between linear and nonlinear thinking, allowing us to approach life with childlike wonder while maintaining a sense of responsibility and purpose.

In relationships, Date flower enhances our desire to connect with others while maintaining a healthy understanding of our own needs. At work, it balances feeling overly responsible with lacking discipline or boundaries.

The Date flower helps us recognize the extreme of worrying too much about what others think. It also helps us acknowledge the opposite extreme of carelessness and lack of responsibility, discipline, and boundaries. The Date Palm flower helps us find the middle ground. We can feel carefree, while remaining aware. This sense of freedom, clarity, and spaciousness allows new ideas and ways of doing things to arise.

Extra Credit

- Notice when you go to extremes in any area of your life, being either overly responsible and tense about something, or careless and lackadaisical about your principles or actions. If you're feeling too tight, relax a little, let go of the tension, and practice being patient and open. This will help you break out of the mold, think outside the box, and find a new paradigm. If you're feeling too loose, get into action in some way. You'll gain momentum. Just keep reminding yourself why it's important to you.

- Too tight? Write your to-do lists and notes in colorful markers. Take classes in painting, sculpture, tai chi, or dance to help you get into your body, feel the space around you and open up different parts of your brain. When you're physically (and mentally) flexible, it will create spaciousness and effortlessness in your daily activities.

- Too loose? Use sharp, thin ballpoint pens to help your mind move toward precision. Adding more structure to your daily routines and activities may help you tighten up the direction you're going in life and be more sharply focused on what's truly important to you.

- Too tight? Take a meditation class, get a massage, sit and do absolutely nothing, or take a leisurely walk in nature.

- Too loose? Attend a boot camp at the gym, start an exercise program, or start volunteering to help someone out—an elderly neighbor, a child in your family, or the nonprofit of your choice.

- Take note of when you tend to care too much for others, ignoring your own needs, and brainstorm about what you can do to block out time for yourself. Or when you indulge to the point of being self-absorbed, practice a random act of kindness.

In Essence

Dissolves

Extremes: Overly responsible vs. undisciplined

Extremes: Self-absorbed vs. enmeshed

Extremes: Careless vs. caring too much

Magnifies

Freedom from extremes, neither too tight nor too loose

Moment-to-moment awareness, free of both worry and daydreaming

Balance between linear and nonlinear thinking

WRITE A FLOWER POEM

First, using stream of consciousness, write down the answers to these questions:

Write down the first flower that comes to your mind.

What color is it, and how does that color feel?

What are five words that describe the flower's personality?

Where would you like to see this flower?

What does this flower embody?

What message does the flower have for you?

What's about to happen?

Now give yourself 3 minutes to write a poem including your answers. It doesn't have to rhyme! Just write a little poem without thinking too much about it. This little creative exercise gets your right brain going, which can help you think creatively about anything in your life.

EUPHRASIA

Euphrasia nemorosa

Activate: Intuition

Message: Be decisive.

When I collected the Euphrasia flower in British Columbia, something strange happened. I don't typically hear flowers talking, but it felt like the flowers were talking to me. I kept hearing the different Euphrasia flowers saying, "Pick me, pick me!" as if they were in a cheerful, joyful scramble to be noticed. I had made the intention to find the flowers that humanity most needed today, and it was as if they were volunteering to be of service.

Sometimes we're presented with situations that we don't understand, yet there is a "knowingness," a sense that we know how to maneuver through the experience. It could be a near-death experience, giving birth to a child, or helping a loved one as they're dying. Sometimes we just know what to do. Euphrasia helps facilitate clear seeing and acting—without hesitation—from that "knowing" place inside us.

Why It's Special

Found in the Americas, Europe, and Asia, Euphrasia grows in alpine meadows where it snows in the wintertime. Also known as Eyebright, this plant is known for healing eye infections, and from a distance the flower looks like an eye with long eyelashes as petals. Herbalists make eye compresses and teas from Euphrasia for eye strain, redness, swelling, irritation, and infections. The tea infusion of the leaves, stems, and flowers can be used as an eyewash, as well as drunk internally to reduce inflammation around the eye. Poultices of Euphrasia can also be applied to wounds and to soothe irritated skin or acne.

What It Reveals

If you're attracted to Euphrasia you may be feeling indecisive lately. For example, you go to a restaurant and can't decide what to eat. You order something, and then wonder if you made the right decision. It can play out in any area of your life. In more serious situations, you could be doubting your parenting ability, or your competence in a new project. Or you may notice that when you make a decision, you second-guess yourself. Whatever it is, you may crave the ability to cut through hesitation and be more decisive.

Alternatively, you may have intuitive abilities that you'd like to develop. Perhaps you get hunches, but are reluctant to fully trust your intuition and go with what you "know."

Ask Yourself

When do I find myself in a state of self-doubt?

In what situations do I become indecisive?

When was the last time I totally trusted my intuition?
What was the outcome?

When do I find myself asking others what to do instead of trusting
my own abilities to figure it out?

What the Elixir Catalyzes

Euphrasia flower elixir helps us trust ourselves and cut through hesitation. It dissolves confusion, self-doubt, and insecurities about being "right" or looking like a fool. When "knowingness" arises, we don't question it.

Euphrasia heightens awareness, making us better listeners; we pick up on more than what is being said. It facilitates effortless knowing and can also enhance psychic or intuitive abilities.

Extra Credit

- To enhance your awareness, give yourself 15 to 20 minutes each morning to sit quietly. Focus on how each inhale and exhale feels in your body. When your mind wanders, bring your attention back to your breathing.

- Take short breaks throughout the day, allowing space for things to come to mind.

- Practice listening to your body's cues. For example, if you have a decision to make, bring it to mind and notice how your body feels. Is there more tension or more freedom in the cells of your body? Is there resistance or expansion?

- Try this exercise: Think of a decision you have to make. For each option in the potential decision, without thinking about it, give it a number on a scale from 1 to 10. Just ask yourself, 1 to 10, what is the number? And whatever number comes to mind first, stick with that. Notice how you feel about the outcome—if it feels right.

- As you're making a decision, notice whether or not there is a lot of mental rumination about it. If you're indecisive about something, with lots of thoughts about it this way and that way, it's likely a "no," "not now," or not worth your time. If there is no mental back-and-forth and your mind is clear, then it's a "yes."

In Essence

Dissolves	*Magnifies*
Self-doubt	Intuition
Indecision	Trust in yourself
Hesitation	Decisiveness

FIRE STAR ORCHID

Epidendrum radicans

Activate: Wild creativity

Message: Think outside the box.

One day I was walking through a flower-filled neighborhood in Santa Monica and came across Epidendrum orchids. I was so excited I knocked on the door of the house. The owner's name was Ratna, and he had some unique and interesting flowers growing in his garden. Ratna was from Sri Lanka; his name means "jewel" in Singhalese.

Ratna and his wife invited me into their home for Singhalese tea and biscuits. I explained what I did, and they graciously allowed me to collect flower elixirs from their orchid garden.

Why It's Special

Most orchids grow purely on air, fastening themselves to a tree. Epidendrums are unique in that they can grow anywhere: on air, in a garden, and even on rocks at high altitude. Over 900 species of Epidendrum grow in the wild on trees from the Carolinas in the U.S. to Argentina. You can find them in jungles, cloud forests, and woodlands, as well as in outdoor pots in Southern California.

Epidendrums are not expensive and they're called the friendship orchid, because baby shoots called keikis—which means baby in Hawaiian—grow out of the mother stalk.[1] When the baby shoots fall off in your hand, they can be planted in their own pots and will bloom within a year. Epidendrum growers share baby offshoots and spread the orchid-growing love.

Of all the orchids, Epidendrums are among the easiest to grow. They tend to be much more forgiving than the average orchid that has more specific needs. Though not typically described as a pioneer species, Epidendrums come to the rescue and grow like crazy in areas of disturbed land.

What It Reveals

If you're attracted to the Fire Star Orchid, you are likely a person who values being on the cutting edge, and you are often ahead of the curve. You tend toward being a rule breaker and a trendsetter. You bring a fresh perspective to the table and seek out innovative ways of doing things. At times, however, you may be shy or timid about going out on a limb and sharing your ideas, because you know they will break cultural norms or established ways of doing things.

You may currently find yourself in a situation in which you are yearning to do things in a different way. You may find it difficult to trust your ideas or sustain the boldness to share them with others and make them happen.

Ask Yourself

When do I notice myself holding back ideas because they seem a little "out there"?

What are some of the most "out of the box"ideas that I've had?

How can I embrace and nourish my fearless creativity even more?

What role models do I have of people who push the envelope, set trends,
or jump on innovations?

What the Elixir Catalyzes

Thought leaders tend to face a certain amount of pushback or criticism in response to their innovative ideas or concepts. Sometimes people around them feel threatened or thrown off kilter by solutions that deviate so much from the norm.

Fire Star Orchid elixir supports us in fearlessly expressing our creative ideas, making suggestions when the timing is right and standing behind them. It gives us a solid foundation of courage. It allows us to think creatively and follow the beat of a different drummer with the intention to create a better world. Fire Star Orchid helps us be more open to sharing ideas in groups that may or may not be supportive.

Extra Credit

- Block out time for creativity each week—work on creative projects purely for fun. Maybe it's a painting class or getting your hands in the clay on the pottery wheel. Learn how to make jewelry, homemade ice cream, or Thai cuisine—whatever suits your fancy—but make sure it's purely for enjoyment! Strengthen your creative juices, which will spill out into other areas of your life.

- Spend time around people who are early adopters, who will be most supportive of your inventive style.

- Start a weekly meetup of creatives, entrepreneurs, and thought leaders, and share ideas over coffee or a meal.

- What are the top three things you love? Start a blog and write, video, photograph, or teach about those three passions.

- Buy an Epidendrum orchid; put it on your desk. Make sure it gets several hours of sun each day and water weekly.

In Essence

Dissolves	*Magnifies*
Fear of what others will think of your ideas	Fearless creativity
Being hard on yourself for being different or thinking differently	Innovation, ingenuity, and ability to brainstorm
Hesitation, holding back, or squelching creativity	Allowing yourself to see beyond what you've seen thus far

PLAYING WITH PETALS:
HOW TO MAKE A FLOWER MANDALA

Whether your intention is to make a flower offering to the divine, for the enjoyment of strangers walking by, or simply to get out in to nature to play with botanicals and get your creative juices flowing, making flower mandalas is a peaceful activity that pulls us into the present moment. By paying attention to what we see around us and recognizing and arranging the treasures we find, we naturally attain one-pointed focus that shuts off the monkey mind. It's a playful, quiet, joyous activity that anyone of any age can get into.

My favorite way to make a flower mandala is to go for a walk and see what flowers speak to me. You can also use sticks, driftwood, pinecones, leaves, stones, shells, or berries if you don't have access to flowers. What catches your eye? What intrigues you? What shapes are interesting or beautiful?

Don't worry about what your mandala will look like or try to pre-create it in your head. Just enjoy yourself on your nature walk, and gather interesting materials from a nature setting nearest to you—the forest, beach, mountains, your garden, yard, or the local park.

When you're happy with your materials and you feel complete, choose a background. You can use a sandy beach, a picnic table, a sidewalk, a pretty table, or even a piece of poster board or foam core.

Choose a center point and build outward from the center. Flower mandalas can be round, square, octagonal, star-shaped, spiral—whatever suits your fancy.

Another simple but elegant way to make a flower mandala is to disassemble an entire flower by removing all of the petals and then reconstruct it in a mandala shape by placing the petals around the center.

When your mandala is complete, take a snapshot and post to Instagram with the #flowerevolution hashtag.

You can sprinkle the treasures back where they came from to compost them or leave the mandala out for other passersby to enjoy. Use free smartphone apps like Stop Motion Studio to make a stop-motion clip of your flower mandala in progress.

FIREWEED

Chamerion angustifolium

Activate: Recovery

Message: Forgive someone now.

Fireweed is a special flower that heals environments, animals, and people after traumatic or disruptive situations. If we were to build a new freeway through the state of Colorado, for example, we'd find Wild Fireweed bursting up around the edges of the freeway to help the environment adjust to the disturbance.

The first time I saw Fireweed, I came across it outside of Whistler near a bike trail that had been forged through the forest. It's a beautiful flower with bright pink and magenta flowers that look like a heart or a butterfly. In its essence, Fireweed is exactly that: transformation of the heart.

Why It's Special

The Fireweed flower got its name because it is the first plant to grow abundantly in areas struck by forest fire. Plants like this are called "pioneer species" because they grow in land that has been disturbed. After trees regrow to shade the area, the Fireweed no longer gets enough sun, but its seeds stay in the ground. When another forest fire passes through, the seeds germinate and the Fireweed flower grows and blooms once again.

Long ago this plant was considered rare in the U.S.; it became common, however, during the expansion of the railroad, which disturbed the soil and disrupted ecosystems. Fireweed is also called "bombweed"; during World War II, it spread quickly and blossomed in the bomb craters.[1] Fireweed benefits all life in environments affected by trauma, including plants, animals, and people.

The fleshy part inside the young stems of the Fireweed is delicious, and the Fireweed leaves can be made into an infusion rich in vitamins A and C. Bees adore Fireweed flowers and produce a liquid gold Fireweed honey.[2]

What It Reveals

If you're attracted to the Fireweed flower, you may have a heartache, painful experience, or trauma that is affecting you, either from a recent experience or from long ago. Most of us have lived through painful experiences at one time or another, and it can even refer to experiences as far back as childhood, infancy, or gestation. There may be a heartbreak that you're not even aware of operating in your subconscious, still running in the background and affecting how you operate in your daily life.

If you can currently identify a specific heartbreak, this may be a good time to work on self-nurturing and forgiveness, freeing the heart of pain and hurt. If it's too difficult to forgive someone else, start by forgiving yourself and making wishes to forgive the other person in the future. Even just having an aspiration for forgiveness is the first step.

Ask Yourself

When has my heart been broken?

When have I been emotionally attacked?

When the thought of forgiving someone arises, who comes to mind?

What things could I forgive myself for?

In what situations do I feel "attacked" energetically or verbally?

What the Elixir Catalyzes

Fireweed flower heals the heart. It transforms painful experiences by dissolving the emotion around them, leaving only the lessons learned. When we have traumatic experiences, they live in the cellular memory of our bodies. The Fireweed flower elixir releases the emotional intensity from old memories of heartbreak and suffering so that we are no longer triggered by current situations that may appear to be similar.

Fireweed enhances our ability to navigate painful situations with strength and grace. It strengthens our capacity to love and forgive ourselves and others.

Extra Credit

- Practice forgiveness in small ways, with the person who cuts you off on the freeway or a colleague who disappoints you.

- List the most painful experiences you've had in life and see if there is any residual emotion still present. Being aware of it is the first step.

- Spend more time with people who love and adore you, and in places where you feel totally safe.

- Grab your notebook and finish this statement: I forgive myself for . . .

- Nourish yourself with self-care—get a massage, take a bath, or do something nice for yourself.

In Essence

Dissolves

Heartbreak, emotional attacks

Fatigue

Magnifies

Feeling that love is all around

Forgiveness

GARDENIA

Gardenia jasminoides

Activate: Shift in perception

Message: Transform your weaknesses into strengths.

I fell in love with the Gardenia after planting one in the front yard. It was such a beautiful dark green leafy plant, and the blossoms were large, heavily fragrant, and luminous in the moonlight. The scent is intoxicating; Gardenia can be infused into a sensuous body oil and its petals can be candied and eaten in desserts.

Why It's Special

The Gardenia belongs to the coffee family, and is native to China and Japan. According to Traditional Chinese Medicine, Gardenia is an herbal remedy for yin deficiency indicated by irritability, restlessness, and difficulty sleeping.[1]

Aromatically speaking, the essential oil of Gardenia is extremely rare. I've only ever seen one authentic distillation of Gardenia petals, and one ounce cost $3,000! Any "Gardenia" fragrance in a store is an artificial fragrance, unless it was specifically made by hand through the botanical perfumery method called enfleurage (soaked in oil or fat), in which case it will likely cost around $500 for an ounce of the diluted oil. A more economical way to capture the fragrance of Gardenias is to grow them and wear them in your hair, or infuse them into an oil for your body, face, or scalp. Historically, French noblemen wore Gardenias as boutonnieres.

Gardenia has a Polynesian sister called *Gardenia taitensis*, which looks like a small white star. It's used for leis in Hawaii and infused in coconut oil for use as a perfumed body oil in Tahiti.

What It Reveals

If you're attracted to the Gardenia flower, there may be an aspect of yourself that you are avoiding. Though all of us have a shadow side, you might be running away from it or preferring not to look at it. You may feel there's something about your character that is not beautiful or not impeccable, something that's too messy, embarrassing, or painful to look at.

What we perceive as weaknesses are often the source of our greatest strengths, and Gardenia is inspiring you to move past those fears and see the beauty of your shadow side.

Ask Yourself

Is there an aspect of myself that I don't like?

What do I consider to be my "shadow" side?

What are my weaknesses?

What do I love most about myself?

What the Elixir Catalyzes

Gardenia elixir helps us look directly at what we perceive as our weaknesses. It enhances our ability to acknowledge our "shadow" side, catalyzing a process of transformation. It helps us gain a deeper understanding of ourselves and what we perceive as negative character traits.

When there's an aspect that we're afraid to look at, we don't feel whole or wholly accepting of ourselves; there's a part that we reject. Just as there's strength in vulnerability, Gardenia helps us see how all aspects of ourselves are human and beautiful.

Exrtra Credit

- Reflect on the biggest challenges you've had in your life and how you got through them.

- Write down what you love most about yourself.

- List on paper what you consider to be your weaknesses. If you were able to transform them into the source of your greatest strengths, what would that look like?

- Find Gardenias that have not been sprayed (florist shop flowers are usually sprayed) and make candied Gardenia petals (see page 204). Remove all the petals and, using a brush, paint them with egg whites that you've whipped with a fork. Sprinkle powdered sugar or evaporated cane juice on the petals.

- Make your own Gardenia-infused body oil. Here's how: Fill a jar with a relatively odorless carrier oil, such as jojoba. Place a fresh Gardenia flower in the oil for 24 hours, covering the top of the jar with cheesecloth. During these 24 hours, the essential oils from the flower will infuse into the oil. Remove the first Gardenia, add another fresh one to the oil, and repeat. Infuse the oil with as many Gardenia flowers as you like, until the oil has the desired scent intensity.*

In Essence

Dissolves

Fear of your "shadow" side

Avoidance of your perceived weaknesses

Judging as negative particular aspects of your personality

Magnifies

Seeing your "shadow" side in a positive light

Transforming your perceived weaknesses into strengths

Embracing all aspects of yourself as beautiful

---

*   This can also be done with Jasmine, Rose, and Chocolate Daisies.

DECADENT CRYSTALLIZED GARDENIA PETALS

If you love Gardenia flowers, you will adore this sweet treat! Imagine snacking on pieces of crystallized Gardenia petals. They're fun to make and absolutely decadent.*

**Important: Only use organic flowers or flowers from a garden. Gardenias from a florist will likely have been sprayed with toxic chemicals and pesticides.

1 egg white
2 tablespoons water
1 handful Gardenia flower petals**
1 teaspoon organic cane sugar

Use a fork to mix the egg white and water in a bowl. Using a small paintbrush or pastry brush, paint each of the petals with the mixture on both sides. Sprinkle sugar on both sides of the petals and let dry for a couple hours.

Eat the crystallized petals like a snack or decorate cakes or special treats. Petals will keep in an airtight container for several days.

---

*   Other sweet florals like Roses, Violets, Pansies, and Johnny-Jump-Ups also work well.

GIANT SPIDER LILY

Crinum asiaticum

Activate: Lightheartedness & lightness

Message: Free your mind.

Every time I see this flower during my travels—usually in jungle-style ornamental gardens—I run toward it. It's one of my favorite scents—a powdery, sweet floral aroma that can rival the most fragrant flowers in a tropical garden. Too bad it's a poisonous plant, otherwise we might just rank this flower's scent right up there with Jasmine.

When I was granted permission to collect flower elixirs at the Naples Botanical Garden in Florida, it was the perfect time to make the Spider Lily elixir. It was a balmy day, and the Spider Lily was shining like a beacon of light.

Why It's Special

The Giant Spider Lily is native to Southeast Asia and grows in wet environments, near lakes, seashores, swamps, or wetlands. It grows in umbrels: each of the six petals of this flower spills downward from the center in the shape of an umbrella, ranging in color from luminous white to deep purple.

As a poisonous flower, the Spider Lily cannot be used for cooking or making an essential oil, but it has tremendous medicinal value. In Indonesia and Malaysia, it's called "Bakong," or poisonous bulb plant, and its leaves and bulb are used for making various herbal medicines. The bulb is crushed and made into an ointment or poultice for rheumatoid arthritis, fevers, and headaches. The succulent leaves are used for sprains, earaches, fractures, swelling, and inflammation. Fresh, bruised leaves serve as an insect repellant, and dried leaves boiled in water make a remedy for hemorrhoids.

In India, the juice of the bulb is used as a substitute for ipecac, to induce vomiting in cases of accidental poisoning. In Australia, Aborigines warm the juice of the bulb to clean and disinfect wounds. Many clinical studies now prove the wondrous anti-inflammatory effects of this plant, in alignment with how the remedies have been used in folk medicine for centuries.[1] However, unless you're very familiar with the plant, it's best to consult with experienced herbalists who have used it successfully.

What It Reveals

If you're attracted to the Spider Lily, you may be craving a sense of freedom, weightlessness, and effortlessness. There may be an area of your life that feels heavy or stagnant, like you're trudging through the mud. You may feel weighed down or dragging, not up for the task at hand. You are likely yearning for lightness, like the natural joy and exhilaration that arise when you jump on a trampoline.

It's also possible that you simply need more air element. You may be imbalanced and have too much Kapha, or Earth/Water element, according to Ayurveda. A Kapha imbalance is caused by eating excess amounts of dairy and white sugar, or living in damp, moist environments. When there's an excess of Earth and Water element in the body, incorporating activities that stimulate or activate the body can create a sense of spaciousness and lightness.

Ask Yourself

Is there anything in my life that is tying me down?

What is weighing on my mind?

In what areas of my life do I feel totally free?

When in my daily life do I feel heavy or stagnant?

What the Elixir Catalyzes

The greatest attribute of the Spider Lily flower elixir is light. It shines light into our blind spots, illuminating areas of our life that are stagnant or in need of fresh energy. It also helps us feel "light," as in light as a feather, weightless, and carefree. When we experience heaviness or feel burdened, it helps us feel light, unfettered, and free.

When life feels arduous and laborious, Spider Lily inspires us to streamline and share our gifts with the world in a simple way. It helps us to look at our lives and projects as a joyful celebration.

Extra Credit

- Make a list of the things you do that make you feel free. Do more of that.
- Jump on a trampoline or rebounder and feel the sense of weightlessness.
- Go swimming and pay attention to how your joints feel underwater.
- Take a photo of yourself jumping in midair and post it in a place you'll see it every day.
- Get a vigorous body scrub and massage to stimulate your circulation.
- For the next week, eliminate white sugar and white flour. See how you feel.

In Essence

Dissolves	*Magnifies*
Feeling heavy or burdened	Feeling light, buoyant, and streamlined
Getting stuck	Effortlessness and simplicity
Worrying so much we stagnate projects	Joy, celebration, ease

GREVILLEA

Grevillea

Activate: Fearless speech

Message: Speak your mind.

I was tickled with delight when I saw Grevillea for the first time in a garden north of San Francisco. The little flowers looked like red snails to me—and they looked like they were giving me the middle finger!

I later saw them in the beautiful Bay Area nursery, Flora Grubb, and was finally able to identify them with their proper name, instead of calling them "red snail flower." I have since found many beautiful versions of this flower, in different colors and varieties, on Australian Instagram profiles.

Why It's Special

Grevillea is native to Australia, Indonesia, New Guinea, and New Caledonia—areas that have both rain forests and wide open habitats. In the U.S. I've seen Grevillea growing in both Northern and Southern California.

Australian Aborigines traditionally loved this plant because the flower is filled with sweet nectar that can be shaken out into one's mouth or hands; the nectar was mixed with water to make a sweet drink. Grevillea flowers are still known as "bush lollies," or lollipops of the wild bush, in Australia. As fun as it sounds, nowadays it's not recommended to drink the nectar directly from the flowers, as some of the cultivars contain toxins.[1]

What It Reveals

If you're attracted to the Grevillea flower, you may have a tendency to hold back your words for fear of hurting someone's feelings. You may have clear insights that don't get expressed for fear of appearing too brash or direct.

In most cases, this kind of hesitation or repression of speech keeps situations stagnant and prevents learning. To constantly hold back in an effort to appear "nice" or be politically correct can keep relationships stuck on a level that lacks compassionate honesty.

Alternatively, there may be a situation in your life in which you are experiencing dread, anger, aversion, or even disgust. You may be unable to voice how you really feel or get to the bottom of why you feel that way.

Ask Yourself

In what situations do I find myself holding back from speaking?

Who am I most able to speak freely with?

When have I experienced that being direct deepens a relationship?

What topics do I find myself suppressing?

What the Elixir Catalyzes

Red snail flower, the name I had given Grevillea, fits the action of the flower, as it helps us come out of our shell and express ourselves, without fear of how someone else will feel about it.

Grevillea gives us the courage to speak up and say directly things that we would usually hold back. It eradicates the habit of hesitation, and we find ourselves with the ability to deliver a clear message and shoot straight from the hip.

Fear of losing a relationship as a result of something we say is eliminated with Grevillea, and we're able to speak calmly and honestly. In turn, people around us respond well to our frankness. It helps us understand difficult situations quickly and not obsess about the details.

When we're able to freely communicate and express our truth without fear of hurting another person's feelings, we can cut to the chase, evolving our relationships faster, and feeling more authentic in everyday interactions.

Once we learn to be direct and honest in our communications, people trust us more. Oftentimes, they actually don't respond in the negative way we imagine they will; our sheer transparency is refreshing and creates more elasticity and spaciousness in our exchanges with them.

Extra Credit

- Spend time around people who speak their minds freely. Avoid relationships in which you cannot speak your mind.
- Ask for constructive criticism or feedback, and give others opportunities to speak freely with you.
- Spend time around children and the elderly, who often have fewer "filters" on their speech.
- Make a list of the things you're typically afraid to say.
- Put more emphasis on being direct and honest.

In Essence

Dissolves	*Magnifies*
Fears around speaking your truth	Fearless speech
Suppression of anger and frustration	Coming out of your shell
Apathy, dread, resistance, aversion, disgust	Expression that enhances engaging with others

HOLLYHOCK

Alcea rosea

Activate: Softness of character
Message: Soft is transformative.

Hollyhocks are one of the most abundant flowers I know. I love to grow them, harvest the seeds, and share them with friends. After the blossoms wilt and die, the seeds emerge in perfect bundles stacked in a circular doughnut-shaped pod. The seeds are hardy and can be mailed to a friend or given away to spread the Hollyhock love. Hollyhocks grow tall, so they're best planted along a wall or near bushes where they'll accent your garden space with vertical rows of flowers.

Why It's Special

The Hollyhock is native to southwestern China. When it was brought to Europe in the 1400s, an herbalist called the flower "holyoke," which led to its name in English today. Hollyhocks come in all the colors of the warm spectrum, including magenta, red, orange, yellow, and even dark maroon to black.

They belong to the Mallow family, in which every plant has leaves that are soft and fuzzy and all parts of the plant are edible. Hollyhock is used in traditional herbal medicine as an emollient, softening and smoothing the skin. The flowers can be used to make teas, facial steams, and washes, and the leaves can be used as poultices. They are also slightly mucilaginous, soothing ulcers, sore throats, and bleeding gums. Hollyhocks are anti-inflammatory, reducing inflammation in the tissues of the body, including the skin.[1]

What It Reveals

If you're attracted to the Hollyhock flower you may have a relationship that is challenging you. You may have felt irritated lately, or powerless to improve the relationship, or worried about being betrayed and left behind. Or you may feel that gentleness, openness, and bonding are absent from the relationship in question.

If you don't have a relationship that's bothering you, you may have another area in your life in which you feel hopeless. You may be telling yourself "There's nothing I can do about it." Perhaps your heart has hardened, since you believe there's nothing you can do to change the situation.

Ask Yourself

Am I irritated lately and if so, why? Is my skin irritated?

Where in my close relationships do I become the opposite of "soft"?

When do I most often find myself in service to others?

Which of my relationships could benefit most from the
transformative power of gentleness?

What the Elixir Catalyzes

Hollyhock flower elixir helps us recognize that we have the power to transform our relationships through gentleness. Instead of being irritable and on the defensive, or creating power struggles, we could be softer in character.

In our relationships, whether with a lover, partner, child, parent, friend, or colleague, Hollyhock helps us be more understanding. It enhances our ability to build and deepen relationships through caring and sharing.

In situations where there is a fear of betrayal, Hollyhock dissolves helpless or hopeless feelings and enhances confidence in ourselves. It also magnifies trust and unconditional love for others.

Extra Credit

- In your relationships, ask more questions and really listen to the answers.
- Notice the deeper motivations of your loved ones, what makes them tick; learn why they are how they are.
- Write down the names of those with whom you have the closest relationships, and next to each write what means the most to that person. If you get stuck, ask.
- Perform a random act of kindness for any loved one with whom you have a difficult relationship.
- Sometimes irritation manifests in your body as irritated or inflamed skin. Take a bath in Hollyhock blossoms.

In Essence

Dissolves	*Magnifies*
Worry about love relationships	Fearless love, compassion, soft heart
Helplessness and hopelessness	Service and caring for others
Skin irritations due to emotional irritability	Abundance in relationships with loved ones

HOLLYHOCK FACIAL STEAM, MASK & BODY WRAP

If you have Hollyhocks in your garden, you can use the flowers and leaves for a facial steam and mask. Collect a handful of flowers for the steam and a handful of leaves for the mask.

Hollyhock Flower Facial Steam
Rinse the Hollyhock flowers and toss them into a large bowl. Boil purified water and pour into the bowl over the top of the flowers. Place a large towel over your face, and gently lower your face over the bowl, taking care to be far enough away from the hot steam that it doesn't burn your skin. The warm steam will open up your pores and leave you feeling refreshed.

Hollyhock Mask & Poultice
If you have oily skin: Blend a handful of Hollyhock leaves with a spoonful of warm water in a blender. Apply directly to your face like a mask.

If you have dry skin: Blend a handful of Hollyhock leaves with a spoonful of oil in a blender. Apply directly to your face like a mask.

Hollyhock Body Wrap
Add water to a large sauce pan. Place a steamer basket or a strainer on top. Bring the water to a boil. When the water is boiling and steam is rising, add a handful of Hollyhock leaves and steam until they are soft and tender. Place the leaves on your body, wrapping any areas where there is irritated or inflamed skin.

HONG KONG ORCHID

Bauhinia blakeana

Activate: Self-acceptance

Message: Express yourself.

The first time I saw the Hong Kong Orchid, I was drawn in by the expressive outward curves of the magenta and red petals, with stamens that seemed to reach out as if wanting to touch someone. The petals reminded me of someone's arched back, their chest and heart opening up to expose their soft inner essence.

Definitely a sensuous-looking flower, the Hong Kong Orchid grows on a tree. The crimson blossoms spread across the entirety of the tree, with leaves that are just as beautiful as the flowers, appearing as rounded hearts or butterflies. When the flowers fall off the tree, they become a carpet of rich red and pink petals.

Why It's Special

A tree flower rather than a real orchid, the Hong Kong Orchid is the national flower of Hong Kong. A hybrid between *Bauhinia purpurea* and *Bauhinia variegata*, it was originally found on the island of Hong Kong and then brought to the Hong Kong Botanical Gardens, from which all other Bauhinia blakeana trees in the world came.

The flowering tree is sterile, and does not produce seeds or fruit. The only way to propagate the tree is to cultivate it through grafting. The buds, leaves, and flowers are exquisite, as if seducing us to help them procreate.

What It Reveals

If you're attracted to Hong Kong Orchid, you likely have high standards. They may make you hard on yourself, or reluctant to be exposed to the world in a way that would make you vulnerable.

If you fear vulnerability, it can lead to feeling hardened, shy, or aloof. It can also manifest as a habit of preventing yourself from forming new friendships or relationships.

You may be secretly wanting to express yourself in new ways, such as speaking, dancing, singing, or artistic endeavors. You may want to accept all aspects of yourself, especially those that have previously been in hiding.

Ask Yourself

When do I find myself holding back? When am I tentative,
afraid of being seen, heard, or exposed?

When am I hard on myself?

What parts of myself do I find myself rejecting?

When do I feel the most beautiful?

What the Elixir Catalyzes

The Hong Kong Orchid flower elixir encourages us to fully accept and love all parts of ourselves. It enhances our ability to express ourselves fully, without hesitation or editing. It coaxes the sincerest aspects of our personality out of hiding and entices us to stretch wide open and expose our hearts. It encourages us to reach outside of our protective shell and expose what's on the inside.

Hong Kong Orchid shows us that being vulnerable enhances our ability to love and be loved, and enriches our experience of the world. If we are usually hard on ourselves, it allows us to be kinder toward ourselves. That loving energy is attractive to others and draws them in, strengthening our magnetic qualities.

Hong Kong Orchid dissolves our fears of being "exposed" as we truly are. It dissolves fear of being seen or heard, including fear of public speaking, being on display, or being observed by others. It shows us that vulnerability can be lovely and even sexy. Embracing all parts of ourselves heals us and everyone we come into contact with. Loving ourselves helps other people around us to feel loved, and gives them permission to love themselves.

Hong Kong Orchid helps us feel comfortable in our own skin, and at ease with the deepest essence of who we are. As we learn to appreciate all aspects of who we are, it allows us to embrace our sensuous side, while embodying a sense of innocence and purity.

Extra Credit

- Practice being vulnerable and out of your comfort zone.
- Tell or show your loved ones how much you love them.
- Put on a little lipstick, wear silk, or dress to the nines just because.
- Go dancing, or crank up the music and dance in your living room.
- Buy some paper and paints and express yourself through color.

In Essence

Dissolves	*Magnifies*
Fear of being "exposed"	Full expression of who you are
Holding back aspects of yourself	Feeling comfortable with yourself
Being hard on yourself	Self-love and appreciation

JADE SUCCULENT

Crassula ovata

Activate: Presence

Message: Go for it!

Beautiful Jade houseplants are common, but never in my life had I seen one bloom until I discovered it in a garden in Los Angeles! The luscious green succulent leaves were tinged bright orange from the sun and the flowers looked like exploding pinkish-white stars. In Hollywood, where everyone is a star, it's a fitting flower.

Why It's Special

The Jade plant, also known as the friendship tree, money tree, or lucky tree, is native to South Africa.[1] The Jade Succulent propagates easily from cuttings; when a branch or leaf falls off the plant, roots will grow right out of the leaves, reaching into the dirt only several weeks later. The Jade plant is easily trained into a bonsai, and it is often the first plant bonsai novices work with.

What It Reveals

If you're attracted to the Jade Succulent flower, there is something inside you that wants to come out. You may be shy, withholding information, or hesitating about bringing forward a talent. You may have a business idea or a secret hobby that no one knows about.

At times you may feel invisible, as if in a room full of people no one sees you. You may wish to have a greater impact, yet feel wary of being the center of attention. You might feel unsure about whether you have what it takes to execute your ideas.

Alternatively, you may be feeling fatigued, weak, or generally low in vitality.

Ask Yourself

Have I been feeling tired lately?

What do I find myself wishing to share with others?
When do I hesitate?

In what situations have I felt invisible?

What is inside me that wants to expand
and be expressed?

What the Elixir Catalyzes

Just as the plant propagates quickly and easily, Jade Succulent gives us a flood of energy and vitality. It recharges our chi and enhances our poise, so that when we walk into a room, we make a strong impression on others with our mere presence.

Jade Succulent flower also brings whatever we are shy about to the surface. If there's something inside us wishing to be recognized and acted upon, Jade Succulent eliminates hesitation and infuses us with a refreshing intensity. It wakes up the stamina and strength necessary to act on our inclinations, along with clarity about where to start. It cuts through our apathy and stimulates a sense of urgency.

Extra Credit

- Take regular tai chi classes to build up your chi.
- Visit a Chinese Medicine Doctor and seek out an herbal formula that builds up your wei chi, or energetic force field.
- Get clear about what you want. Write it down, and be specific.
- Wear the color red to stimulate blood flow and energy. From an outside perspective it's also a power color.
- Practice the art of nonconformity. If you feel like wearing sequins, emerald-green shoes, or a crazy hat with peacock feathers, do it. Explore different aspects of yourself and your preferences.

In Essence

Dissolves

Feeling invisible

Ambivalence about what you want

Hesitation and shyness

Magnifies

Vitality, presence, strength

Clarity about what you want

Expansion of chi energy

JASMINE

Jasminum sambac

Activate: Self-appreciation

Message: You are beautiful.

One of my all-time favorite flowers is the Sambac variety of the Night-Blooming Jasmine. The flowers open in the evening and bloom all night, reflecting the light of the moon. Walking by the plant at night, you're enveloped in a heady cloud of beautiful floral scent that fills up every pore of your being with moonlight magic.

For over a decade, I've cultivated Jasmine plants at my office and at home. One of my favorite things to do in the summer is to gather Jasmine flowers and use them in recipes, smoothies, and teas, or just put a couple of blossoms on my desk to enjoy the smell. The scent of a fresh Jasmine flower is intoxicating!

Why It's Special

Though the night-blooming Sambac variety of Jasmine is commonly known as Arabian Jasmine, it doesn't originate from the Middle East. Instead it is native to Bhutan, India, and parts of Southeast Asia.

Highly fragrant, Jasmine is considered sacred in Indonesia, and is strung into garlands for the bride's hair in wedding ceremonies. In Hawaii, the flowers are woven into leis, and in Thailand, Cambodia, and Sri Lanka, Jasmine garlands are offered in Buddhist temples. In the Philippines, Jasmine garlands are used on altars or to honor special guests.

Because Jasmine is both an edible flower and exquisitely fragrant, it's used for both perfumery and food and beverages. In China, the flowers are used to make Jasmine tea, and Jasmine ice cream is common in the Philippines. All over the world, Jasmine is distilled to obtain the essential oil commonly used in botanical perfumery and aromatherapy.

What It Reveals

If you're attracted to the Jasmine flower you may be shy and want to express more confidence. You may want to feel beautiful and sensual. Or you may catch yourself getting caught up in external appearances, feeling discontented with your body, and wishing to change some of your features. At times you may feel lonely, as a result of subconsciously pulling back from other people. You may also be hard on yourself or experience jealousy from time to time.

Ask Yourself

Have I felt shy, insecure, lonely, or jealous lately? Which one? When?

Am I radiating my full light, or holding back?

What gives me a boost of confidence?

When do I feel beautiful?

What the Elixir Catalyzes

Jasmine flower elixir helps us appreciate our own unique beauty. It enhances the radiance of the face and heart area, and eliminates the desire to change our features. Jasmine helps us focus on inner beauty, instead of judging ourselves solely on our physical appearance.

Jasmine enhances our ability to recognize our own beauty while dissolving insecurity and self-hatred. It also dissolves jealousy and loneliness, and can help with weight issues related to loneliness. Finally, it helps us accept friendship from others.

Extra Credit

- Surround yourself with beautiful things—your favorite crystals, nature photos, pottery, art. Seeing beautiful things can make you feel more beautiful.

- Out with the frumpy pajamas or sweatpants! Only wear those clothes that make you feel beautiful.

- Take a Japanese Ikebana flower-arranging course or learn to make flower crowns. Adorn yourself and your space with the beauty of flowers.

- Head to the spa, sit in the sauna, soak in the hot tub, and get a body scrub. Come out glowing.

- Wear Jasmine essential oil as a perfume.

In Essence

Dissolves

Desire to change your appearance

Insecurity, jealousy, or self-hatred

Magnifies

Appreciation of your own beauty

Magnetism and attraction

MAGNETIC JASMINE-INFUSED MAPLE SYRUP
AND JASMINE FOAM CAPPUCCINOS

Jasmine flowers are edible; you can use them to make oil, extract, and tea; bake a cake; blend a smoothie; and more! When you eat them fresh, they're a touch bitter and they cool down the body when they bloom in the summertime. My favorite thing to do is make Jasmine-infused maple syrup, which can be used as a sweetener in coffee drinks. To make it at home, you will need a Jasmine plant that produces flowers for you every morning. If you don't have one, go to a nursery and see if Jasmine grows in your area. There are many varieties of Jasmine and some of them, like Star Jasmine or Pink Jasmine, may only bloom for two weeks at a time. If you catch the Jasmine while it's blooming, two weeks will be enough time for you to make this syrup.

I love to use this as a sweetener for Jasmine Foam Cappuccinos.

Jasmine-Infused Maple Syrup

Each morning, pick the Jasmine blossoms that have just opened the night prior. Clean the blossoms of any dirt or bugs, and place the blossoms in a glass jar. Cover with maple syrup until all of the blossoms are completely covered. Seal the jar and store in the refrigerator. The next day, remove the old blossoms using a pair of wooden chopsticks and replace them with freshly collected blossoms. Over time, the original amount of maple syrup will decrease, but the remaining syrup will transform into a heady floral Jasmine syrup. Repeat this for as many days as you like for the desired intensity of jasmine scent/flavor in the syrup. For a heavily scented syrup, 20 to 30 days is recommended.

Jasmine Foam Cappuccinos

Heat 1 cup of dairy or nut milk in a small saucepan over medium-high heat.

After the milk has been heated, use a handheld milk frother to froth the milk. (Dairy milk will get the best foaming action for a cappuccino, but you can make a latte with a little bit of foam using nondairy milks.)

Brew the espresso or coffee according to instructions. Pour the milk foam over the espresso or coffee. Pour 1 teaspoon Jasmine maple syrup into a spoon and gently fold it into the foam.

LILAC

Syringa vulgaris

Activate: Flexibility

Message: Adapt quickly to changes.

Many people adore Lilacs, and for some it's their favorite flower. Part of the magic is that they only bloom for a short time in the early spring, when the days are finally growing warmer after the cold winter and excitement about springtime is in the air. Lilacs also bloom near Mother's Day and tend to remind people of their mothers and grandmothers.

I never would have expected to find Lilacs in the high desert, so I was surprised when I discovered them on a trip to Santa Fe, New Mexico, at an altitude of over 7,000 feet. Originally brought to the area in the 1850s, Lilacs now grow wild there. The flowers look the same, but the plant itself is not as tall and bushy; it's more delicate than the Lilacs in the north.

Why It's Special

Lilacs are native to Asia and Eastern Europe. They were brought to the Americas in the 17th century. Like many plants that were transported across the oceans to the Americas, the first Lilacs were planted in botanical gardens. Both Thomas Jefferson and George Washington grew Lilacs in their personal gardens.

Surprisingly, there are 1,000 different varieties of Lilac bushes and trees and they all belong to the same family as the Olive tree. Lilac bushes grow from 6 to 20 feet tall; however, the Peking Lilac Tree and the Japanese Lilac Tree in Asia both grow over 30 feet tall.

Most people think of Lilacs as a deep violet color, but they can also be white, pink, red, lavender, yellow, and blue! Many people believe that the deep purple flower clusters tend to have the strongest fragrance, but really it depends on the species of the plant, along with its terroir: the conditions of its environment, including moisture, soil, location, climate, and weather.

Butterflies are the pollinators of Lilacs, so anytime you're around these colorful beauties, expect to see the gentle fluttering of butterflies. Though the flower is delicate, the Lilac plant is extremely hardy, surviving temperatures as low as -60°F! The wood is extremely dense, and has been used to create musical instruments and knives. And their longevity is impressive: lilac bushes can live for hundreds of years.

What It Reveals

If you're attracted to the Lilac flower, you may be clinging to things being a certain way. There may be a situation in which you want to control the outcome. You may wish for things to be different, and when your expectations are not met, find yourself feeling uncomfortable or depressed. When plans unexpectedly change, you may find it difficult to adapt quickly enough.

There may be areas in your life in which you've become controlling, or rigid in your ideas. You may find yourself being hard on yourself for this reason, or judging what is best for others. At times you may feel there's only one right way, which closes you off to other possibilities.

Ask Yourself

In what situations do I find myself becoming controlling or rigid in my beliefs and ways?

In what areas of my life could I be more flexible?

How does having expectations lead me to disappointments? What might the outcome be of not having any expectations at all?

When has spontaneity and being open to surprises worked in my favor?

What the Elixir Catalyzes

Lilac bushes have tremendous strength and fortitude, with flowers that teach us how to accept the impermanence of life. Everything changes, and the Lilac flower elixir helps us loosen up and free ourselves from clinging to things being a certain way.

Lilac helps us embrace change and go with the flow, while letting go of rigid ideas and the desire to control outcomes. If a situation is beyond our control, Lilac helps us let it be; it makes us more flexible with what arises. If something is within our control, then it can help us make an effort to change it from a place of equanimity.

Lilac helps us cherish the way life is presenting itself to us, instead of wishing things were another way. Life is so fleeting; Lilac helps us adapt quickly to surprises with a flexible, accepting heart.

Extra Credit

- Stretch your body daily—a flexible body can help the mind be more flexible.
- Identify anyone in your life that you wish would change, and practice accepting them the way they are 100 percent.
- Whenever you feel rigidity or neediness arising, take a step back and spend some time alone. Doing breathing meditation each day can enhance our ability to let go of expectations and be more flexible.
- Try breaking up your routines now and then and approaching things in a different way, to train your mind to embrace change.
- Remember impermanence: Things are always changing. Cherish and enjoy things as they are, right now, knowing they will change.

In Essence

Dissolves

Desire for things to be a certain way

Expectations of a person, place, or condition

Rigidity or control, believing there's only one way

Magnifies

Flexibility, freedom from rigid or fixed structures

Acceptance of things and people as they are

Ability to embrace change

AROMATIC LILAC POMADE

Though Lilac is a popular fragrance for soaps and lotions, any "Lilac scent" you see on the market is made from artificial, petroleum-based chemicals that may cause attention deficit issues and serious reproductive issues.

In fact, it is impossible to extract natural essential oils in a way that allows for mass production. Lilac flowers are far too delicate.

The only way to make a true Lilac perfume is to make it yourself at home during Lilac season.

One artisanal way to extract the precious fragrant oils from the Lilac flowers is the age-old perfumery method called enfleurage. This involves placing the delicate flowers into trays of fat. Traditionally in France, animal fat was used; however, you can make an aromatic Lilac pomade using solid coconut oil or a soft salve made from beeswax and oil. Place the flowers facedown in the fat and let the fat extract their delicate oils. After one day, remove the flowers, add more fresh flowers, and repeat numerous times until the flower balm has the desired intensity of scent.

This scented pomade can be scooped into a jar to use to apply to your skin. Or you can soak the infused balm in alcohol for three months, allowing the alcohol to slowly extract the delicate Lilac essential oils from the buttery goodness.

MANDEVILLA

Mandevilla sendari

Activate: Acceptance

Message: Fall in love with what is.

My mother has the proverbial green thumb; she can get any plant to grow. She even has a huge tropical Mandevilla vine blooming in the high desert of northern Arizona. The soil is rocky and dry, so she planted the Mandevilla in a big pot with a tall trellis. In a year the vine grew up the trellis and climbed two stories up to her deck!

Why It's Special

Mandevilla blooms in pink, red, white, and yellow varieties and loves warmer climates. The flowers on the vine start out as oversize pink buds that are tightly curled into a spiral pattern. Native to Central and South America, this showy flower vine can be trained to grow up a trellis or garden wall by using twist ties to guide the vines where you want them to grow, either horizontally or vertically. One species of Mandevilla from Chile, *Mandevilla laxa*, even smells like gardenias!

Not an edible flower, Mandevilla is a part of the dogbane family; all members of this family are toxic to people and animals. Mandevilla itself is not as poisonous as other flowers in its family, such as oleander and periwinkle, but if ingested, it does cause indigestion. Mandevillas are considered a low-maintenance vine, and pruning from time to time makes them flourish.

What It Reveals

If you're attracted to the Mandevilla flower, you may recently have felt a twinge of fear at the prospect of losing something. It's natural to feel attachment to the way things are—to people, places, or things that we love. Yet the nature of life is that things are constantly changing, and thus you may have recently felt anguish or worry about losing something or someone you love. The more you cling, the less empowered you feel.

Being drawn to Mandevilla can also indicate impatience or rushing, which can lead to physical tension and discomfort.

Ask Yourself

When do I find myself rushing? Feeling impatient?

When do I experience attachment, or fear of loss?

What do I hold on to too tightly?

What is my greatest fear if I let go?

What the Elixir Catalyzes

Mandevilla helps us feel secure in the love that we possess inside us, rather than needing something from the outside to feel complete and whole. This leads to peacefulness, contentment, and the liberation of creative energy. When we're not holding on too tightly to something or someone, we have more energy at our disposal to appreciate the unfathomable rightness of how things actually are.

Mandevilla flower elixir helps us to be profoundly at peace with the way things are, without wanting to change them or wishing for another outcome. It opens us up to being more present with what is, dissolving attachment and fear of loss.

Extra Credit

- Notice when you experience attachment or clinging on any level. Pay particular attention to the presence of any tension in your body. Try breathing and relaxing into the tight places.

- If it's difficult to say good-bye to people, instead of focusing on their absence, put your focus on your gratitude for the opportunity to know them and spend time with them.

- Notice when you find yourself hurrying, and slow down. Or if you're always running late, try to rework your schedule so that you never have to hurry or rush.

- Be open to surprises. Invite a wild spaciousness into your life.

- Make a date with a friend and decide at the last minute what you're going to do.

In Essence

Dissolves

Fear of loss regarding people or possessions

Anger, anguish, or sadness as a result of clinging

Fear of abandonment or rejection

Magnifies

Deep appreciation of the present moment

Peace, patience, and contentment

Freedom and creativity

NASTURTIUM

Tropaeolum majus

Activate: Spontaneity

Message: Spice up your life.

I love everything about the Nasturtium: the brightly colored flowers with rounded petals and little hairs in the middle that lead to what looks like a bright green vase funneling to a point. The leaves are just as gorgeous as the flowers, shaped like miniature lily pads with the same elegant beauty.

While inspecting a Nasturtium flower closely, you feel a bright whimsical essence with a touch of fierceness. If you munch on it, the smooth, rounded leaves surprise you with a spicy bite.

Why It's Special

Nasturtiums are native to Central and South America, the flowers ranging from fiery orange to crimson and sunny yellow. This plant is ideal as a floral ground cover or garden flower. Nasturtiums are hardy and easy to grow, whether in a pot or in the ground, flourishing in moist climates.

The meaning of Nasturtium is "nose-twister" or "nose-tweaker." Even though the plant is not technically related to the genus *Nasturtium* (watercress, mustard, wasabi, and other spicy plants), it was given the name Nasturtium because of its peppery bite.

Though it's a common garden flower, many do not know that it is edible and can be added to salads and savory dishes for a spicy twist. What's more, it's packed with nutrients, containing large amounts of vitamin C and the highest amount of lutein it's in any edible plant. Infused in vinegar, the seeds can even be eaten like capers.

In herbal medicine, Nasturtiums are used as a remedy for chest colds and to enhance new blood cell growth. The spicy kick of the flower warms up the body and gives it a jump start.

What It Reveals

If you're drawn to Nasturtium you may feel that life has become too routine. You might be craving more spiciness and flavor in your daily activities. Perhaps you feel your day-to-day schedule has gotten stale or stagnant, or that you're trapped in the drudgery of the daily grind, yearning for freedom and exploration.

Alternatively, you may have felt down lately, feeling plain, ordinary, or doubtful of yourself. You may be craving you-know-who's attention or have a strong desire to feel "special." Or you may simply be experiencing the blues for no apparent reason.

Ask Yourself

What wakes up joy inside me?

What can I do to spice up my life a little?

What routines can I break up?

What is unique or extraordinary about me?

What the Elixir Catalyzes

When life begins to feel routine, boring, or bland, Nasturtiums help us add more spice to life! They enhance joy and contentment, and make us feel like we're in the right place at the right time.

When we feel sad, left out, or unwanted, Nasturtium helps us be more spontaneous and rely less on attention from others. When we feel plain or ordinary, Nasturtium highlights our strengths and helps us refine our own unique way of being ourselves. Dancing to our own beat never felt so good!

Extra Credit

- Join a hiking club or head to a home-brew meetup—explore new interests and shake up your activities a bit. Move toward anything that inspires wonder.

- Get out into the community, volunteer—find ways to reach out of your comfort zone and be a part of a fun group of folks with positive intentions.

- Refresh your surroundings—go through your closet and pull out anything that says "ordinary," "bland," or "boring" to you. Look for ways to add color and pizzazz to your wardrobe.

- Eat fruits and vegetables with bright colors. Eat spicy or exotic-to-you foods and cook with ginger, turmeric, galangal, cinnamon, and other spices. Drink chai tea or ginger tea.

- Head to the spa and get a body scrub or start dry brushing and get your circulation moving.

In Essence

Dissolves	*Magnifies*
Sorrow	Joy and spontaneity
Feeling plain, ordinary, or unwanted	Contentment and variety
Seeking attention	Being in the right place at the right time

DELIGHTFUL GOLDEN NASTURTIUM SALAD

Jump-start your body with loads of vitamin C, lutein, and a spicy kick, while enjoying a gorgeous flower-filled salad!

To make the Nasturtium Vinaigrette: Fill a jar 3/4 full with fresh Nasturtium blossoms. Then top with 1/2 cup white rice vinegar or white wine vinegar. Store in a dark place for three weeks. Add a sprig of fresh rosemary, a handful of fresh chives, or a couple crushed cloves of garlic to enhance the flavor. Rinse fresh flowers and leaves with water and dry with a paper towel. Combine Nasturtium vinegar with 1/2 cup olive oil, 3 tablespoons maple syrup, 2 teaspoons Dijon mustard, ½ teaspoon pink Himalayan salt, and 2 large handfuls of Nasturtium flowers and leaves. Shake well. Allow the flavors to marry for a couple minutes and violà! Store in the refrigerator and use within five days.

To make the salad: Combine 1 large handful of salad greens and 8 Nasturtium flowers and leaves in a large bowl. Top with Nasturtium Vinaigrette and toss to combine.

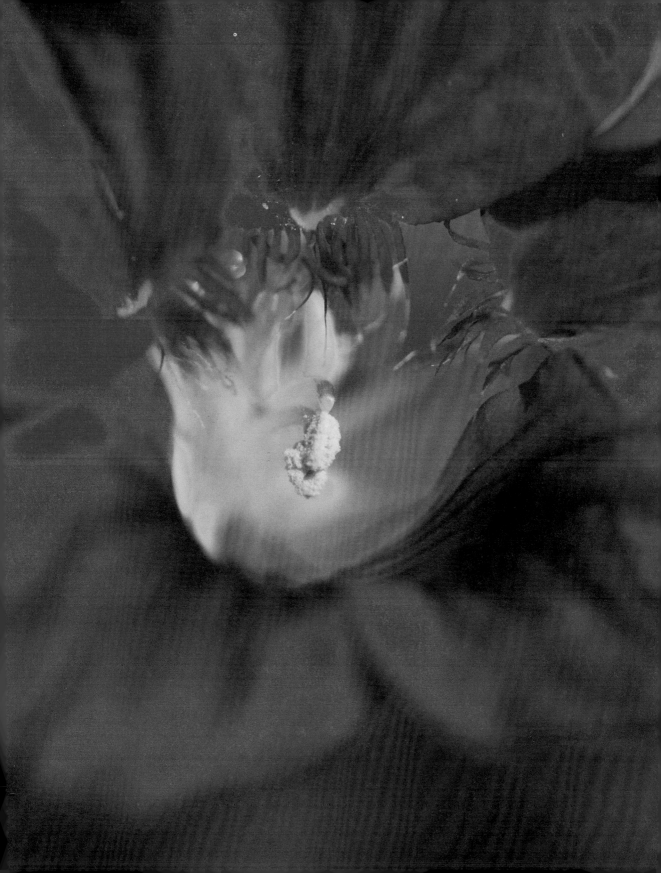

NECTARINE BLOSSOM

Prunus persica, var. *nectarina*

Activate: Sweetness

Message: You're among friends.

One of my favorite fruits is the Nectarine, and the sweetest Nectarines I ever tasted were plucked right off a tree in our backyard. I've always adored this tree, with its beautiful craggy limbs and gorgeous flowers. The blossoms have a delicate quality similar to cherry blossoms, but the flowers are larger and hardier.

I wanted to give a gift to a dear friend who lives north of San Francisco, so I gave him the best thing I could think of: a Nectarine tree! Auspiciously, the species variety was called "Katie." Before giving it to him, I had a talk with that tree. I infused it with prayers and wishes for him and requested a future of wish-fulfilling fruit. Now he says that each year, out of all his fruit trees, this tree produces the most fruit.

Why It's Special

Nectarines emerged from a long lineage of peach trees going back to 2,000 B.C. in China, where peaches were considered an auspicious symbol of long life. The Nectarine is a miraculous fruit, having appeared spontaneously as a "bud sport" from a peach tree several hundred years ago. When a plant or tree sprouts an offshoot that is totally different morphologically, it's called a bud sport. Peaches have a dominant gene for fuzzy skin, while in Nectarines that gene is recessive.[1]

What It Reveals

If you're attracted to the Nectarine blossom, you may be experiencing low-level annoyance, or feel that the energy in your environment is inflammatory, aggressive, or uncomfortable. You are likely experiencing tension in your body and neck, and you may feel nervous about being berated. When people around you are harsh-mannered and you feel you're in the presence of adversaries, your inner balance is easily disturbed, causing you to pull back and clam up. You may be feeling vulnerable at the heart level, wanting to crawl under the covers or make a safe escape.

Lately you may only want to interact with people whose demeanor is gentle, sweet, and soft. You deeply appreciate friendliness, camaraderie, and a sense that loved ones are "on your side." You'll go out of your way to do nice things for people who are kind to you, while with those who are inflammatory, you may pull back out of lack of trust.

Ask Yourself

What is causing me tension right now? What is annoying me?

What situations am I experiencing that are inflammatory?

When do I feel like doing sweet things for other people?

When do I experience camaraderie and trust, and when do I feel a lack of safety?

What the Elixir Catalyzes

Nectarine flower relaxes tension caused by being on edge and feeling like we can't trust the people or situations around us. It dissolves annoyance, hatred, and resentment, making room for tenderness.

Nectarine blossom magnifies tolerance, affection, and thoughtfulness, enhancing the desire to be of service and perform random acts of kindness. It softens our character and brings out our good intentions. It helps us feel that, instead of being surrounded by people we can't trust, we are among friends.

Extra Credit

- Engage in a random act of kindness once daily for the next week.
- Put a piece of rose quartz in your pocket to remind you of gentle loving support. When you feel stressed, reach into your pocket and squeeze the pink quartz, remembering that the entire Earth is supporting you.
- Nectarine fruits emerge from the flower—eat as many Nectarines as you want. Buy organic! Nonorganic Nectarines measure high in pesticide residue.
- Recognize the effort others make—especially people who annoy you or who are aggressive; try to see them in a different light.
- Make a stone fruit salad—using plums, peaches, cherries, apricots, nectarines, and almonds.

In Essence

Dissolves	*Magnifies*
Hatred or annoyance	Gentleness, sweetness, softness
Feeling attacked, or that people around you can't be trusted	Camaraderie, friendliness
Neck pain or tension	Desire to be of service or do nice things for others

PLANT A LEGACY TREE

The best time to plant a tree was 20 years ago. The second best time is now.

CHINESE PROVERB

The first time I heard this phrase was from my teacher. I helped him plant trees and watched how he tended and cared for trees for over 15 years. Now many of those trees are two to three stories tall and he's created a lush green oasis in the desert. The amount of love, watering, pruning, nourishing, and time infused into the trees makes a property priceless.

We can buy many things, but we can't buy love—or old-growth trees. We can't speed up time. When I see big trees giving shade, moisture, fruit, and good vibes, I am so inspired by the love and time the caretaker spent tending them. The time spent—and the tree—are gifts that keep on giving.

One of the best ways to leave a legacy on this Earth is to plant a tree. When you plant the tree, you can infuse it with your dreams and wishes. If you gift a tree to a loved one, you can infuse it with your wishes for the other person. You can even have a tree-planting ceremony with a group. Anytime you see the tree, you'll feel a deep connection to it and remember the ceremony that you had. When we see how much the tree has grown, it reminds us of impermanence—that things are always changing—and that we can leave a legacy behind us after we've gone.

Additionally, if you plant a fruit tree, it'll offer sweet nourishment. Children and grandchildren can climb the tree, hide in the green leaves, and learn where fruit comes from (not the grocery store!). The juicy, sweet fruit can be enjoyed fresh or given to friends and neighbors if there's an abundance. If you move to another house, you'll leave behind a beautiful legacy for the future owners of the home.

NIGHT-BLOOMING CEREUS

Echinopsis candicans

Activate: Fearlessness

Message: Take the leap!

This is the Night-Blooming Cereus that I wrote about in Chapter 8, the flower that radically changed my business and my life almost overnight. It gave me the energy and fearlessness to catapult myself from quiet one-on-one consultations to formulating a product line for the flagship spa of the world's largest hotel chain. It helped me scale my business to produce thousands of products and make hundreds of custom perfumes for special guests, including the President of the United States. Since then it has helped many other people to dig deep and dissolve fears and self-imposed limitations in order to sky-rocket to the next level of their growth.

Why It's Special

Native to the Americas, it is also called Moonlight Cactus, or Queen of the Night.

There are about 20 different kinds of Night-Blooming Cereus growing in jungles and deserts. This particular species is known as the Argentine Giant, and it blooms in the desert, usually in springtime, on the full or new moon. It blooms at night—for one night only—and by midmorning has already begun to wilt.

The Night-Blooming Cereus flower is six to seven inches in diameter. At about 9 or 10 P.M. it starts unfolding its creamy white petals and its intoxicating fragrance. Inside the shimmery, featherlike petals are green and yellow pollen-filled stamens that are pollinated by sphinx moths.

What It Reveals

If you're attracted to the Night-Blooming Cereus flower, on some level you're yearning to make a huge leap in your personal growth. There may be fears or self-limiting patterns that will need to be worked through, however, as you make that leap. They likely reside in your subconscious, so you may be unaware of how they affect your actions or how they could create obstacles toward reaching your goals.

Being drawn to the Cereus flower indicates that you are ready to see those fears or limitations as illusory appearances and move past them to accomplish your highest expression. You have the courage to sift through your fears and old patterns to free the part of yourself that wants to propel you forward in a big way.

You may also notice that you sometimes fall into the extremes of feeling either inferior or superior.

Ask Yourself

What is the biggest expression I can imagine of what I'm doing?

What fears or limitations am I ready to dissolve?

How have I held myself back in the past?

What is one way I could make a huge leap toward expressing my full potential?

What the Elixir Catalyzes

Night-blooming flowers shine light on shadows and illuminate aspects of ourselves that we haven't seen or paid attention to. This species of the Night-Blooming Cereus digs deep into fear patterns. It unearths self-limiting habits and conscious or subconscious fears that are running in the background and affecting our behavior.

Fear holds us back from being our greatest selves. It prevents us from getting out of our comfort zone and taking a big leap toward our full potential. Night-Blooming Cereus brings up our fears and makes them apparent so we can look at them and release them. It also shows us when we are going to extremes—feeling inferior, combined with feeling superior—and through awareness, helps us dissolve those patterns.

Night-Blooming Cereus offers a boost of courage and bold determination. Not about baby steps, rather Cereus helps you take a huge leap in your growth or in the expression of your talent. It pushes you past any preconceived self-limitations, moving you into new territories, new expressions of your gifts. When you fearlessly go out on a limb after your dreams, you can achieve what you may have previously thought was unattainable.

Extra Credit

- Make a list of the ways you hold yourself back, and become aware of when they manifest in your life.
- Notice when you feel like you're in the right place at the right time. What causes and conditions led you to that experience, and how can you repeat them?
- Make a list of the most exciting ways you could see living your highest potential in the world.
- What are you afraid of? What makes you hesitant?
- What are you really amazing at? If you continued devoting time to one area of your life, what could you master?

In Essence

Dissolves

Fears, negativity, self-limitations

Old habits, patterns, and illusions

Extremes of inferiority and superiority

Magnifies

Fearlessness, courage, and great leaps toward reaching your full potential

Deeper understanding of your shadow side and illusions

Realization of your true gifts and how to expand on them

GROW A MOONFLOWER GARDEN

Moonflowers are any flowers that bloom in the evening or at night by the light of the full moon. Typically they are white flowers in order to attract moths for pollination, though some are colorful night-bloomers that open earlier in the evening.

To grow a moonflower garden, consider these exquisite and highly fragrant flowers:

*Night-Blooming Cereus, *Night-Blooming Jasmine, *Brugmansia, *Chocolate Daisy, *Pink Primrose, *Gardenia, Moonflower Vine, Datura "Angel's Trumpet," Tuberose, Flowering Tobacco, Dragon Fruit Cactus, "Casa Blanca" Lily, "Easter Lily" Echinopsis Cactus, Rain Lily, Night-Blooming Water Lily, Night Jessamine, Banana Yucca

Night-blooming flowers usually bring aspects of ourselves to the surface that we don't ordinarily see. As you plant your garden, you can make the intention that the flowers help you bring light to your greatest potential.

*Featured in this book

PAPAYA FLOWER

Carica papaya

Activate: Receptivity

Message: Gentle is powerful.

The first time I saw Papaya flowers growing in the jungles of Mexico I was amazed. I was familiar with Papaya, but to see the tree from which this large orange fruit came was a surprise. And they were just growing alongside the road!

The trees are tall, like palm trees, and the leaves shoot out from the top in a perfect radius, reaching for the sun. In the center under the leaves hang huge green Papaya fruits that appear suspended in midair, like a bunch of green balloons.

Why It's Special

Though now grown in tropical areas around the world, the Papaya tree is native to southern Mexico and Central America. There are three different kinds: male, female, and hermaphrodite. The male produces starlike flowers, the female gorgeous flowers that look like fallopian tubes. Whereas the female tree needs the male tree's pollen in order to produce fruits, the hermaphrodite tree can self-pollinate.

The Papaya's green fruit and the tree's latex are rich with an enzyme called papain, which helps us digest food, acts as a natural skin exfoliant, and tenderizes meat. In herbal medicine, Papaya leaves are infused as a tea for malaria and dengue fever.

Papaya fruits are used in cooking, both the green unripe and the sweet ripe ones. In Indonesia, Papaya flower buds are used in a vegetable dish.

What It Reveals

If you are attracted to the Papaya flower, you may be exerting a lot of effort and overextending yourself. You may feel the desire to collaborate instead of compete, yet find it difficult to accept help. You may wish to dismantle hierarchy and operate more from an interconnected community mind-set, yet feel like you need to be a superwoman or superman.

Being drawn to Papaya may indicate that you are reevaluating your relationship to masculine and feminine qualities within yourself. You may have had a difficult relationship with your mother or a mother figure, or simply wish to express more tenderness and vulnerability. You may crave to rely more on intuition and listening versus being heard or expressing your energy outwardly.

If you are in a relationship, you may not be sure of your compatibility. You may be seeking a sign that you are compatible, or that you are not, so that you can split amicably.

Ask Yourself

When has my vulnerability and tenderness been my greatest strength?

How was my relationship with my mother? How does that affect my
style of "mothering" others or myself?

When do I find myself engaging in competition where collaboration might be more effective?

When do I allow myself to follow my intuition?

What the Elixir Catalyzes

Just as the enzyme in the fruit is known for its ability to tenderize and soften, the Papaya flower plays a special role in helping our planet recognize the power in being tender and soft.

As we enter into a time of increasing female leadership, Papaya flower elixir prepares our collective consciousness for honoring the feminine just as much as the masculine. It makes the collective more open to what are traditionally known as "feminine," or yin, qualities: receptivity, listening, nurturing, intuition, collaboration, compassion, and tenderness.

Papaya flower teaches us how to flourish by attaining a healthy balance of both yin and yang qualities in ourselves and our culture. Both are necessary and vitally important; however, if we are to find a balance, it is now time to enhance the yin qualities that have been historically devalued. Cultural indicators that we have gone too far to one end of the spectrum include the following: a sense that menstruation, birthing, and breast-feeding are dirty or strange; the absence of maternity/paternity leave; an environment that's highly competitive, not collaborative; and soft character traits like tenderness being commonly perceived as "weakness."

By honoring the feminine, the Papaya flower elixir helps us perceive events such as menses, birthing, breast-feeding, and menopause as sacred and divine—activities that relate to giving life and supporting the sustainability of humankind. It also helps women accept support and assistance from men with grace and tenderness. It inspires both men and women to re-create the healthy and harmonic balance of feminine and masculine aspects in our world.

Papaya flower elixir also assists greatly in any type of relationship by clarifying compatibility, sexual orientation, and our ability to love ourselves and others with the unconditional love that a mother shows her child. Beyond romantic relationships, it also helps us understand our relationship with our mother and anyone that we "mother."

Extra Credit

- Notice when you respond in a "hard" way to situations in life or refuse help from others.

- Spend more time with your mother, sister, girlfriends, or children.

- Notice when you find yourself doing too much or overextending your energy.

- Support people and systems that are collaborative, receptive, nurturing, and community-minded.

- Make a list of the communities that you're a part of. Which ones are supportive, collaborative, receptive, and nurturing? Eliminate any communities you're a part of that are competitive or lack the kind of nurturing and listening you require for thriving.

In Essence

Dissolves	*Magnifies*
Hardness of character, envy, or refusal to accept help	Balance of feminine and masculine aspects
Past trauma with mother or mothering	Collaboration, receptivity, community mind-set
Discord within romantic partnership	Compatibility within relationships
Confusion regarding sexuality or sexual orientation	Harmony within relationships with mother or children
Fears about pregnancy, breast-feeding, motherhood, menopause	Clarity regarding sexuality/sexual orientation

PASSIONFLOWER

Passiflora incarnata

Activate: Healing sleep

Message: Rest more.

The Passionflower has one of the most exotic shapes of any flower. I always felt that it looked somewhat like a dish antenna, sending or receiving messages from outer space. I once found an entire wall of them, thriving and buzzing with bumblebees, their delicate inner petals quivering under the weight of the bees.

Over the years I have noticed that most people love how the Passionflower looks and many of us need it in our daily lives. When I started doing one-on-one consultations over fifteen years ago, sleep was not a common topic of conversation. Now when I give talks or classes, over half of the participants say they don't sleep well. This flower offers a huge benefit to us, with our frazzled, busy lifestyles, helping us let go of stress and sleep more deeply.

Why It's Special

There are about 500 different kinds of Passionflower, most growing in tropical areas of South America and Asia. Passionflower is a vine and each flower blooms for only one day.

Some of the Passionflower vines have delicious edible fruits, and for many centuries the leaves of Passionflower were traditionally infused as a medicinal tea for insomnia and epilepsy. In 2001, a study showed Passionflower to be just as effective as anxiety medications, but without side effects.[1]

What It Reveals

If you are attracted to the Passionflower, you may have felt like you're moving so fast you're not operating on all cylinders. You may be overworking, or on the go so much that your nerves are frazzled. You need more rest, naps, or minibreaks throughout the day.

You may also suffer from restless sleep, disturbing dreams, or inability to sleep throughout the entire night. Conversely, you may have difficulties in winding down at night before bed. You may tend to think about something over and over, either before sleep or upon waking in the middle of the night.

Ask Yourself

When do I experience anxiety, restless sleep, or mental chatter?

How can I block out more time for rest and naps?

What projects or activities could I let go of to experience more ease and relief?

How can I enhance my bedtime ritual?

What the Elixir Catalyzes

Passionflower elixir helps us let go of mental chatter, anxiety, and thinking too much and too fast. It encourages deep sleep, and facilitates the effortless resolution of issues on a subconscious level through slumber.

During the day, Passionflower slows us down ever so slightly so that we can be more effective. When we think too much, it leads to stress, depletion, and eventually to adrenal fatigue or burnout.

When we make it a habit to take breaks during the day, and possibly even naps or power naps, we're sharper and more decisive.

Passionflower induces a sense of deep peace and helps us take deeper breaths. It inspires us to feel not only more grounded, but also more plugged in to what's sacred to us, enhancing both awareness and intuition.

Extra Credit

- Make sure you're getting enough sleep: go to bed an hour earlier than usual.

- Take a daily power nap to let your nervous system reset: set your cell phone alarm to go off in 15 to 20 minutes, lie down or recline the seat in your car, and take a little snooze during your lunch break.

- Limit coffee to 1 to 2 cups each day, or replace coffee with yerba maté for energy without the adrenal overstimulation.

- Consider taking supplements to support and nourish your adrenal glands. Visit with a Doctor of Oriental Medicine and have a pulse and tongue reading to check for adrenal exhaustion. Get an acupuncture treatment.

- Eliminate technology use a couple hours before going to sleep. Make sure your cell phone is not plugged in close to your head where you sleep at night, and power it down at night. Consider installing "demand switches" in your house so you can turn off the electricity in your room while you sleep.

- Enhance your bedtime ritual. Try meditation or a hot bath. Drink a cup of Passionflower tea before going to sleep. Create a relaxing music playlist that you can put on as you're getting ready for bed. Make sure you absolutely love your sheets, pillows, and mattress, and that your sleeping area is fluffy, relaxing, and inviting.

- Carve out time first thing in the morning for meditation, prayer, or quiet reflection. Put a meditation app on your phone so you can do short meditations while waiting in line, on the train or public transport, or before bed.

In Essence

Dissolves

Muscular tension, frazzled nerves, adrenal overuse, depletion

Restless sleep, mental chatter

Anxiety, panic, or fear

Magnifies

Deep calm, peace, steadiness

Ability to let go, relax, rest, and sleep soundly

Awareness, intuition, and spiritual connection

271

PEONY

Paeonia lactiflora

Activate: Magnetism

Message: Attract abundance.

While researching the Peony, I found out that it's actually a myth that Peonies can't bloom without the help of the ants; on the contrary, the Peony flower buds release a sweet, sticky nectar that attracts the ants. As you'll read below, the Peony flower is the perfect floral role model—showing us how to attract an army of assistance to help us achieve our vision.

Why It's Special

Though the Peony is native to Asia, Europe, and North America, it is in Asia that it seems to have made its biggest impression. In Chinese culture, the Peony flower is the "King of All Flowers." I personally tend to think of it more as the "Queen of All Flowers," because it's so feminine and ruffly.

In any case, the Peony has long been a deeply significant flower for Chinese culture, cultivated all the way back to 900 B.C. It's also known to the Chinese as the "Flower of Riches and Honor." It is common to see Peonies in paintings, on ceramics, and on other household items in Asia. Together with the Lotus, it is the flower most often painted as a sacred offering flower in *thangkas,* or Tibetan paintings.

There are about 30 different varieties of Peony flower, ranging in color from pale pink to magenta to yellow or white. The flowers are huge and highly fragrant, flowering in late spring to early summer.

Though it is virtually impossible to make an essential oil from the Peony flower, in Asia the fresh petals are used to flavor tea. In China, the petals were boiled and sweetened into a kind of treat to be eaten with tea. If you have any Peony flowers growing in your garden that are free of pesticides, you can add the fragrant petals to salads or beverages.

The Peony is also highly regarded as a medicinal herb. The roots are used in Chinese, Japanese, and Korean traditional herbal medicine systems; depending on the color of the roots (white or red), the health benefits differ.

What It Reveals

If you are drawn to the Peony flower, you may be overextending yourself or overworking. In the process of making big goals happen, sometimes you may push too hard when a softer approach might be more effective. At times you may feel limited, afraid that there is not enough to go around or that you may miss out on something. Fear of loss can sneak in, causing you to scramble more than is necessary. You may feel like you have to work hard for everything, when, in fact, it could be more effortless, if only you called on your magnetic powers.

Alternatively, you may at times feel insecure, embarrassed, or shy, leading you to hold back or be overly cautious. You may worry about what others think, or you may tend to feel ashamed of whatever makes you different.

Ask Yourself

When do I catch myself working too hard, overextending in vain for the things I want to accomplish?

What kinds of resources are already within my reach to help me actualize my aspirations?

What are three things that are going really well this week and why?

If I could attract any opportunity, what would it be?

When have I felt totally satiated and fulfilled in life? What was I doing?
How can I invite more of that into my life?

What the Elixir Catalyzes

Have you ever buried your face in a Peony flower? It's easy to be completely enveloped by how huge, soft, ruffly, and unabashedly itself it is. There is no ounce of "meek" in this flower. It's all in. It's sexy in an elegant yet down-to-earth way.

Loved by so many, the Peony flower magnifies our sense of abundance. It makes us feel full, whole, grateful, and that mentality just attracts more. Peony flower dissolves any sense of lack or "I don't have enough" or "I'm not enough." "Lack" does not exist in the Peony world. Peony is like a gorgeous woman with huge ruffly skirts dancing—exquisite, graceful, and full of life. Peony flower elixir eliminates shame or bashfulness. It magnifies feeling uninhibited and sensuously whole.

Peony makes us feel luscious, wild, delicious—like everything is at our fingertips and everything is possible. With Peony flower elixir, we magnetize what we need. Instead of striving and working too hard and overextending, it comes to us.

The quality of Peony is to attract and magnetize. This is an active process—it's not about sitting back and waiting for things to happen. It's wise to take the necessary steps that get us closer to our goals; however, we must make sure we aren't forcing anything.

We can allow ourselves to savor and appreciate whatever fortunate circumstances we are in, and any positive domino effects we have put into action. We can let our minds run wild with what's possible when there are no limitations. Then we can discover ways and resources to make those new possibilities a reality.

Also, being open, relaxed, and receptive will help us recognize opportunities when they come to us. We may need to slow down a beat and be more present in order to be receptive to the opportunities that will reveal themselves. Enjoying the present moment leaves us open to being approached, so it's wise to indulge in moments of absolute gratitude and appreciation for everything in life.

Extra Credit

- Start your day thinking about what three things you're grateful for. Each night before you go to bed, write down three things that are going well and why. This practice alone attracts more abundance of everything you want.

- Buy yourself a bouquet of flowers. Treat yourself.

- Take a moment now to recognize all the blessings in your life.

- Go through all of your clothes and get rid of anything that doesn't make you feel lovely, luscious, or joyful.

- Read the book, *The Life-Changing Magic of Tidying Up*, by Marie Kondo—even though it's about streamlining, it's also about fully appreciating all the things you have in your life that you love, which makes you feel abundant.

In Essence

Dissolves	*Magnifies*
Shame, embarrassment, shyness	Abundance, prosperity, ability to magnetize
Perception of lack	Gratitude, appreciation, contentment
Habit of overextending	Elegance, gracefulness, innocence

LUSCIOUS PEONY FACIAL MIST

Capturing the fragrance of the Peony flower is something you can only do at home. You'll never be able to find its elusive fragrance in any product in a store. If you have Peony flowers growing in your garden or know someone who would give you a few blossoms, you can make a facial mist of the Peony flower:

Gather two large handfuls of fresh Peony flower petals, bruise them slightly by squeezing them, and add them to a cup of cold water in a pan. Heat the flower petal water on a low flame, very gently, and then strain the flower petals out of the water after 10 minutes.

Transfer the Peony water to a spray bottle and store in the refrigerator for up to one week. Feel free to mist the Peony water on your face as many times as you can each day, because you've got to use it up within the week! If you find that you have a lot left over at the end of the week, pour yourself a nice hot bath and add the rest of the Peony water to the bath.

In keeping with the quality of the Peony flower, each time you use the facial mist or take a Peony water bath, reflect on what you're grateful for and what you'd like to attract more of.

Important Note: Peonies are poisonous to cats, so don't let the cats drink it.

PINK LOTUS

Nelumbo nucifera

Activate: Divine wisdom

Message: Look within.

Once, while traveling in Korea, I spent time around enormous expanses of Pink Lotus flowers. The blossoms are huge and fragrant, and they instantly make you feel energized and alive, yet supremely relaxed. The leaves are gigantic, some of them resting on the surface of the water, with dragonflies zooming around, others growing and curling up toward the sky.

In Korea there is a special Lotus flower ceremony, in which an entire Pink Lotus flower is placed into a bowl of hot water. A wooden ladle scoops out the Lotus tisane for each person at the ceremony. A beautiful tradition, the hot Lotus infusion is simultaneously energizing and calming.

Why It's Special

Considered a sacred symbol in Asia, the Lotus flower is native to the Asian tropics, and typically grows in marshy, swampy areas. It is often confused with the Water Lily, though the two plants are unrelated.

Amazingly, the Lotus is one of only three plants in the world that can regulate its temperature like humans do! Researchers in Adelaide, Australia, found that though the ambient temperature dropped to 50°F, Lotus flowers maintained their temperature around 90°F![1]

Another aspect unique to the Lotus is that the leaves and flowers are always impeccably clean. Most engineers know about the magical "lotus effect"—exquisite microscopic formations on the surface of the leaves act as a brilliant self-cleansing technology; not one speck of dust is able to rest on them.

The Lotus is also a precious source of food and natural remedies. The roots are used in herbal medicine in Asia as well as cooked as food. Lotus roots have a beautiful shape, somewhat like the snow-flakes we cut out of paper as children. They can be sliced and fried like potato chips or added to stews and savory dishes. Lotus seeds are boiled and mashed with sugar to make a sweet lotus seed paste that is used to fill moon cakes, mochi, and other Asian desserts.

The Lotus flower is a plant of ancient wisdom. One of the oldest known viable seeds was a Lotus flower seed identified as 1,300 years old, and when it was germinated, it bloomed!

What It Reveals

The Pink Lotus flower is a catalyst, precipitating or encouraging a change. If you're attracted to the Pink Lotus flower, you either live by or yearn for a spiritual path and way of life. If you don't practice meditation, it may be time to start. If you do meditate, perhaps it's time to expand your practice or recommit to making it your top priority. Maybe your cell phone or busy mind is interfering with having a truly focused practice.

If you already meditate, find a way to practice with more diligence or to incorporate it into your everyday life, like maintaining breath awareness while walking the dog or washing the dishes. Create more mindful moments during your day. Find triggers in your daily life to remind you to rest in the pres-ent moment and relax the tension in the back of your neck. Focus on your breathing at stoplights, or on the train or bus to work. Develop special rituals for last thing at night and first thing in the morning that remind you of your intention to continue to develop spiritually.

It may be time to put your spiritual practice into action. Think about visiting one of your teachers, requesting a certain practice, or simply asking in your mind for a teacher's help. If you don't have a teacher and you'd like one, make wishes that an authentic spiritual teacher appear at the right time. Or perhaps something is occurring in your life that is acting as a teacher for you, imparting lessons that will be of value to you for a long time.

If Pink Lotus is speaking to you, it can also be a reminder to look within. There is an inner wisdom and knowingness that you may be overlooking. If you find yourself looking for answers outside of yourself lately, give yourself the luxury of mental spaciousness that will make room for your own inner wisdom and insights to arise.

Ask Yourself

What kind of change is occurring in my life?

What new perspectives and wisdom are arising from within?

When am I allowing myself to be distracted, though mindful awareness is a value for me?

How might I take my spiritual practice to the next level?

What the Elixir Catalyzes

In the Far East, the Lotus has long been a symbol of purity and enlightenment. The muddy swamp where the Lotus grows is akin to the craziness of daily life—and we can use that chaos to wake up and bloom into our purest self. We can use the wildness of our own minds to refine ourselves over time into more compassionate, loving beings.

The Pink Lotus awakens spiritual insight and understanding from a part of us that is not dependent on our mental thinking. "Figuring out" is not necessary—this kind of wisdom appears more like an "aha" moment. It comes to us in the middle of the night, or first thing when we wake up in the morning, during our meditation, or at other random moments. It slides into our consciousness effortlessly when we're not thinking—when there's space in between the thoughts.

The Pink Lotus flower also dissolves stagnant or stuck energy, weakness, and apathy. Tapping into the Lotus flower is like hooking up jumper cables to give us a "jump" or a spark, to inspire us to action. It wakes up the part of us that perceives the sacredness of daily life. It reveals our own inner wisdom, deepening our understanding of life.

Pink Lotus elixir is also a "catalyst," which refers to any botanical, herb, or flower that strengthens the overall effectiveness and synergy of the other remedies they are formulated with. For example, in herbal medicine, licorice root and cayenne are examples of herbal catalysts, strengthening the overall herbal formula. When preparing combinations of flower elixirs, adding Pink Lotus not only strengthens the overall effectiveness of the formula but also boosts each of the other flowers' individual qualities. Pink Lotus elixir may be added to other flower elixir formulas and herbal formulas as a catalyst.

Extra Credit

- Take more quiet time for yourself and watch the sun set or rise.

- Practice mindfulness meditation. If you already meditate, find ways to incorporate mindful awareness practices into other activities throughout the day.

- Make time for prayer, to reflect on what you're grateful for, or to connect with what you consider sacred.

- Wake up early, between 4 to 6 A.M., when the energy of the Earth is most conducive to meditation, to facilitate clarity, insight, and wisdom.

- Take short breaks often to check in with yourself.

In Essence

Dissolves

Stagnant or stuck energy

Weakness

Apathy

Magnifies

Spiritual insight and understanding

Revitalized but calm energy

Catalyst effect for all flower elixirs and plant remedies

HOW TO MAKE FLOWER OFFERINGS

Making flower offerings is a practice that dissolves the habit of attachment and helps us practice generosity. Flowers are chosen for offerings because of their unsurpassed purity, the fact that they bring tremendous joy to the world, and because of their myriad qualities of fragrance, softness, shape, and color. They also remind us of the ever-changing, impermanent nature of life—that all things come to an end or change form.

Flowers for making offerings can be picked from a garden or purchased from a shop or nursery. In either case, try to choose flowers that are not poisonous flowers, and take care to choose the most vibrant, beautiful flowers from a clean location.

Wash your hands and your face before picking or obtaining the flowers. Most importantly, do not sniff the flowers that you use for making offerings, as it symbolizes taking away the precious essence for yourself instead of generously making an offering of the entire essence of the flower in all its purity.

Hold the flowers in your hands (with stems, or you can take off the tops), visualizing that they multiply and fill the entire sky. Dedicate the flowers and your visualization to the happiness of all beings in the world. Place the flowers on your altar. When the flowers are spent, toss them outside or in the compost—do not throw them in the trash. Replace with fresh flowers and repeat.

PINK MAGNOLIA

Magnolia liliflora

Activate: Self-care

Message: Take exquisite care of yourself.

When I first saw the Pink Magnolia tree I was enchanted; its blossoms look like large pink cups making offerings to the sky. The softness of the flowers contrasts with the strength of the tree.

After making a flower elixir of the Pink Magnolia, I played around with the blossoms on a black cloth, snapping photographs. It is one of the most photogenic flowers there is. If you pick a flower, it retains its beautiful shape for hours.

Why It's Special

The Pink Magnolia is a small tree native to southeast China that has grown all over China and Japan for hundreds of years. This flower is a hermaphrodite (it contains both male and female organs) and like the White Magnolia, it is pollinated by beetles.

The flowers and buds are used medicinally, as a general tonic to alleviate pain, relax the body, induce sleep, and break fevers. The flower alone is commonly used as an herbal remedy for runny noses, colds, and allergies.[1]

This is a tree for modern times; because it can tolerate atmospheric pollution, it is the perfect tree for urban living. As larger populations move into cities around the world, this tree supports us even in polluted environments.[2]

What It Reveals

You may be experiencing a period in which you're giving all of your time, energy, and love to others, while forgetting to take care of yourself. When parenting, caregiving, or working on big projects, we often pour our energy into doing the best we can.

Whether it's your family, friends, children, or colleagues that are requiring your attention, you may have a tendency to lose yourself in all the giving. You could find yourself empty or run down later, if you don't take time for self-care now.

If you're attracted to Pink Magnolia, this is an indication—and a permission slip—for you to take a little break. Do something to take care of yourself: walk in nature, take a bath, go to the spa, listen to music, or crawl in bed for a nap. Do whatever works best to give yourself some well-deserved love and care.

Remember, your ability to care for others is only as good as your ability to care for yourself. If you deplete your energy to the point of exhaustion, you won't have anything left to give. Take time now to do something nice for yourself.

Ask Yourself

When do I take care of others to the extent that I forget to take care of myself?

What efforts am I really proud of?

How often do I schedule in self-care or breaks to recharge?

Who is my biggest support?

What the Elixir Catalyzes

Just as cities fill up with people and become polluted, our lives may become polluted with static, distractions, and stress. We may attempt to be superhuman: to answer every e-mail, check social media, find solutions for others' problems, and give love wherever it's needed. The danger of not weaving self-care into our routine is that we may burn out, becoming resentful and joyless. We can give and give until there's nothing left to give.

Pink Magnolia helps us give ourselves a break. Its elixir helps us value our needs just as much as everyone else's, without perceiving that as selfish. Making time to recharge is vital for maintaining our ability to give to others, and Pink Magnolia encourages us to make time for self-care.

For this reason, Pink Magnolia is an important flower elixir for parents, hospice workers, and caregivers.

Extra Credit

- Treat yourself to a recharge: massage, sauna, bath, or whatever is a treat.
- Take an adrenal tonic or tea daily to nourish your nervous system.
- Eat more dark chocolate (for magnesium, iron, antioxidants, and happiness).
- Make sure you're getting enough to eat, and eating often enough, to nourish your body and keep your energy level high.
- Know your own personal signs of burnout and take action the moment they appear.

In Essence

Dissolves

Giving away too much energy to others

Self-sacrifice

Harming oneself in the name of helping others

Magnifies

Feeling complete, whole, and worthy

Retaining your energy for your own needs and purposes

Protection from burnout or resentment

PINK MAGNOLIA SELF-CARE FLOWER CROWN

Making flower crowns is outrageously fun and easy—and wearing them makes you feel special (because you are!). If you wear it in public people around you will feel happy and inspired. Since fresh Pink Magnolia's superpower is self-love and self-care, this flower crown is a celebration of you! You can also make one for a loved one and crown them with love.

Materials

Twine-covered wire
Flower clippers or sharp scissors
Floral tape
3 to 4 Pink Magnolia Blossoms* (if you're cutting them from a tree, keep an inch of the green stem)
Pretty piece of ribbon

Cut a piece of twine-covered wire long enough to wrap around your head, plus a little extra. Make a loop at each end of the bendable twine.

Using the floral tape, wrap the Pink Magnolia flower several times around the green stem base and then wrap around your piece of twine. You want the flowers to be in the front of the crown, so put them in the middle of the twine. Add the other blossoms to the twine crown in the same way.

Using the piece of ribbon, tie the two loops together and adjust to the size of your head.

---

*   Other flowers can be used if you don't have access to Pink Magnolias.

PINK PRIMROSE

Oenothera speciosa

> **Activate:** Rapid growth
>
> **Message:** Make it effortless.

I first discovered and collected the Pink Primrose flower south of the border—in Tecate, Mexico. I was at a special place called Rancho La Puerta, a wellness-focused destination resort with more than 3,000 acres of flowers, trees, mountains, and a riparian reserve. It was fall, and I was there for a spa industry event—my first one ever. I was a bit nervous, because I wasn't sure if I would fit in with the spa world, but I wanted to expand from individual consultations to making a product line that could reach more people.

While at Rancho La Puerta, I made an elixir of a flower that I noticed growing all around the property. Although Pink Primrose typically only blooms in spring and summer, I found it blooming in the fall. It was perfect timing for the flower, and for me to use the elixir; after launching the product line, my business more than doubled annually for the next few years.

Why It's Special

The Pink Primrose flower is native to the Southwest and Mexico. The pastel pink flowers bloom in the evening and nighttime, and close when the sun's rays are the strongest during the day. The flowers glow at dusk, and though they don't have much of a scent, you can sometimes detect a faint whiff of an aroma like bubble gum or Earl Grey tea.

What's most amazing about this flower is how prolifically it grows. Despite how delicate the flower looks, when the plant gets water, it springs up fast and is strong and hardy, growing in dry, rocky, and nutrient-poor soil. When planted in areas where the soil is nutrient-rich, it takes over rapidly and confettis the area in an explosion of pink. It doesn't choke out other plants or harm them, but fills in the spaces with pastel pink.

For that very reason, Pink Primrose, also known as Mexican Primrose, is good for inexperienced or low-maintenance gardeners. Each root grows another 30 rootlets so the plant spreads very fast. If you're looking for easy ground cover, this is it. It thrives in all conditions, even if you forget to water it.[1]

What It Reveals

If you are attracted to the Pink Primrose, you may have a big project that you're teeing up or a big vision of what's possible in your future. When this is the case, subconscious fears often arise in the form of a subtle resistance, distraction, or procrastination. Or the project starts to feel like "work": lots of effort, pushing a rock uphill, a chore or a drain on your energy. When this happens you start to feel stuck.

You've probably also had the experience of being "on," when you could work for hours and hours without fatigue, moved by some force within you that infuses your experience with ease and effortlessness. Everything flows like a steady river, resistance disappears, and your mind is able to access wild creativity and fresh ideas. You may currently be vacillating between this stage and feeling stuck, overwhelmed, or resistant.

Ask Yourself

Are there any areas of my life that are stagnant or disharmonious?

What things feel like a chore or a drain on my energy?

When do I feel the most at ease in my life?
What am I preparing for?

What the Elixir Catalyzes

Pink Primrose flower elixir helps to prepare us for rapid growth—often personal growth, but it can also refer to business/career growth or creative growth. Primrose helps us identify any areas of disharmony in our lives, so we can eliminate them or remove bumps in the road that would become bigger obstacles down the line.

Primrose dissolves fear, hesitation, and holding back, and enhances a sense of readiness for big changes in our lives or work. It also cuts through the belief that daily activities are draining or a chore. It gives us a sense of effortlessness and ease, along with the ability to think creatively to come up with out-of-the-box solutions. Primrose helps us adjust to major transitions in life, helps us birth new projects, and moves us swiftly though phases of feeling stuck, stagnant, or resistant during the creative process.

Primrose can also help us prepare for birthing a baby and all the changes involved with being a new parent.

Extra Credit

- Start preparing now for the outcome of your biggest dreams.
- Lay the proper foundation for what you want to create.
- Eliminate anything from your life that is not harmonious.
- Work a little bit each day on your project; start with the areas that are the most fun or full of ease.
- Remind yourself that it can be effortless.

In Essence

Dissolves	*Magnifies*
Fears, resistance, hesitancy, holding back	Effortless and easeful ideas and action
Perceiving things as a chore	Fearless readiness and sense of being called to action
Feeling unprepared, stuck, or stagnant	Creativity, thinking outside the box, innovation

WISH-FULFILLING FLOWER BOMBS

Visionary Japanese farmer in sustainability, Masanobu Fukuoka, came up with the idea of seed bombs 40 years ago as a way to plant new crops without disturbing the beneficial nutrients left by the previous crops. It's a smart way to garden if you don't want to till the land or dig, and it's a fun way to beautify empty city lots. Seed bombs, or flower bombs, are chocolate truffle–sized balls of clay and dirt rolled with seeds inside.

This is a fun project that's quick, easy, and gets your hands in the dirt. Simple enough that kids can participate, it's a valuable learning experience for them. Throwing flower bombs means you are planting wildflowers, resulting in more food for bees, butterflies, and hummingbirds, who keep our world alive with their pollination efforts. When the flowers bloom, it beautifies the environment, spreads good flower vibes, and makes people happy.

How to Make a Flower Bomb

Ingredients
1 part Wildflower seeds (native to your growing zone)
5 parts peat-free compost
3 parts potter's clay (earth-friendly, naturally colored clays)

Mix everything together in a bowl and slowly add water until the consistency allows you to roll the mixture into balls the size of chocolate truffles. Put the flower bombs on a tray outside to dry in the sun or on a sunny windowsill for about 3 hours.

When you are ready to plant, soak the seed truffle in water to soften it first. As you plant the seed bombs, reflect on what seeds you'd like to plant in your life, your community, or the world. Dedicate the flourishing of your seeds to that vision.

PINK SPIREA

Spiraea douglasii

Activate: Laughter

Message: Let your inner child play.

When I was on my first flower elixir collection trip in British Columbia, I made the intention to find the flowers that were most needed by people today. I asked for signs. A butterfly appeared and fluttered in a circle around my head three times, then landed on Pink Spirea, long luscious stalks of tiny pink flowers that look like they're having a party. The tiny petals and stamens seemed to be exploding with joy. Just looking at the flowers made me smile.

Why It's Special

Pink Spirea is a part of the Rose family and grows in wetlands like bogs, swamps, and riparian areas. They grow in Alaska, southwestern Canada, and the Pacific Northwest of the U.S. Their nectar attracts bees and butterflies.

Pink Spirea is a valuable astringent remedy for diarrhea and dysentery, as well as a tonic for the resulting weakness and fatigue. A bitter infusion that smells like black tea is made from the leaves and woody stems.[1]

What It Reveals

If you're drawn to Pink Spirea flower, you may be feeling a bit serious, down, or stressed. You may have a wrinkle between your eyebrows that will become permanent if you don't have some fun. The idea of "play" may seem superficial when there's so much work to be done and so many pressing things going on. You may find that you avoid or dislike the question, "What do you do for fun?"

Alternatively, you may feel tired of the seriousness of life and wish for a little more fun. Your inner child wants to come out and play, but you may not know where to start. Or you may feel lonely and yearn for fun companionship.

Ask Yourself

Have I felt serious lately or noticed myself furrowing my brow?

What kinds of activities bring me joy? How can I invite more of that into my life?

When was the last time I belly laughed?

When was the last time I let my inner child play?

What the Elixir Catalyzes

Pink Spirea heals old wounds of the heart and fills the heart with joy. It dissolves excessive seriousness and heaviness. It encourages our inner child to come out and play, stimulating laughter and lightheartedness. It dissolves burdens of the heart, enlivening us with a sense of freedom.

Laughter and play are important for creativity, productivity, and overall well-being. Laughter loosens up the body, releases endorphins, and helps us relax and recharge. Laughter heals our hearts.

Extra Credit

- Surround yourself with colors, food, and music that bring you joy.
- Make a music playlist full of songs that you love—that inspire you to sing and feel like doing a happy dance.
- Spend time with a friend who makes you laugh.
- Play with pets or kids. If you don't have any, go hang out with friends who have some.
- Throw a party! Play charades, Pictionary, or some other crazy game that makes you all laugh.

In Essence

Dissolves

Old wounds of the heart

Sadness or loneliness

Undervaluing or squelching your inner child

Magnifies

Joy, laughter, lightheartedness

Permission for your inner child to play

Feeling free, yet supported

POMEGRANATE FLOWER

Punica granatum

> **Activate:** Strength
>
> **Message:** Detox and reenergize.

One day my teacher asked me to buy several Pomegranate trees to plant in the front yard. I was unfamiliar with them, and delighted to discover bushes with emerald-green leaves that bloom in the spring with orange-petaled flowers. By fall, the flowers transform into round red fruits. During winter, the plant goes into hibernation and reserves its energy for the next growing season.

At the time, I was working as a crisis counselor while building my flower elixir practice. I worked 10-hour shifts and often at night. Whatever could not be resolved by the county phone crisis line would be turned over to us and we'd be sent out: two counselors with clipboards, radios, and flashlights in a minivan. We went to people's homes, shelters, parks, and the street. At times the job was dangerous and unpredictable, but the hardest part was the energetic saturation that occurred from lengthy hours of listening to people. Often I would come home speechless, managing only to take a shower and go straight to bed, thoroughly drained.

After the Pomegranate trees took root and grew taller, my teacher gave me a tip: pull off one leaf from the tree and put it in your pocket. The leaf absorbs toxic energies. Later, after work, on your way home, in a place where there are no people, throw the leaf out the window as you're driving. Before every shift I would pluck an emerald leaf; at the end of the day, I tossed the leaf. Having a way to rid myself of all the wacky vibes I was exposed to helped protect me from the mental and emotional intensity of the job.

Why It's Special

Pomegranates, native to India and the Middle East, thrive in dry regions and are now cultivated in Asia, the Mediterranean, California, and Arizona. The flower has bright orange petals with waxy, coral-colored, triangular sepals in between the petals. The flower transforms into a yellow or red fruit with seeds that are red and white. The seeds are either sweet or tart, and are used for making juice, and also in salads and cocktails (the original grenadine was made with Pomegranate juice). The seeds are used for making chutneys and curries in India and Pakistan, and soups and other savory dishes in the Middle East.

Many skin-care formulations now use Pomegranate seed oil for tonifying and tightening the skin. In Ayurvedic medicine, the Pomegranate rind and bark are used for their astringent qualities, like tightening tissues and treating diarrhea, nose bleeds, and hemorrhoids.[1] The juice of the Pomegranate and its flower balance the constitutions of people who like to eat sweet, fatty (Kapha) foods.[2]

Historically in China, paintings with Pomegranates were hung in homes to support fertility and bless the family with children.[3]

What It Reveals

If you're attracted to the Pomegranate flower, you may either be doing a lot of creative projects, requiring extra creative energy, or feel slightly stuck and blocked, needing an electric jolt of creative juice to give you strength so you don't peter out.

You may also feel like you easily take on the stress of other people. If a colleague or family member walks in the room angry or upset, afterward you also feel upset. You may have either strong empathic qualities or an energetic weakness that lowers your resistance to others' vibes. This can lead to fatigue and exhaustion.

Or you may be exposed to external toxins, such as pollution, artificial fragrances, pollen, or other physical irritants. You may need a boost of energy to help your body detoxify. You may have experienced allergies recently or felt fatigued and tired, lacking energy to accomplish your projects.

If you're a woman, being drawn to Pomegranate can mean that your reproductive system needs a boost. Perhaps you get cramps or PMS. If you have irregular cycles, you may want to regularize your cycles so that you can become pregnant or avoid becoming pregnant.

Ask Yourself

Do I feel susceptible to taking on others' stress? Have I felt energetically vulnerable?

Have I recently had allergies or felt irritated by pollutants?

Is my immune system weakened?

Do I need an extra creative boost?

If I am a woman, are my menstrual cycles irregular or painful?

What the Elixir Catalyzes

When we find ourselves dragging, fatigued, or needing more vitality to get us through the day, Pomegranate flower elixir offers a gentle cleansing of the body, strengthening the body's natural detoxification systems and ridding the body and energetic system of toxins and irritants.

Pomegranate strengthens our energetic system so that we are no longer so vulnerable to taking on other people's emotions. We can be compassionate and still be shielded from making other people's stress our own.

The result of better physical and energetic detoxification is that the female reproductive system becomes more balanced. Using Pomegranate elixir regularly over time can eliminate painful cramps, PMS, or irregular cycles within one to three cycles' time.

Additionally, Pomegranate flower activates our creative juices, giving us a creative boost of energy.

Extra Credit

- Get a gym or spa membership and regularly sweat out your toxins at the sauna. If you feel up to it, alternate hot sauna sessions with cold showers and then back to the hot sauna. This detoxifies you and strengthens your immune system over time. Alternatively, take detox baths at least once each week (see page 80 from Chapter 6).

- Drink more water. Get a beautiful water bottle if it helps you feel more inspired. Add flower elixirs to the water to increase your desire to drink it. Squeeze a bit of lemon or lime juice in the water to support your body's natural detox.

- For irregular or painful menstrual cycles, start taking Pomegranate flower elixir every day.

- For energetic vulnerability, practice 5 to 10 minutes of meditation or breathing daily, or plant a Pomegranate tree and try out the method described above.

- Reduce toxins in your food and personal care. Look up the Clean 15 and Dirty Dozen, and eliminate processed foods from your diet (most anything in a box, bag, or can). Eat whole foods. Avoid GMO foods and all forms of refined sugar and flour. Read the book, *No More Dirty Looks*, by Siobhan O'Connor and Alexandra Spunt, and eliminate toxic chemicals from your beauty routine.

In Essence

Dissolves

Irritation, both physical and emotional, as a result of toxic overload

Irregular or painful periods

Lack of creative energy

Magnifies

Vitality through cleansing body and energy

Balancing of reproductive system

Creative energy and self-expression

RED BIRD OF PARADISE

Caesalpinia pulcherrima

Activate: Focus

Message: Get it done.

The Red Bird of Paradise is a fiery gem. The flowers look like exploding orchids, bursting open into flames of orange, red, and yellow. The electric-red stamens reach out in long beautiful strands, and the leaves range from the deepest of greens to blue. This is one of those plants that you could dismiss from a distance, but up close its striking beauty will blow you away.

It flourishes in intense environments like the Sonoran Desert, where the summertime temperatures can rise to over 115 degrees, making everything—from humans to birds, animals, and plant life—weary from the heat. However, the Red Bird of Paradise is unfazed by the heat, transforming it into floral fire. Instead of withering, it channels the hot sun and unfurls into a passionate display.

Why It's Special

The Red Bird of Paradise is native to the tropics and subtropics of the Americas, with widespread cultivation across Asia. During warm weather the plant can grow to a lush 12 feet high. In winter, it likes to be cut back to hibernate or go dormant, waiting for the intensity of the sun and heat to inspire it to grow and bloom. In Asia it's called the Peacock Flower, and in the West Indies, the Dwarf Poinciana.

What It Reveals

If you are drawn to the Red Bird of Paradise, there may be something on your to-do list that you've been avoiding. Even though it may be high priority and important to you, you find yourself procrastinating. You may be going astray, working on inconsequential, easy tasks while leaving your foremost priorities for last.

If there is something you're avoiding, ask yourself why. If it's something that you love, but there's a subtle resistance, it's time to block out other demands, remove all distractions, and get to work. Roll up your sleeves and get it done. Oftentimes we just need a push to start, and once we've started, we enjoy it.

If the sheer volume of what you need to get done sends you spinning into overwhelm, the antidote is to break the task or project into smaller pieces and focus your energy on those actions that will create the highest impact. Redirecting your energies to what's most vital will breathe new life into the "doing" and make it effortless.

Ask Yourself

What truly important items on my to-do list am I avoiding?

When do I procrastinate? How do I distract myself?

Do I feel uninspired or overwhelmed?

What deserves my undivided attention and focus right now?

What the Elixir Catalyzes

Red Bird of Paradise elixir motivates and inspires us to get things done. It fills us with passion and drive, and makes projects that we've previously put off effortless to finish. It dissolves struggle, resistance, and procrastination and helps us act with ease.

From big undertakings that both excite and scare us, like writing a book or applying for a new job, to things that we're dreading, like doing taxes or cleaning closets, Red Bird of Paradise sparks us and ramps up our passion and drive. It helps us understand timing, allowing us to let go of those things whose time has not yet come and jump into action when the time is right.

Extra Credit

- Look at your to-do list and see what items you can delegate, get help with, or defer.

- Write down the three most meaningful things on your to-do list, and focus only on those until completion. Choose those things that will make the biggest impact. Make sure you do something every day that moves each of those three goals forward.

- Make a playlist of music that inspires you and gets you going.

- Identify the physical location where you are most focused and inspired to get things done, and address your priorities there at the same time every day.

- Remind yourself of the why behind your highest priorities, and let that constantly fuel you.

- Dive into reading the book, *Big Magic*, by Elizabeth Gilbert.

In Essence

Dissolves

Procrastination

Overwhelm

Distraction or avoidance

Magnifies

Motivation, drive, passion

"Get it done now" attitude

Effortless action

RED HIBISCUS

Hibiscus rosa-sinensis

Activate: Fresh perspective

Message: Hit the refresh button.

The first time I went to India, an Indian friend of mine asked his sisters to give me a scalp massage. They used an oil that was a dark red in color and smelled of herbs and spices.

I was intrigued by the color, which had been infused from Hibiscus flowers. They gave me the bottle to take home and every time I smell the oil it takes me back to India, where I gained a totally new perspective on life.

Why It's Special

The Hibiscus flower is in the Mallow family, and this variety, *Hibiscus rosa-sinensis*, is also known as the "Chinese rose" or "Chinese hibiscus." This Hibiscus comes in many colors, usually warm colors like yellow, orange, red, and pink. It is beloved in gardening and landscaping for its bright colors and swirling shapes.

In Ayurvedic medicine, the *Hibiscus rosa-sinensis* is used for hair loss and graying of the hair. Hibiscus flowers are boiled and combined with other herbs and spices in oil as a hair and scalp treatment. Studies show that the extract absorbs ultraviolet light, making it an important sun-protective ingredient in skin care.

Note: This Hibiscus flower is different from the one commonly used in teas and beverages like Agua de Jamaica, a refreshing hibiscus drink made in Mexico. That is *Hibiscus sabdariffa*, a sister to the flower featured here.

What It Reveals

If you're drawn to Red Hibiscus, you may have recently experienced a series of stressful events. You might feel exhausted by emotional stress, having had "one thing after another" occur. Perhaps by now you feel totally overwhelmed and overstimulated, and unsure of what to do. You may be craving a light at the end of the tunnel, a sigh of relief, and a fresh perspective for the future.

Ask Yourself

What stressful events have occurred in my life lately?

What am I learning from them?

What new perspective am I gaining?

What would give me a sense of hope and relief?

What the Elixir Catalyzes

Hibiscus helps us regain hope and experience relief after a string of stressful events. It brings in light at the end of the tunnel, and supports us in recognizing how these situations contribute to our personal growth.

When we have several life-changing events in a row, these events can re-create or mold us into a different person. This has a positive side; it can give us the sense of having a fresh start.

Hibiscus flower helps us turn over a new leaf into a new chapter of our lives, while retaining the wisdom we have gained from challenging situations. It allows us to start anew with a fresh perspective.

Extra Credit

- Write down a list of the stressful events you've experienced in the last few months, and what you've learned from them. Give yourself credit for all you do.

- Time for a spa day! Get a massage; head to the nearest sauna or hot tub to relax for a while.

- Find a way to offload some chores. Hire a housecleaner, order out, get food delivered, or find other ways to get help.

- Take vitamins or drink green juices to nourish your body and prevent stressors from wearing you down physically.

- Take a day off and do whatever nourishes you.

In Essence

Dissolves	Magnifies
High stress	Hope, relief, and fresh perspective
Overwhelm	Light at the end of the tunnel
Sense of being challenged for a long period of time	Sense of a new start

RHODODENDRON

Rhododendron ferrugineum

Activate: Compassion

Message: Be kind to yourself.

The first time I fell in love with Rhododendron flowers I was in Seattle, Washington, for a conference called Seeds of Compassion with His Holiness the Dalai Lama. Since Rhododendron activates compassion, I thought it was fitting that so many Rhododendron flowers were blooming at the time.

I later found out that the Rhododendron is Washington's state flower. I find it interesting that there are so many nonprofits in Washington, all dedicated to promoting the practice of compassion in action.

Why It's Special

The name Rhododendron comes from a Greek word meaning "rose tree," and this plant is known for its clusters of bright-colored flowers. There are about 1,000 different species of Rhododendron, found mainly from the Himalayas to Southeast Asia. Some Rhododendrons are also found in North America—on West Coast or Appalachian mountains.

In the state of Himachal Pradesh in India, wines are made with the fruits of the Rhododendron. In India and Burma, among the Zomi indigenous people, the word for the Rhododendron flower can be used in place of the word for "woman."

What It Reveals

If you're attracted to the Pink Rhododendron flower, it may be time to practice compassion with yourself. You may have felt out of place, unprotected, or vulnerable. Or you may be feeling lonely or having doubts about someone's love for you. You may have had a misunderstanding in a relationship that left you feeling despair, anguish, or worry that your love is not reciprocated.

If you find yourself annoyed with others, finding fault with their mannerisms, or judging them, it may be related to being hard on yourself. Your capacity to care for others is enhanced by developing compassion for yourself. Softening, and taking a gentle approach with both yourself and others can melt glaciers of ice and move mountains.

Ask Yourself

In what situations could I be more loving and kind to myself?

Have I recently experienced fear of not being loved? When?

What relationship has been strained? What am I learning from it?

When do I feel critical of others and judge their actions?

What the Elixir Catalyzes

Rhododendron flower embodies the rich warmth, love, and understanding that a mother has for her child. It is the stable, enduring, unconditional love that dissolves fear and loneliness.

The quality of the Rhododendron flower is like being inside a big soft pink cloud of love and comfort. It helps you treat yourself with compassion and genuine care. This means you don't have to look for love outside of yourself, so you are not experiencing yearning, loneliness, or lack.

Rhododendron strengthens all kinds of relationships, especially where there is doubt about the reciprocal nature of love. It helps you feel included and valued. Rhododendron enhances bonding in all types of relationships, with a special impact on babies and mothers during pregnancy and between children and parents during adoption.

Extra Credit

- If you feel anguish, sit with whatever is arising in your mind in a nonjudgmental way and watch it transform into insights.

- Within any relationship, especially one that is currently strained, constantly put yourself in the other person's shoes to inspire empathy with their perspective.

- Notice when you judge yourself or your feelings and reactions. Give yourself a break and be gentle with yourself.

- Warm up your heart, toward both yourself and others around you. A soft heart capable of vulnerability softens the harder edges of life. People will respond to you with that same softness, because you'll inspire it in them.

- Turn inward and give yourself unconditional love and compassion.

In Essence

Dissolves	*Magnifies*
Feeling cold, alone, out of place, vulnerable	Understanding, compassion, empathy
Jealousy, insecurity, despair	Motherly love, comfort, warmth, and protection
Fear of misunderstanding or betrayal	Steadiness, equanimity

ROSE

Rosa spp.

Activate: Tenderness

Message: Nurture yourself.

As I mentioned earlier in these pages, during one of my trips to India, I was invited to the wedding of two American friends who wanted a traditional Indian wedding. I brought a bouquet of red roses with me, thinking it would be novel to pull off the rose petals and toss them over the bride and groom.

I was shocked when I entered the space: There was a large mandala of flowers on the ground where the ceremony was to take place. There were beautiful baskets filled with rose and marigold petals. I realized that throwing flower petals was a custom in India, and felt a little silly about the roses I had brought.

This was by far the most exquisite wedding I'd ever been to. During the ceremony, the couple was tied together with a large flower garland that connected them to each other. As they circled around inside the huge flower mandala, we grabbed handfuls of petals and threw them up into the air, letting blossoms rain down into their hair.

Why It's Special

Rose is one of the most popular and beloved flowers in the world. There are around 100 different species of Roses, with thousands of hybrids and cultivars. Most roses originate from Asia, and they are the quintessential flower for weddings in the U.S.

The scent of Rose is soothing and to some intoxicating, with love-inducing effects. Its essential oil is one of the most expensive and sought-after oils. The distillation process requires at least 60 Roses in order to get just one drop of precious Rose oil.

Rose was the most popular flavoring in Europe and North America until the 19th century, when vanilla was discovered. It remains a popular flavoring in India and the Middle East, with Rose water splashed into beverages and desserts.

Whether drunk as a tea, inhaled in an essential oil, or taken as a flower elixir, Rose is a general tonic that soothes the heart. Roses cool the body and decrease inflammation, making them a popular choice for skin care.

What It Reveals

If you're attracted to the Rose flower, you may need some extra love and comfort. Create an environment around you that is nurturing, supportive, and sweet. As you soften your heart and offer compassion to yourself, it will naturally be returned to you. As you treat yourself with more kindness, that naturally extends toward others as well.

If you feel under psychic or emotional attack, or if someone in your home or work space has been harsh with you, make time to nurture yourself. Soften into your own vulnerability, to heal your heart and protect you from bitterness and resentment.

Ask Yourself

When do I feel myself harden, or become cold or aloof?

In what areas of my life do I feel unloved or in need of more nourishment?

When do I feel like life is a struggle?

How could I nurture myself more?

What inspires me to be more loving toward myself? Toward others?

What the Elixir Catalyzes

Rose elixir magnifies unconditional love and tenderness. It inspires us to nurture and care for ourselves and others. One of the best flowers for healing the heart, Rose cools the temper and triggers forgiveness, healing emotional wounds and scars. It softens our hard edges and enhances compassion and empathy.

Rose flower elixir unravels the causes of a hardened heart—not just a broken heart, but also our disappointment and stubbornness, our feeling that we are being ignored or that life is full of struggle. It warms us up when we feel aloof or cold, and sweetens us when we feel bitter.

Rose is also a protective agent, keeping us safe from angry vibes and harmful thought forms. It shields us from negativity and promotes a gentle strength.

Extra Credit

- Hop into bed and snuggle with your pet, child, or loved one.
- Practice heart opening stretches or yoga poses: roll up a blanket or pillow and place it under your shoulder blades or along your spine; stretch out your arms and open up your chest and rest that way for a few minutes.
- Eat more dark chocolate—it's good for heart health.
- Make sure your bed is soft and comforting. Use soft sheets and a comfortable blanket that you can wrap up in.
- Put a piece of rose quartz in your pocket or wear rose quartz jewelry.
- Anoint yourself with real Rose essential oil.
- Spend time in a Rose garden or buy yourself a bouquet of Roses.
- Make yourself a cup of Rose petal tea.

In Essence

Dissolves	*Magnifies*
Disappointment	Attentiveness, sweetness
Feeling ignored or unloved	Kindness and caring for yourself and others
Belief that life is full of struggle	Healing emotional wounds and scars

ROSE PETAL BATH TO NURTURE THE HEART

Collect nine roses and soak them in a large clear glass bowl filled with water. Place the bowl in direct sunlight, leaving the petals intact. After several hours, the water will be super-charged with the healing powers of Rose. Pour into a bathtub filled with warm water.

For a beautiful aesthetic effect, remove all the petals from each Rose and sprinkle them into the bathwater. Immerse yourself in the Rose bathwater.

ROSE HOUSE CLEANSING RITUAL

If you or anyone in your house has gotten into an argument, with shouting and fighting, or if a negative person came to visit you and left remnants of their bad mood in your house, here is a ritual to clear out any negative vibes from the house.

Collect six Roses and soak five of them in a large clear glass bowl filled with water. Place the bowl in direct morning sunlight for several hours.

Using the sixth Rose, dip the tips of the petals into the Rose water, gently splashing Rose water around each room of the house. Include corners and above doorways and windows, being careful not to get anything important wet.

You can also strain out Roses and transfer the Rose water to a spray bottle and mist around the house. The mist will last up to one week when refrigerated. It will not have a strong scent, but it will spread love and warm feelings throughout the house.

ROYAL POINCIANA

Delonix regia

Activate: Conviction

Message: Ask for what you want.

During a business trip to the island of Bermuda, I discovered one of the most beautiful flowering trees I'd ever seen. From a distance it looked like a massive tree on fire. Covered in explosive red flowers, it was almost too bright to look at.

As I was gazing at the tree, a couple drove up on a motorbike, and the gentleman said he had grown up on the island. This was his first time back to visit in 20 years, and he had brought his girlfriend along to show her this tree—that's how significant this tree was to him.

Why It's Special

Also known as the Flame Tree, Royal Poinciana is native to Madagascar, where the wild tree is endangered as it is being cut down for firewood. Luckily it's cultivated all over the world, not only in Bermuda but also in Asia, where it has names like "Phoenix Tail" and "Peacock Tree." In Central America, it's "Call of the Forest." In the Caribbean it's called "Flamboyant"—a synonym for exuberant, confident, lively, animated, vibrant, stylish, and vivacious—which opens a window into this flower's special qualities.

The flowers are wildly beautiful, with colors ranging from the brightest of yellows to the most fiery scarlet and crimson. The trunk of the tree twists around into humanlike poses, imitating the sensuous curves of a woman's hip, with branches that look like arms and legs. The leaves are bright green in a lacy, fernlike formation, draping down toward the ground. At dusk the delicate leaves fold up for the night.

If you live in a warm climate where the temperatures don't fall below 45°F, this is a hardy tree that will grow 20 to 40 feet tall, creating tons of shade, along with an occasional carpet of fiery flowers. If the tree is in the proper climate, it requires little care, except watering during very dry periods and pruning when it's young, so that it grows taller and fuller. It's surprisingly easy to grow from seed, and if you live in colder areas, you can make the tree into a strikingly beautiful indoor bonsai tree.

What It Reveals

If you're attracted to the Royal Poinciana flower, there may be times that you keep quiet or settle for less than exactly what you want. You may feel shy or hesitant, or beat around the bush. If you don't get what you want, you may feel apathetic, thinking to yourself, "Oh well, next time."

Now is the time to get out of your own way and cut through fears and hesitations, or insecurities about whether or not you "deserve" it. Ask for what you want. Worst-case scenario, you get a "no." And then you can ask again and again until you exhaust all possibilities. Be persistent. Tap into your conviction and what you know to be true. Then, if you still get a "no," implement plan B.

Be direct. Ask for things that would normally be way out of your comfort zone. Refuse to allow any mundane policies, gatekeepers, naysayers, or small thinkers to say no or create obstacles to achieving what you want. Talk to the highest-level person, and if you experience resistance, keep moving up the ladder. Respectfully, don't take no for an answer.

If there's something you've been thinking about, now is the time to go for it. If you need support on a project, an interview with a high-level person, a new team member to help you with your work, help cleaning the house, or mentoring to take what you're doing to the next level—do it now. Allow yourself to be driven by your conviction and your wish to benefit others. Dismiss negative thinking on your part or anyone else's.

Ask Yourself

In what situations do I play small? What would it look like if I were playing big?

What's distracting me from going after my biggest dreams by making an action plan?

What are some ways I can eliminate distraction?

What's my best strategy for declining others' requests on my time?

If I were absolutely FEARLESS, what would I do?

What the Elixir Catalyzes

Royal Poinciana flower enhances certitude, assurance, and confidence. It eliminates doubt and hesitation by awakening clarity and an earnest conviction about the choices we make. It helps us to go out on a limb and request things we normally wouldn't request. Instead of being nervous or feeling like we're "making a big deal," Royal Poinciana allows us to feel that we deserve the best and more—and gives us the strength to go after it.

This fiery flower also helps with setting boundaries, making sure we don't play small or get taken advantage of. It encourages us to be direct, forthright, and bold in our communication and actions. It sharpens our focus for engaging in constructive action, while enhancing our ability to think big and take on projects that are challenging. It helps us be more in tune with our wildest aspirations, and awakens a deep conviction that we can make them real.

Royal Poinciana transforms dullness, lackadaisical (or lazy) attitudes and lack of motivation into clarity and decisiveness. It dissolves shame, meekness, timidity, lack of self-worth, and deep-seated patterns of feeling undeserving or uncertain. When we experience absolute conviction, there is no room for hesitation or doubt. We simply act.

Extra Credit

- Make a list of your most convincing, compelling reasons for doing what you want to do. Post it in your bathroom, car, on your laptop, or as your cell phone wallpaper.

- Make a list right now of the top five things that you'd like to accomplish in the next five years. These would be your wildest dreams (so wild you probably keep them secret), your biggest vision, and your boldest, most audacious projects. Put this list somewhere that you'll see every day, so that it's uppermost in your mind. Make sure your daily actions build a foundation for those top priorities.

- For the next month, anytime a customer-service person says something is not possible, ask for their manager and keep asking until you don't get no for an answer.

- If you have any credit cards, call them and ask for a lower interest rate.

- Ask someone for help. Find ways to stretch your "ask-for-what-you-want" muscle.

- Reach out to someone you admire and ask for a mentoring session.

In Essence

Dissolves	*Magnifies*
Meekness, shyness	Clarity, decisiveness, laser focus
Unworthiness, shame	Asking for what you want without hesitation
Lackadaisical attitude, lack of motivation	Thinking big, taking on challenges, "whatever it takes" conviction

SILK FLOSS

Ceiba speciosa

Activate: Confidence

Message: It's time to shine.

In my neighborhood, one tree stands out as different from the rest. When all the other trees have a rich green hue to their leaves, the Silk Floss is covered in blossoms, ablaze in shocking pink! When you approach the tree, you notice something else that's different: its trunk is covered in conical spikes.

Why It's Special

Silk Floss is a tree native to South America. Its flowers are magenta, with a creamy center and a huge pistil popping out from the center. The blossoms are large, about the size of your hand. One of the only pollinators successful with this flower is the monarch butterfly.

Silk Floss produces long seedpods that contain a fluffy, silklike plant matter that can be used in making paper. Like the kapok tree, it's also used to stuff pillows and life jackets for boats. When the Silk Floss tree is young, its trunk is green and capable of photosynthesis; as the tree gets older and has more leaves, the trunk matures into a beautiful gray.[1]

What It Reveals

If you find yourself attracted to the Silk Floss flower, you may be in a new situation that is making you feel out of your element. When you feel self-conscious, it takes your focus away from being present in the moment. There may be times when you worry about what others think, or you feel weird and different, which makes it difficult to let loose. You could be feeling wary, small, and insignificant, or simply awkward.

Alternatively, feeling uncomfortable in your own skin can be particularly distressing or troublesome during the aging process.

Ask Yourself

In what areas of my life do I lack confidence?

When do I feel weird, different, awkward, or out of my element?

In what circumstances do I feel like I allow myself to shine?

What would it feel like to fully accept myself?

What the Elixir Catalyzes

The Silk Floss flower enhances our ability to be at ease in our own skin, no matter what situation we are in. It dissolves shame, embarrassment, or awkwardness, and helps us embrace our uniqueness.

When we're wound up in self-consciousness, we tend to close ourselves off from enjoying the moment and experiencing what's around us. Silk Floss helps us fully accept ourselves, and shine. It helps us stand tall, exude confidence, and feel at ease with who and how we are.

Regarding aging, Silk Floss encourages us to shine from our inner essence, and not get caught up in how our appearance is changing with time and gravity. It magnifies self-assuredness and ease.

Extra Credit

- Dress to the nines even if you have nowhere to go.

- Express confidence with your posture. Lift up your heart to the sky and straighten your spine. Point your nose straight ahead of you without looking down. Smile and make eye contact with people you meet.

- Take a ballroom dance class to improve your posture, balance, and grace.

- Remind yourself of the many reasons you have to be confident. Appreciate yourself for what you're good at, and when you've been a kind person.

- Ask five people who cherish and love you to give you five words that describe your greatest strengths.

In Essence

Dissolves

Feeling out of your element, awkward, embarrassed

Feeling small, insignificant

Feeling ashamed, weird, different

Magnifies

Confidence and comfort with who you are

Ability to shine and be proud of yourself

Self-expression, self-assuredness

SQUASH BLOSSOM

Cucurbita pepo

> **Activate:** Liberation
>
> **Message:** Feel free in your body.

When I lived in Mexico, I loved the way that delicate Squash blossoms were made a part of Mexican cuisine. As every flower typically transforms into the fruit of the plant, I always thought that eating the Squash blossoms meant there would be one less squash, making them even more precious as a delicacy.

On the squash plant, however, there are both male and female flowers, and only the females turn into squashes. The female flowers grow close to the center of the plant and have a swollen fruit instead of a stalk as their base, whereas the male flowers grow on longer, skinnier stalks that extend farther out from the plant. The male flowers fall off the plant anyway, so as long as the female flowers are pollinated, the male flowers can be used for cooking.

Why It's Special

Squash blossoms are native to the Americas. The flower is cooked and eaten all over Latin America, often stuffed and fried, or gently steamed inside a pocket of light tempura batter. Though we typically consider it a vegetable, botanically it is a fruit, one that's often made into sweet breads like zucchini bread.

What It Reveals

If you're attracted to the Squash blossom, you may feel creatively stagnant, shut down, or blocked. A subtle resistance may be preventing you from tapping into your usual innovative ideas.

Another possibility is that intimate relationships may feel difficult or challenging. This can also manifest as a general hesitancy regarding close romantic or sexual relationships, as a fear of not being beautiful, or a feeling of shame about one's body.

Yet another possibility is that you may be afraid of one of the following: getting pregnant, not getting pregnant, having a miscarriage, or motherhood. If you are pregnant, you may have inexplicable fears around pregnancy and childbirth, the possibility of the baby's being born with health issues, or of not having sufficient mothering skills.

Ask Yourself

When have I recently felt creatively blocked?

What are my fears around intimacy and relationships? Around motherhood?

In what ways could I enhance my intimate relationships?

What could I do to feel freer in my body?

What the Elixir Catalyzes

Squash blossom liberates our creative energy, promoting a prolific imagination. It leaves us inspired and able to inspire others. It cuts through blocks and stuckness to help us create.

It also enhances fertility, balances a woman's reproductive system, and regularizes menstrual cycles. It enhances our maternal instincts, and helps us understand and dismantle our fears related to pregnancy and childbirth. It dissolves our fear of losing control and our fear of our own bodies. Squash blossom can be helpful for challenging conceptions and pregnancies.

Squash blossom also unravels and heals trauma from feeling exploited or abused in the past. It clarifies any confusion, shyness, or apprehension we may have regarding our sexuality.

Extra Credit

- Blast through any creative blocks by writing a one-minute poem, messing around with watercolors for 20 minutes, or building a mandala with flower petals, leaves, and twigs you find outside.

- Gather up a group of creatives and keep each other motivated by sharing quick and easy creativity prompts with each other.

- Whether you're a man or a woman, find ways to get in touch with your feminine, receptive, and tender side.

- If you're considering pregnancy or are already pregnant, find a supportive midwife and doula in your area.

- Spend time around mothers with small babies.

In Essence

Dissolves

Limiting patterns regarding sensuality and sexuality, trauma from past sexual abuse

Fear of losing control, fear of labor and childbirth

Lack of creativity, feeling stagnant or shut down

Magnifies

Fertility, easeful labor, and childbirth, women's reproductive balance

Healthy expression of sensuality and sexuality

Prolific creative expression, birthing new ideas

SAVORY SQUASH BLOSSOMS

The delicate flavor of Squash blossoms is a nice surprise when discovered within the salty and savory taste of tempura batter fried in oil. This recipe's batter is not only gluten-free, but it's infused with kombucha, an effervescent fermented tea. Choose your favorite kind of kombucha to give it your own personal flavorful twist. Combine that with melted goat cheese, and it's basically the ultimate comfort food.

The typical season for Zucchini Squash blossoms is May to September. If you grow your own zucchini squashes, pick the flowers that are farthest from the center of the plant, as those are the males and will not turn into squashes, as will the female flowers tucked in close to the center of the plant. If you don't have a garden, the best place to find Squash blossoms is at a farmers' market or organic market. Squash blossoms are very delicate; use within 24 hours of obtaining them.

Ingredients

12 Zucchini Squash Blossoms, stamen removed

Savory Goat Cheese Filling
8 ounces goat cheese
Juice from 1/2 lemon
3 tablespoons minced blend of cilantro, chives, and garlic
1/4 teaspoon cayenne pepper (optional)

Gluten-Free Bubbly Batter
1/2 cup white rice flour
1/2 cup kombucha
2 teaspoons salt

2 cups vegetable oil
Maple syrup (optional)

Gently remove the stamen from the center of each Zucchini Squash blossom, and set aside.

To make the Savory Goat Cheese Filling: Mix together all the filling ingredients and scoop them into a zip-top bag. Snip one corner of the bag, so you can squeeze the cheese mixture into the center of each Zucchini Squash blossom.

Fill each Zucchini Squash blossom and delicately twist the flower shut.

To make the Gluten-Free Bubbly Batter: Mix together all the batter ingredients in a shallow bowl, and set aside.

Dip the filled Zucchini Squash blossoms into the batter. Heat the vegetable oil in a frying pan or wok. Place the battered Zucchini Squash blossoms in the frying pan, and fry for 2 to 3 minutes. Flip to the other side and repeat until they are a nice golden color. Use a pair of tongs or a slotted spoon to remove the battered flowers from the oil. Transfer to a plate lined with a paper towel to absorb the excess oil. Drizzle with maple syrup, if using, and serve.

STRAWBERRY BLOSSOM

Fragaria

Activate: Optimism

Message: Expect the best.

Who doesn't love strawberries? Especially wild strawberries! It's such a delicious and joyous explosion of flavor—sweet and fruity. Finding a patch of wild strawberries is like finding treasure!

Why It's Special

In the 15th century, monks in Europe wrote in their manuscripts about the medicinal properties of wild strawberry plants as a treatment for depression. By the 16th century, mainstream culture in Europe began using them for their medicinal value. During this time, strawberries were only available in the wild and the only way to obtain them was by foraging.

The modern strawberry that we know today was cultivated in the late 18th century, when a new species occurred between two plants that were imported into France, one from North America and one from Chile.

Fast-forward to today, when the top five strawberry growing countries in the world produce almost 5 ½ million tons of strawberries annually. Strawberries, now a popular ingredient in desserts, are commonly added to smoothies, gelato, ice cream, milk, and yogurt.[1]

Herbalists have worked with strawberry leaves for centuries as an invaluable remedy to improve digestion, purify the blood, soothe the stomach, reduce aches and pains, support natural weight loss, diminish menstruation, and dissolve tension and stress. Strawberry leaf tea is gentle, appropriate for both pregnant women and children. Strawberry plants also have one of the highest naturally occurring rates of vitamin C.

Strawberry blossoms are white or pink, and the flowers are edible—but of course if you eat the flower, you won't get the fruit!

What It Reveals

If you're attracted to the Strawberry blossom you may feel like you're waiting for the other shoe to drop. You may notice your mind making up scenarios about the future and expecting the worst outcome.

There may be an area of your life that fills you with dread, or has you spinning with negative possibilities. You might catch yourself feeling like "Negative Nelly," either complaining or anticipating unfavorable circumstances.

You may feel in need of fresh energy and opportunities.

Ask Yourself

When do I find myself expecting the worst?

When do I find myself expecting the best?

What opportunities am I wide open to right now?

In what ways might I be closing myself off to opportunities?

What the Elixir Catalyzes

Imagine the feeling we get, in the forest or in a garden, when we see a strawberry patch full of ripe strawberries. It's like a miracle! We feel so lucky. And when we reach down to pick and eat these ruby-red jewels it's like a secret treasure that we were lucky enough to find. That sense of good fortune is the feeling that Strawberry blossom imparts.

It dissolves the habit of expecting or preparing for the worst, and gives us a fresh outlook, a sense that anything is possible. It cuts through pessimism, worry, and negative thoughts. It helps us have a deeper understanding of ourselves and our infinite possibilities for personal growth.

Extra Credit

- List all the wild possibilities that might be available to you now.
- If you catch yourself experiencing dread, immediately flip your mind toward a possible positive outcome.
- Write down all of the opportunities you have been given in the past.
- Write down all the opportunities that you are currently open to right now.
- What's the best possible outcome for every area of your life? Remember you don't have to know "how" to get there—just focus on the end goal.

In Essence

Dissolves

Blindness to possibilities and opportunities

Pessimism, expecting the worst

Dread, negativity, drudgery

Magnifies

Optimism, sense of possibility

Openness to growth and opportunities

Fresh perspective

TRUMPET VINE

Campsis grandiflora

Activate: Effortless speech

Message: Free your voice.

Trumpet Vine has little tendrils that grab on to anything and climb up walls. Bees buzz in and out of the flowers, and hummingbirds zoom through space, poking their long slender beaks into the trumpets for nectar. The flowers open their mouths in song with voluptuous, caricature-like lips. Since I was a child who had a tendency to be shy and found it difficult to speak my mind, this flower often called my name.

Why It's Special

There are two kinds of Trumpet Vine, one that's native to China (*Campsis grandiflora*) and one that's native to the eastern United States (*Campsis radicans*). Also known as Trumpet Creeper, this vine grows vigorously and blossoms into large trumpet-shaped flowers in the brightest of reds, oranges, and yellows.[1]

The Chinese variety has the largest flowers and is not quite as invasive as its American sister, which has been known to swallow entire buildings and trees if not guided through pruning. To avoid damaging houses or strangling trees, you should plant this variety away from them. Their green tendrils grab on to surfaces and quickly turn into a woody vine. After the flowers die, long seedpods emerge and fall off the vine. When you prune the plant, gloves are recommended, as it can be irritating to the skin.

What It Reveals

If you're attracted to the Trumpet Vine flower, you may be struggling to speak with ease. You may feel blocked in the throat or hesitant in your speech. Perhaps you need to have a difficult conversation that you've been avoiding, or you tend to avoid difficult conversations altogether.

Being drawn to Trumpet Vine usually indicates a general fear of speaking and public speaking. You may want to develop your singing voice and your vocal projection.

Ask Yourself

When do I have a hard time speaking my mind? Speaking in public?

In what situations has it been easier to express myself?

What's my favorite form of self-expression?

Are there any difficult conversations I avoid?

What the Elixir Catalyzes

The Trumpet Vine flower dissolves blockages and self-limiting patterns regarding speech and communication. It cuts through fears of speaking up, while magnifying our ability to speak freely about what's inside us, even if it's a difficult conversation.

Trumpet Vine also helps us develop and refine our singing voice. It enhances our comfort with being heard and being seen by other people, and even by large audiences.

Extra Credit

- Take a public speaking class or apply to do a public talk.
- Take voice or vocal projection lessons.
- Join a community choir, sing in the shower, or learn a chanting meditation.
- Often when you don't want to be seen, your shoulders curve downward. Improve your posture and free your voice by lifting your heart to the sky.
- Refrain from speaking for one day to build up your speech energies.
- Go to a party or gathering and vow to strike up a conversation with five strangers.

In Essence

Dissolves

Fear of speaking and being heard

Communication issues

Avoidance of saying what needs to be said

Magnifies

Ability to speak freely about what's inside you

Effortless communication even during difficult conversations

Enhanced singing voice

WHITE MAGNOLIA

Magnolia grandiflora

Activate: Spiritual fulfillment

Message: You are divine.

I fell in love with the White Magnolia in San Francisco, when I took a perfumery intensive in the attic of the legendary Jeanne Rose, fashion designer for Janis Joplin and other rock stars. In addition to designing clothes, over her lifetime Jeanne became a walking encyclopedia of gardening, herbal, distillation, essential oil, and botanical perfumery knowledge.

While creating perfumes one after another in her attic, we frequently had to step outside to take breaks, as the space filled up with aromatic molecules from over 100 different oils. I would stick my head out the front window of her house, only to inhale an intoxicating scent from the trees down below—White Magnolias. Later, at tree level, I reached up, pulled down a blossom, and buried my face in it, breathing deep and feeling drunk on the rich, spicy aroma.

Years later, I made a flower elixir of the White Magnolia on the subtropical island of Bermuda. To me, the Magnolia has always looked like a tree full of white Lotus flowers. Like the Lotus, White Magnolia embodies ancient wisdom and purity.

Why It's Special

The Magnolia flower is so old, it was alive on Earth before the bees appeared, with some fossils identified to be over 95 million years old! That's why the Magnolia flower is so tough, because this ancient flower was pollinated by beetles.

The Magnolia tree survived the ice ages and the formation of new mountains. It also survived continental drift—one of the possible scenarios explaining why some of the 200 species of Magnolia grow in Asia and others grow in the Americas.

The *Magnolia grandiflora*, which is the huge creamy White Magnolia, is native to the Americas. The leaves are a rich green on top with dark brown velvet on the undersides. The flower is supremely fragrant with a spicy floral scent.

What It Reveals

If you feel attracted to Magnolia, you may feel like something in your life is changing in a big way. Magnolia offers a chance to slow down, feel more in tune, accept the unknown, and trust that all will be well. Magnolia clears away negativity, darkness, extraneous thoughts, and fears (including fears about death and the afterlife).

There may be a natural process that's happening in your life that you are fighting. Aging, for example, is something that we often resist. Instead of recognizing that our bodies change over time, we wish them to be as they were in our younger years, and we either live in a fantasy world or push our physical limits too far—even to the point of injury.

You may notice that you've recently been afraid of change, or of losing something that's important to you. You may be fearful of being separated from a loved one. You may find yourself worrying about the future, which may cause you to miss out on the present, inviting disappointment or a sense of missed opportunity. If you can relax into the way things are and how they are evolving, you can find peace and magic in the moment, no matter what might change in the future.

Ask Yourself

When do I find myself thinking too much or worrying about the future?

When do I get so distracted that I'm not present with the people I love?

When do I perceive my loved ones as divine? When do I experience myself as divine? In what situations have I felt the most connected or fulfilled spiritually?

What the Elixir Catalyzes

The White Magnolia holds itself open like a gentle cup from which to drink, inspiring us to look beyond the obvious and see what's deeper. Magnolia helps us to experience profound peace and spiritual fulfillment. It frees us from worry, and awakens the part of us that is all-knowing and aware of divine timing.

Magnolia helps us come to peace with the way things are and what's to come, making for gentle transformations. For that reason, Magnolia flower is supportive for major transitions like birth and death, or for those times when we feel that an aspect of ourselves is dying or being reborn.

Like the Pink Lotus, White Magnolia is a catalyst flower elixir, strengthening the effectiveness and synergy of all other flower elixirs and botanical remedies with which it's combined.

Extra Credit

- Be in the present moment by being aware of your breath and how your body feels. When you're in the present moment you will automatically have a more acute sense of how meaningful life is.
- When faced with transitions, move through them gently by using mindful-awareness techniques like the one above.
- Make time for meditation, prayer, nature walks, or whatever makes you feel more in tune with the profoundness of life.
- Tonight before you go to bed, make a short list of those people you feel most grateful for in your life.
- Notice whether you see the cup as half full or half empty; consciously choose how you want to see it.

In Essence

Dissolves	*Magnifies*
Negativity, darkness	Awakening, highest aspirations
Extraneous thoughts	Deep peace, spiritual fulfillment, acceptance
Fears, including fears about death	Ability to sense the divine in every moment
	Catalyst for all flower elixirs and plant remedies

WHITE WATER LILY

Nymphaea odorata

Activate: Awareness

Message: Sharpen your senses.

Who doesn't love Water Lilies? With all their beautiful colors and magic carpet pads that float on the water's surface, they transform tea-colored ponds into a kaleidoscopic paradise.

When I encountered the White Water Lily, I was in awe, walking around the property of a green-thumb landscaper in the Arizona desert. He had grown a paradise—a micro-climate that included bamboo, comfrey plants, mulberries, kumquats, and Water Lilies. Plants of all different environments co-existed in the world that he created, the elegant Water Lily so much the opposite of what we usually see in the desert.

Why It's Special

During the summer months, Water Lilies bloom for several days, opening their delicate petals in the morning sun and closing back into buds in the evenings. Even the night-blooming Water Lilies need the hot sun as a catalyst to open at night.

Water Lilies are one of the oldest aquatic plants, and some Water Lily fossils have leaf pads that are four feet wide! Though they are cultivated all over the world, Water Lilies are native to Europe and North Africa.

Water Lilies are rooted into the mud in a pond, with the flowers floating on the surface of the water. White Water Lilies have many petals, sometimes with a pinkish tinge, and bright yellow stamens in the middle.

After the Water Lily has blossomed, the flower stalk coils itself like a corkscrew and drags the flower under the water to develop the fruit. When the seeds are ready, they float back up to the surface so they can travel around the pond, finally sinking and burying themselves in the muddy bottom.[1]

Medicinally, the rhizome and seeds are used for cooling and moistening the body and removing toxins from the tissues; they are indicated for a variety of infections, inflammations, irritations, and heat in the body. For wounds or sunburns, the leaves and flowers can be bruised and applied directly to decrease swelling and inflammation and cool the skin.[2]

What It Reveals

If you are attracted to White Water Lily you may feel as if there are invisible walls around you, preventing you from really seeing. Or you may feel like you're under water. There are times in our lives when we feel that nothing is clear and nothing is happening, which usually couldn't be further from the truth.

If you've been hibernating, it may simply be because you are growing something bigger than yourself. Oftentimes we need to dissolve or unravel everything in life in order to reconstruct it in a whole new way that will better support what's to come.

Just as the Water Lily winds itself into a corkscrew and pulls the flower stem under water in order to create the fruit, when we perceive that things aren't clear, it is due to old structures dissolving in order to make way for new ones. These new ways cannot emerge without complete dissolution of the old.

If things have not been going as expected on a project you're working on, see it as a gestation period. Something is getting ready to be birthed, and it may be completely different from (and better than) your expectations.

Ask Yourself

In what area of my life do I feel unclear?

What is gestating right now in my life?

What old ways of doing or being am I altering in order to bring in new ways?

When do I feel like I'm in the right place at the right time?

What the Elixir Catalyzes

Just as the White Water Lily drags itself under water, the elixir has the effect of bringing us into a world of deeper sensitivity. It enhances an inner stillness that is undisturbed by external factors. It expands our ability to feel deeply connected to others through compassion and synchronicity.

White Water Lily also helps us feel more in tune with the world we live in by heightening our senses of hearing, smelling, seeing, tasting, and feeling. It enhances our ability to perceive more deeply what's around us, transforming our ordinary perception into seeing the magic of the world we live in.

Water Lily magnifies clarity and acuity of vision, dissolving dullness and the walls around us. It lessens the intensity of the feeling that there's something we don't know or can't see, heightening our senses and our awareness.

Extra Credit

- Wait to make any big decisions until the muddiness settles and you can see clearly.
- Take advantage of this time as a period of observation in which you don't yet have to act or make a decision; rather, deepen your awareness of the situation first.
- Spend more time with loved ones.
- Tune in to your surroundings. Take note of the people around you and what they're experiencing or reflecting back to you.
- Remember to be patient with yourself.

In Essence

Dissolves	Magnifies
Lack of awareness or clarity	Awareness, sensitivity to others' needs, compassion, synchronicity
Ignorance or feeling dull	
Walls around you that prevent you from seeing	Feeling more connected to everyone and everything around you
	Sharper senses and perception: hearing, smelling, seeing, feeling, tasting

YARROW

Achillea millefolium

Activate: Recharge

Message: Do a digital detox.

The first time I saw Yarrow I didn't know what I was looking at. A shiny snake had slithered out of the embankment and glided in a squiggly line right in front of my toes, sneaking out of sight under a patch of plants with beautiful white flowers. The snake led me to the renowned Yarrow plant, of which I made an elixir.

During the first five years of using this flower in formulations, few Americans were visually drawn to it. When I went to Japan in 2013, however, I was astounded to see that nearly every person I asked in Tokyo picked Yarrow among the top 3 flowers (out of 24) they were attracted to. I hypothesized that low levels of radiation present in the environment since the Fukushima disaster had created a greater need for Yarrow flower elixir in Japan.

In the last year I've noticed that many people in the United States are now attracted to this flower, too. My theory in the U.S. is that our love for electronic devices is finally catching up with us, resulting in a greater need for Yarrow's specialty: energetic balancing and revitalization.

Recent studies show that we check our smartphones over 150 times each day and spend on average 3 hours daily on the phone. This happens anywhere, including in our beds, in the bathroom, or when we're having a meal with someone. In addition, the average person spends about 5 hours each day on some kind of screen, totaling around 150 hours per month, almost equivalent to a full-time job. Whether surfing the Internet, posting on social media, streaming movies, or reading on a device, most of us are "plugged in" much of the day.[1]

Why It's Special

Yarrow flowers are highly fragrant clusters of tiny white flowers with bright yellow centers. Yarrow is native to the Northern Hemisphere, including Europe, Asia, and North America.

Among Yarrow's many virtues, it has deep roots and mineral-rich leaves that prevent both soil erosion and the loss of nutrients in the soil. It's also a good companion plant, attracting insects that prey on pests that destroy neighboring plants. Yarrow is a favorite flower for butterfly gardens; butterflies love it.

Yarrow's Latin name, *Achillea millefolium*, refers to a mythical Greek character named Achilles who used Yarrow to heal battle wounds. Yarrow is known not only for healing broken tissues and abrasions, but also as a valuable medicinal herb that reduces fevers, encourages clotting, lowers blood pressure, stimulates circulation, and acts as a diuretic and a digestive tonic. Yarrow is a catalyst herb, enhancing the medicinal qualities of all the other herbs with which it is compounded.[2]

Native Americans used Yarrow for pain, such as toothaches and fever aches. The Zuni peoples made a poultice with Yarrow and water as a preparation for fire walking or fire eating, to reduce inflammation and heal burns.

Yarrow is considered a sacred herb, protecting those who carry it from negativity, and even birds line their nests with it to prevent parasites. Additionally, Yarrow essential oil, obtained from steam distillation, is the most exquisite royal blue color and is used in skin care as a powerful anti-inflammatory agent.

Though historically Yarrow is most widely known as a medicinal herb, it was also used as a food, beloved in the 1600s. The leaves were cooked as a vegetable or made into a soup that had a slightly bitter taste.

***WARNING: Be very cautious if foraging Yarrow in the wild. Do not confuse it with the highly poisonous Water Hemlock—which looks similar, like an umbrella of white flowers. If you want to cook with Yarrow, it is safest to grow it yourself.

What It Reveals

If you are attracted to Yarrow, you may find yourself working long hours on the computer and cell phone, which may cause fatigue and drain your energy levels. Or if you have been traveling long distances by airplane, you may experience a lack of vitality due to the natural radiation in the upper atmosphere. Another reason for being attracted to the Yarrow flower is exposure to other kinds of radiation, in cancer treatments or nuclear reactor sites.

If the drain on your energy has nothing to do with electronics or radiation, you may live in a large city or work in an environment packed with people that leave you energetically saturated. This is especially true for empaths; for people in high-touch professions, such as massage therapists, estheticians, hair stylists, and barbers; and for people whose professions include extensive listening, such as therapists, counselors, or customer-service representatives.

Ask Yourself

How many hours each day do I spend on my smartphone, laptop, or desktop? Watching TV?

Have I been feeling drained at the end of the day?

What are my revitalization practices after long airplane flights?

What has been my most effective method for cleansing my energy after large events, parties, or other times when I've been in contact with many people?

What the Elixir Catalyzes

Yarrow flower elixir cleanses the body's energetic field of the static and fatigue that occur after spending long hours in front of any kind of electronic screen (desktop, laptop, tablet, television, smartphone) or in the upper atmosphere on airplane flights. Yarrow boosts the body's natural energy after exposure to these subtle forms of radiation, as well as nuclear radiation that occurs in cancer treatments and near reactor sites.

Yarrow also clears the excess or foreign energies that build up in the energetic field from urban life, being around a lot of people, and excessive physical contact with others, such as shaking hands or hugging. In these situations, the body's energetic field gets saturated or clogged, leading us to feel dull, stagnant, or irritable. Yarrow clears our energetic field, so we can access our natural clarity and vitality.

Extra Credit

- Add up the hours you spend on technology in one week; commit to exchanging a few hours of tech-time for nature time. Have more work meetings outdoors. Get together with friends for a picnic lunch in the park.

- Do a digital detox: commit to not using your smartphone or computer for a determined period of time—even if it's only several hours. Better yet, try a one-day digital fast: turn off your smartphone, computer, and television for an entire day. Best yet, go on a digital detox retreat out of the country or off the grid. Set up an e-mail autoresponder and unplug for an entire week!

- Minimize flight time by using Skype or phone conferencing as much as possible for meetings.

- After you've had a lot of physical contact with many people (shaking hands, hugging, etc.), take a sea salt bath or rub your body down with sea salt in the shower to clear foreign energies. At the very least, splash your face with water.

- Eat more seaweed (that has been checked for radiation) and know where your ocean fish comes from.

In Essence

Dissolves

Toxic, negative, or foreign energies in your energetic field

Fatigue from computer and cell phone use, television, and air travel

Energetic saturation from urban lifestyle, office work, crowds, or high-touch profession

Magnifies

Revitalization of body and mind after exposure to any kind of radiation

Energy and clarity of mind

Radiance of the skin

UNPLUG AND RECHARGE WITH A DIGITAL DETOX

Spending so much time with electronics can result in fatigue, dullness of the skin, distraction, not being present, and feeling like time moves very quickly. Physical imbalances can also ensue, as a result of a sedentary lifestyle.

If you're drawn to the Yarrow flower, it's time to recharge! Here's how.

Find one day in your calendar when you can refrain from technology for an entire day (perhaps Sunday). If one day feels impossible, start out with a 4-hour detox.

Power down your smartphone completely and leave it at home. If that is not possible for your lifestyle, carry your phone with you, but use it only for emergency calls or taking photos.

Do not use the iPad, tablet, laptop, desktop, television, games, or other technology for that one day.

As you commit to an entire day without technology, notice your internal response. It can range from freedom and relief—to panic and anxiety. Whatever arises, just notice it and keep going. You may need to let family and friends know you'll be offline for a day. If you run a business, create an e-mail responder, schedule your social media posts, or do what you need to do to give you peace of mind while you're away.

Loosely plan what you'll do that day or explore the options. Notice if it feels like time slows down or feels more spacious without digital distractions.

Take it to the next level: Calendar in a digital detox once each week or month. Notice the positive effects of an entire day without technology. How does it affect your vitality, creativity, and sense of freedom? Find ways to plan longer and longer digital detoxes, such as during a vacation or taking a trip off the grid.

Besides experiencing more vitality and radiance, the benefits of a digital detox can also lead to an increase in adventures, reading books, painting, meaningful connections with others, deep listening, and being more mindfully aware.

MASTER KEY TO THE ELIXIRS

What do you want to experience more or less of? Find the right flower elixir for your mood!

A

Abundance
Hollyhock (prosperity) (page 215)
Peony (gratitude) (page 273)

Acceptance
Bodhi Tree (acceptance of others) (page 159)
Gardenia (vulnerability) (page 201)
Grevillea (speaking your mind) (page 211)
Hong Kong Orchid (self-acceptance; self-love) (page 221)
Jasmine (self-appreciation) (page 229)
Lilac (flexibility, nonjudgment) (page 235)
Mandevilla (nonattachment) (page 241)
Papaya Flower (compatibility in relationships) (page 263)
Silk Floss (confidence; self-acceptance) (page 331)
White Magnolia (acceptance of transitions, change, even death) (page 349)

Accomplishment
Bamboo (determination) (page 133)
Banana Yucca (revealing hidden talents) (page 141)
Black Bat Flower (advocacy) (page 153)
Giant Spider Lily (simplicity) (page 207)
Night-Blooming Cereus (realization of full potential) (page 257)
Papaya Flower collaboration) (page 263)
Pink Primrose (effortlessness, ease) (page 291)
Red Bird of Paradise (motivation, drive) (page 307)

Adoption
Arctic Lupine (peaceful, supportive transition) (page 129)
Papaya Flower (compatibility) (page 263)
Rhododendron (motherly love) (page 315)

Affection
Bodhi Tree (devotional love, gentleness) (page 159)
Hollyhock (fearless love, compassion, softness) (page 215)
Nectarine Blossom (sweetness, camaraderie) (page 251)
Papaya Flower (compatibility, tenderness) (page 263)
Rose (attentiveness, caring) (page 319)

Agility
Bamboo (gracefulness) (page 133)
Giant Spider Lily (feeling light or light on your feet) (page 207)

Anger
Black Bat Flower (anger) (page 153)
Bodhi Tree (aggression and violence) (page 159)
Grevillea (repressed anger, dread, aversion) (page 211)
Mandevilla (impatience, attachment) (page 241)
Nectarine Blossom (attacked) (page 251)

Anguish
Bee Balm (past or current traumatic experiences, dramatic change, or broken heart) (page 145)
Grevillea (fear about how your words will affect others) (page 211)
Mandevilla (result of attachment, impatience, clinging to a certain way) (page 241)
Rhododendron (feeling unloved or undervalued) (page 315)

Annoyance
Grevillea (holding back verbally; unable to speak freely) (page 211)
Nectarine Blossom (attacked or pressured) (page 251)
Rhododendron (critical or criticizing) (page 315)

Anxiety
Arctic Lupine (overwhelm, lack of support) (page 129)
Banana Blossom (time-based anxiety, feeling rushed, or

running out of time) (page 137)

> Bee Balm (traumatic experiences or dramatic life changes) (page 145)
> Black Bat Flower (fear, phobia, paranoia) (page 153)
> Bodhi Tree (disconnected) (page 159)
> Brugmansia (worry about taking time off, relying on others or letting others down) (page 165)
> Passionflower (mental chatter, frazzled nerves, panic, inability to let it go) (page 269)

Apathy

> Grevillea (ambivalent to speak the truth) (page 211)
> Jade Succulent (hesitation, shyness, or low vitality) (page 225)
> Nasturtium (monotony, boredom) (page 245)
> Pink Lotus (distraction or stuck/stagnant energy) (page 279)

Appreciation

> Chocolate Daisy (cheerfulness, lightheartedness) (page 171)
> Gardenia (embracing all aspects of yourself) (page 201)
> Hong Kong Orchid (self-love, self-appreciation) (page 221)
> Jasmine (feeling beautiful) (page 229)
> Mandevilla (deep appreciation of present moment) (page 241)

Assurance

> Royal Poinciana (playing big, asking for what you want) (page 325)
> Silk Floss (confidence, comfort with who you are) (page 331)

Attachment

> Bodhi Tree (negative fixation or obsession) (page 159)
> Brugmansia (overly responsible/workaholism) (page 165)
> Date Palm Flower (rigid behaviors, going to extremes) (page 181)
> Lilac (expectations, rigidity, or control) (page 235)
> Mandevilla (fear of loss, clinging, or fear of abandonment/rejection) (page 241)
> Night-Blooming Cereus (self-limitation, old habit/patterns) (page 257)
> Passionflower (difficulty letting go) (page 269)
> White Magnolia (fear of death) (page 349)

Attentiveness

> Bodhi Tree (patience and acceptance of others) (page 159)
> Nectarine Blossom (desire to be of service) (page 251)
> Rose (kindness and caring for yourself and others) (page 319)

Attraction

> Hong Kong Orchid (sensuality) (page 221)
> Jasmine (magnetism) (page 229)
> Nectarine Blossom (sweetness) (page 251)
> Peony (elegance, beauty) (page 273)

Awareness

> Bamboo (spacious, expansive mind) (page 133)
> Bird of Paradise (quiet mind) (page 149)
> Dandelion (where stress is stored in the body) (page 177)
> Date Palm Flower (freedom from extremes) (page 181)
> Euphrasia (intuition) (page 187)
> Night-Blooming Cereus (understanding of shadow side, fears) (page 257)
> Passionflower (mental awareness) (page 269)
> White Magnolia (highest aspirations, spiritual fulfillment) (page 349)
> White Water Lily (sharper senses, sensitivity to others' needs) (page 353)

B

Balance

> Arctic Lupine (calm, sense of support) (page 129)
> Bee Balm (during dramatic change and traumatic events) (page 145)
> Brugmansia (allowing others to assist you) (page 165)
> Date Palm Flower (between two extremes) (page 181)
> Papaya Flower (masculine and feminine energies) (page 263)
> Passionflower (peacefulness) (page 269)
> Pink Magnolia (self-care) (page 285)
> Pomegranate Flower (woman's reproductive system) (page 301)
> Yarrow (after computer/cell phone use and air travel) (page 357)

Beauty

> Gardenia (embracing all aspects of yourself) (page 201)
> Hong Kong Orchid (self-love and acceptance, magnetism) (page 221)
> Jasmine (radiance) (page 229)
> Peony (femininity, magnetism) (page 273)

Bitterness

> Fireweed (need for forgiveness) (page 197)
> Hollyhock (betrayal) (page 215)
> Mandevilla (abandonment or rejection) (page 241)
> Nectarine Blossom (feeling attacked) (page 251)
> Rose (emotional wounds and scars) (page 319)

Boredom

Nasturtium (spontaneity) (page 245)
Pink Lotus (catalyst) (page 279)
White Water Lily (synchronicity) (page 353)

C

Calmness

Arctic Lupine (peacefulness) (page 129)
Banana Blossom (slow down a little) (page 137)
Bee Balm (relief and perspective) (page 145)
Bird of Paradise (quiet mind) (page 149)
Brugmansia (let go) (page 165)
Passionflower (peacefulness, deep sleep) (page 269)

Carefree

Banana Blossom (spacious mind) (page 137)
Chocolate Daisy (simplify, streamline) (page 171)
Date Palm Flower (freedom from extremes) (page 181)
Giant Spider Lily (buoyancy, weightlessness) (page 207)
Nasturtium (spontaneity) (page 245)
Pink Primrose (effortlessness) (page 291)

Celebration

African Daisy (joy, laughter) (page 125)
Giant Spider Lily (lightheartedness) (page 207)
Nasturtium (curiosity, wonder) (page 245)
Pink Spirea (letting your inner child enjoy) (page 297)
Strawberry Blossom (optimism) (page 341)

Centeredness

Arctic Lupine (peace, stability, support) (page 129)
Brugmansia (balance) (page 165)

Certitude

Euphrasia (decisiveness, trusting your intuition) (page 187)
Royal Poinciana (self-assuredness) (page 325)
Silk Floss (confidence, comfort being yourself) (page 331)

Change

Arctic Lupine (overwhelm) (page 129)
Bee Balm (trauma) (page 145)
Lilac (rigidity) (page 235)
Mandevilla (attachment) (page 241)
Pink Lotus (stuck, stagnant) (page 279)
Pink Primrose (rapid growth) (page 291)
White Magnolia (major transitions, including death) (page 349)

Chi

Jade Succulent (radiance, vitality) (page 225)
Pink Lotus (energizing) (page 279)
Yarrow (revitalizing after computers, air travel) (page 357)

Clarity

Bamboo (strength, determination) (page 133)
Bird of Paradise (mental clarity) (page 149)
Black Bat Flower (fearlessness) (page 153)
Chocolate Daisy (keeping it simple) (page 171)
Euphrasia (decisiveness) (page 187)
Grevillea (speech) (page 211)
Jade Succulent (expansion) (page 225)
Royal Poinciana (certitude) (page 325)
White Water Lily (perception) (page 353)
Yarrow (energetic) (page 357)

Collaboration

Banana Yucca (networking, leadership) (page 141)
Papaya Flower (community mind-set, compatibility) (page 263)

Comfort

Arctic Lupine (sense of support) (page 129)
Hong Kong Orchid (self-expression) (page 221)
Mandevilla (acceptance) (page 241)
Passionflower (peacefulness) (page 269)
Rhododendron (compassion) (page 315)
Rose (nurturing) (page 319)
Silk Floss (being yourself) (page 331)

Communication

Banana Yucca (collaboration with women) (page 141)
Black Bat Flower (healthy expression of anger) (page 153)
Grevillea (fearless speech) (page 211)
Royal Poinciana (asking for what you want) (page 325)
Trumpet Vine (speaking freely, singing) (page 345)

Compassion

Bee Balm (self-compassion) (page 145)
Black Bat Flower (fierce compassion, advocacy) (page 153)
Grevillea (speaking the truth) (page 211)
Hollyhock (tenderness, softness) (page 215)
Hong Kong Orchid (self-acceptance and acceptance of others) (page 221)
Papaya Flower (gentleness) (page 315)
Pink Lotus (wisdom) (page 279)
Rhododendron (understanding, empathy) (page 315)
Rose (attentiveness) (page 319)
White Water Lily (awareness of others' needs) (page 353)

D

Discipline

Bamboo (perseverance, determination) (page 133)
Date Palm Flower (responsibility, boundaries) (page 181)
Red Bird of Paradise (motivation, drive) (page 307)

Discontent

Gardenia (disappointment in oneself) (page 201)
Mandevilla (attachment, impatience) (page 241)
Nasturtium (boredom, stagnancy, regret) (page 245)
Peony (lack) (page 273)
Pink Lotus (disconnection, apathy) (page 279)
White Magnolia (fear of loss) (page 349)
White Water Lily (out of tune) (page 353)

Disgust

Grevillea (aversion) (page 211)

Distraction

Bee Balm (extreme stress) (page 145)
Bird of Paradise (overthinking) (page 149)
Passionflower (frazzled) (page 269)
Pink Primrose (resistance) (page 291)
Red Bird of Paradise (procrastination) (page 307)

Dread

Bee Balm (trauma) (page 145)
Black Bat Flower (worry, fear) (page 153)
Gardenia (avoidance of perceived weaknesses) (page 201)
Grevillea (aversion) (page 211)
Strawberry Blossom (pessimism) (page 341)

Drive

Black Bat Flower (advocacy) (page 153)
Red Bird of Paradise (motivation) (page 307)

Dullness

Royal Poinciana (feeling undeserving) (page 325)

E

Efficiency

Banana Blossom (prioritization) (page 137)
Bird of Paradise (mental clarity) (page 149)
Euphrasia (decisiveness) (page 187)
Passionflower (mindful awareness) (page 269)
Pink Primrose (responsiveness) (page 291)
Red Bird of Paradise (productivity) (page 307)

Effortlessness

Giant Spider Lily (lightheartedness, buoyancy) (page 207)
Nasturtium (spontaneity) (page 245)
Pink Primrose (ease, effortless action) (page 291)
Red Bird of Paradise (motivation, drive) (page 307)

Elegance

Bamboo (gracefulness) (page 133)
Hong Kong Orchid (magnetism) (page 221)
Peony (attraction) (page 273)

Embarrassment

Gardenia (shadow side) (page 201)
Hong Kong Orchid (of being seen or heard) (page 221)
Peony (shame, bashfulness) (page 273)
Silk Floss (discomfort in one's own skin) (page 331)

Emotional Detox

Bee Balm (past trauma) (page 145)
Black Bat Flower (anger) (page 153)
Dandelion (physical tension) (page 177)
Fireweed (past bad memories) (page 197)
Night-Blooming Cereus (self-limitation and fears) (page 257)
Passionflower (frazzled, overdrive) (page 269)
Pomegranate Flower (taking on others' stress) (page 301)

Empathy

Nectarine Blossom (desire to be of service) (page 251)
Rhododendron (compassion) (page 315)
Rose (kindness) (page 319)
White Water Lily (perception) (page 353)

Energy

Bamboo (strength, determination) (page 133)
Jade Succulent (vitality) (page 225)
Jasmine (radiance) (page 229)
Pink Lotus (catalyst) (page 279)
Pink Magnolia (self-care) (page 285)
Pomegranate Flower (cleansing) (page 301)
Red Bird of Paradise (motivation) (page 307)
Yarrow (revitalization after technology) (page 357)

Enlightenment

Bodhi Tree (devotional love) (page 159)
Pink Lotus (inner wisdom) (page 279)
White Magnolia (purity) (page 349)

Enmeshment

Bamboo (codependent) (page 133)
Date Palm Flower (merged with another) (page 181)
Lilac (expectations, fixation) (page 235)
Mandevilla (clinging, attachment) (page 241)

Envy

Jasmine (insecurity, jealousy) (page 229)
Nectarine Blossom (resentment) (page 251)
Papaya Flower (competition) (page 263)

Euphoria

Banana Blossom (timelessness) (page 137)
Bee Balm (new perspective) (page 145)
Date Palm Flower (carefree) (page 181)
Giant Spider Lily (buoyancy) (page 207)
Nasturtium (spontaneity) (page 245)

Exhaustion

Pink Magnolia (giving all energy away) (page 285)
Pomegranate Flower (taking on stress of others) (page 301)

Expression

Fire Star Orchid (out-of-the-box ideas) (page 191)
Grevillea (fearless speech) (page 211)
Hong Kong Orchid (self-expression, being heard) (page 221)
Silk Floss (letting it all hang out) (page 331)
Trumpet Vine (effortless communication) (page 345)

Extremes

Date Palm Flower (rigid vs. loose, linear vs. nonlinear thinking) (page 181)

F

Fatigue

Jade Succulent (weakness) (page 225)
Pomegranate Flower (taking on others' stress) (page 301)
Yarrow (excessive air travel or computer/cell phone radiation) (page 357)

Fear

Arctic Lupine (general worry, anxiety) (page 129)
Bamboo ("I can't do it," playing small) (page 133)
Banana Blossom (running out of time) (page 137)
Black Bat Flower (spiders, snakes, public speaking, being exposed, going crazy) (page 153)
Bodhi Tree (of being unsafe) (page 159)
Fire Star Orchid (of being ostracized for ideas) (page 191)
Gardenia (of shadow side) (page 201)
Grevillea (of one's words destroying a relationship) (page 211)
Hong Kong Orchid (of being seen, heard) (page 221)
Mandevilla (of loss) (page 241)
Nectarine Blossom (emotionally attacked) (page 251)
Night-Blooming Cereus (self-limitation, fear of success) (page 257)
Papaya Flower (sexual confusion) (page 263)
Passionflower (of psychosis) (page 269)
Pink Primrose (resistance) (page 291)
Squash Blossom (of sexuality, pregnancy) (page 335)
Trumpet Vine (of communication) (page 345)

White Magnolia (of change, transitions, death) (page 349)

Fearlessness

Bamboo (playing big) (page 133)
Banana Blossom (expansive) (page 137)
Black Bat Flower (courage) (page 153)
Date Palm Flower (fresh perspectives, freedom from extremes) (page 181)
Fire Star Orchid (sharing out-of-the-box ideas) (page 191)
Gardenia (transforming weaknesses into strengths) (page 201)
Grevillea (speaking the truth) (page 211)
Lilac (flexibility, allowing) (page 235)
Mandevilla (nonattached) (page 241)
Night-Blooming Cereus (free of self-imposed limitations) (page 257)
Pink Primrose (growth) (page 291)
Royal Poinciana (conviction) (page 325)
Silk Floss (confidence) (page 331)
Squash Blossom (sexuality, birthing) (page 335)
Trumpet Vine (communication) (page 345)
White Magnolia (transitions, death) (page 349)

Femininity

Banana Yucca (collaboration with women) (page 141)
Papaya Flower (honoring feminine energy, behaviors, roles) (page 263)
Pomegranate Flower (balancing woman's reproductive system) (page 301)

Flexibility

Bamboo (gracefulness) (page 133)
Lilac (adaptability) (page 235)

Focus

Bee Balm (staying present despite high stress) (page 145)
Bamboo (determination) (page 133)
Chocolate Daisy (streamlining life) (page 171)
Red Bird of Paradise (productivity) (page 307)
Royal Poinciana (certitude) (page 325)

Forgiveness

Bodhi Tree (love) (page 159)
Fireweed (past or current heartache) (page 197)
Rose (disappointment) (page 319)

Freedom

African Daisy (joy) (page 125)
Chocolate Daisy (simplify) (page 171)
Dandelion (relaxed muscles) (page 177)
Date Palm Flower (from extremes) (page 181)

Grevillea (fearless speech) (page 211)
>> Trumpet Vine (effortless communication) (page 345)

Honor

Black Bat Flower (advocacy) (page 153)
Papaya Flower (feminine energy, roles) (page 263)

Hope

Bee Balm (during or after traumatic events) (page 145)
Red Hibiscus (fresh perspective after stressful events)
(page 311)

Hopelessness

Hollyhock (relationships) (page 215)

Hurry/Rushing

Banana Blossom (perceiving a lack of time) (page 137)
Mandevilla (impatience) (page 241)

I

Ignorance

White Water Lily (lack of awareness) (page 353)

Illumination

Gardenia (seeing and transforming shadow side) (page 201)
Giant Spider Lily (shining light into blind spots) (page 207)
Night-Blooming Cereus (identifying self-limitations)
(page 257)
White Water Lily (heightened perception) (page 353)

Impatience

Banana Blossom (running out of time) (page 137)
Mandevilla (rushing) (page 241)

Impotence

Bamboo ("I can't do it") (page 133)

Inadequacy

Jasmine (insecurity) (page 229)

Indecisiveness

Euphrasia (hesitancy) (page 187)

Individuality

Date Palm Flower (independence) (page 181)

Inferiority

Night-Blooming Cereus (self-limitation) (page 257)

Innovative Thinking

Banana Yucca (hidden talents) (page 141)
Date Palm Flower (wild creativity) (page 181)
Fire Star Orchid (forward thinking) (page 191)
Pink Primrose (effortless ideas) (page 291)
Royal Poinciana (conviction) (page 325)

Insecurity

Banana Yucca (capabilities) (page 141)
Black Bat Flower (fear) (page 153)
Euphrasia (indecision) (page 187)
Jade Succulent (holding back) (page 225)
Jasmine (self-loathing) (page 229)
Night-Blooming Cereus (self-limitation) (page 257)
Rhododendron (feeling unloved) (page 315)

Insomnia

Bird of Paradise (mental chatter) (page 149)
Brugmansia (inability to let go) (page 165)
Dandelion (physical tension) (page 177)
Passionflower (on overdrive, restless sleep) (page 269)

Inspiration

Banana Blossom (euphoria) (page 137)
Banana Yucca (revealing hidden talents) (page 141)
Date Palm Flower (breakthroughs) (page 181)
Fire Star Orchid (creativity) (page 191)
Giant Spider Lily (exhilaration) (page 207)
Nasturtium (spice up your life) (page 245)
Night-Blooming Cereus (taking big leaps) (page 257)
Pink Lotus (inner wisdom) (page 279)
Pink Primrose (birthing of new projects) (page 291)
Red Bird of Paradise (motivation) (page 307)
Squash Blossom (imagination) (page 335)
Strawberry Blossom (openness to opportunities)
(page 341)

Intuition

Banana Yucca (vision) (page 141)
Bird of Paradise (follow heart, not head) (page 149)
Euphrasia (trust your intuition) (page 187)
Papaya Flower (receptivity) (page 263)
Passionflower (in tune) (page 269)
White Water Lily (enhanced sensory perception)
(page 353)

Irritability

Hollyhock (frustration) (page 215)
Pomegranate Flower (taking on others' emotions)
(page 301)

J

Jealousy

Jasmine (insecurity) (page 229)
Rhododendron (feeling unloved) (page 315)

Joy

African Daisy (enjoyment) (page 125)
Chocolate Daisy (cheerfulness) (page 171)

Giant Spider Lily (lightheartedness) (page 207)
    Nasturtium (spontaneity, wonder) (page 245)
    Pink Spirea (playfulness) (page 297)
    Strawberry Blossom (optimism) (page 341)

K

Kindness
    Bodhi Tree (love) (page 159)
    Hong Kong Orchid (toward ourselves) (page 221)
    Nectarine Blossom (desire to be of service, sweet words) (page 251)
    Pink Magnolia (self-care) (page 285)
    Rhododendron (compassion, motherly love) (page 315)

L

Laughter
    African Daisy (playfulness) (page 125)
    Pink Spirea (open heart) (page 297)

Lazy
    Red Bird of Paradise (procrastination, avoidance) (page 307)
    Royal Poinciana (apathy) (page 325)

Loneliness
    Banana Yucca (hiding) (page 141)
    Jasmine (solitary, aloof) (page 229)
    Rhododendron (unreciprocated love) (page 315)

Loss
    Bee Balm (traumatic experiences) (page 145)
    Lilac (unexpected outcome) (page 235)
    Mandevilla (fear of loss, clinging) (page 241)

Love
    Bodhi Tree (devotional love) (page 159)
    Fireweed (forgiveness) (page 197)
    Hollyhock (gentleness, tenderness) (page 215)
    Hong Kong Orchid (self-love, magnetism) (page 221)
    Nectarine Blossom (sweet words, service, friendship) (page 251)
    Peony (gratitude, attraction) (page 273)
    Pink Magnolia (self-care) (page 285)
    Rhododendron (motherly love) (page 315)
    Rose (attentiveness, nurturing) (page 319)

M

Magic
    Banana Blossom (timelessness) (page 137)
    Date Palm Flower (breakthroughs) (page 181)
    Giant Spider Lily (carefree) (page 207)

Nasturtium (wonder) (page 245)
    Peony (magnetism) (page 273)
    Pink Lotus (catalyst) (page 279)
    Pink Primrose (effortlessness) (page 291)
    White Magnolia (divine present moment) (page 349)
    White Water Lily (synchronicity) (page 353)

Magnetism
    Hong Kong Orchid (attraction) (page 221)
    Jasmine (beauty) (page 229)
    Peony (abundance) (page 273)

Motherhood
    Arctic Lupine (peacefulness, support) (page 129)
    Papaya Flower (appreciation of feminine roles) (page 263)
    Rhododendron (motherly love) (page 315)
    Squash Blossom (conception, birthing, pregnancy) (page 341)

Motivation
    Bodhi Tree (purity) (page 159)
    Black Bat Flower (courage) (page 153)
    Pink Primrose (effortlessness) (page 291)
    Red Bird of Paradise (drive) (page 307)
    Royal Poinciana (conviction) (page 325)

N

Negativity
    Black Bat Flower (anger and fear) (page 153)
    Bodhi Tree (anger, violence, compassion) (page 159)
    Gardenia (perceived weaknesses) (page 201)
    Night-Blooming Cereus (self-limitation) (page 257)
    Rose (bitterness) (page 319)
    Royal Poinciana (apathy) (page 325)
    Strawberry Blossom (pessimism) (page 341)
    White Magnolia (fighting transitions) (page 349)

Negligence
    Date Palm Flower (carelessness) (page 181)
    Red Bird of Paradise (procrastination) (page 307)

Nurture
    Bodhi Tree (devotional love) (page 159)
    Hollyhock (bonding, gentleness) (page 215)
    Nectarine Blossom (affectionate, of service) (page 251)
    Papaya Flower (tenderness) (page 263)
    Pink Magnolia (self-care) (page 285)
    Rhododendron (motherly love) (page 315)
    Rose (attentive, of service) (page 319)

O

Obsession
Black Bat Flower (deepest fears) (page 153)
Bodhi Tree (negativity) (page 159)
Brugmansia (workaholism) (page 165)
Chocolate Daisy (overcomplication) (page 171)
Date Palm Flower (extremes, rigidity) (page 181)
Lilac (controlling) (page 235)
Mandevilla (clinging) (page 241)
Pink Magnolia (giving all of our energy away) (page 285)

Organization
Brugmansia (delegation) (page 165)
Chocolate Daisy (streamline) (page 171)
Red Bird of Paradise (taking action) (page 307)

Openness
Grevillea (speaking the truth) (page 211)
Night-Blooming Cereus (full potential) (page 257)
Peony (gratitude) (page 273)
Strawberry Blossom (opportunities) (page 341)

Optimism
Strawberry Blossom (expecting the best) (page 341)

Overthinking
Bird of Paradise (mental chatter) (page 149)
Chocolate Daisy (overcomplication) (page 171)
Giant Spider Lily (something weighing on mind)
(page 207)
Grevillea (fear about what others think) (page 211)
Passionflower (monkey mind) (page 269)

Overwhelm
Arctic Lupine (lack of support) (page 129)
Chocolate Daisy (overcomplication) (page 171)
Peony (cautious) (page 273)
Red Bird of Paradise (resistance) (page 307)
Red Hibiscus (succession of stressful events) (page 311)

P

Panic
Arctic Lupine (overwhelm) (page 129)
Black Bat Flower (paranoias, fears) (page 153)
Passionflower (anxiety) (page 269)

Paranoia
Arctic Lupine (overwhelm) (page 129)
Black Bat Flower (phobias) (page 153)
Jasmine (jealousy) (page 229)
Night-Blooming Cereus (self-limitation) (page 257)
Passionflower (obsessive mental activity) (page 269)

Passion
Hong Kong Orchid (magnetism) (page 221)
Red Bird of Paradise (motivation, drive) (page 307)
Squash Blossom (ease with sexuality) (page 335)

Patience
Banana Blossom (timelessness) (page 137)
Bodhi Tree (acceptance) (page 159)
Lilac (flexibility) (page 235)
Mandevilla (nonattachment) (page 241)

Peace
Arctic Lupine (stability) (page 129)
Banana Blossom (in the flow) (page 137)
Bee Balm (relief) (page 145)
Bodhi Tree (devotion) (page 159)
Brugmansia (let go) (page 165)
Mandevilla (patience) (page 241)
Passionflower (calm) (page 269)
Red Hibiscus (fresh perspective) (page 311)
White Magnolia (transitions) (page 349)

Perception
Euphrasia (intuition) (page 187)
White Water Lily (sensory) (page 353)

Persistence
Bamboo (determination) (page 133)
Red Bird of Paradise (drive) (page 307)
Royal Poinciana (conviction) (page 325)

Perspective
Red Hibiscus (reframing) (page 311)
Strawberry Blossom (expecting the best) (page 341)

Phobia
Black Bat Flower (fears) (page 153)

Playfulness
African Daisy (enjoyment) (page 125)
Pink Spirea (fun) (page 297)

Possessive
Hollyhock (fear of betrayal) (page 215)
Jasmine (jealousy) (page 229)
Lilac (controlling, rigid) (page 235)
Mandevilla (clinging) (page 241)

Power
Bamboo (strength) (page 133)
Banana Yucca (liberating hidden talent) (page 141)
Black Bat Flower (courage) (page 153)
Night-Blooming Cereus (liberating potential) (page 257)
Royal Poinciana (asking for what you want) (page 325)

Spontaneity

Chocolate Daisy (simplicity) (page 171)
Nasturtium (wonder) (page 245)
White Water Lily (synchronicity) (page 353)

Stagnancy

Giant Spider Lily (burdened) (page 207)
Nasturtium (bored, underengaged) (page 245)
Pink Lotus (stuck) (page 279)
Pink Primrose (resistance) (page 291)
Red Bird of Paradise (lazy, procrastination) (page 307)

Stamina

Bamboo (endurance) (page 133)
Jade Succulent (vitality) (page 225)
Red Bird of Paradise (drive, follow through) (page 307)
Yarrow (energy) (page 357)

Stillness

Arctic Lupine (steadiness) (page 129)
Bee Balm (calm) (page 145)
Bird of Paradise (quiet mind) (page 149)
Passionflower (awareness) (page 269)
White Water Lily (enhanced sensory perception) (page 353)
White Magnolia (ease with change) (page 349)

Strength

Arctic Lupine (steadiness) (page 129)
Bamboo (determination) (page 133)
Black Bat Flower (courage) (page 153)
Jade Succulent (vitality) (page 225)
Pomegranate Flower (women's reproductive health) (page 301)

Stress

African Daisy (too many responsibilities) (page 125)
Arctic Lupine (overwhelm) (page 129)
Bee Balm (big changes or traumatic experiences) (page 145)
Black Bat Flower (anxiety, fear, anger) (page 153)
Dandelion (physical tension) (page 177)
Pink Magnolia (giving all your energy away) (page 285)
Red Hibiscus (series of stressful events) (page 311)

Stubborn

Dandelion (hardheaded) (page 177)
Lilac (inflexible) (page 235)
Rose (struggle) (page 319)
Strawberry Blossom (expecting the worst) (page 341)

Struggle

Arctic Lupine (overwhelm) (page 129)
Pink Magnolia (fatigue) (page 285)

Pink Primrose (resistance) (page 291)
Red Bird of Paradise (procrastination) (page 307)
Rose (bitterness) (page 319)

Suppression

Date Palm Flower (extremes) (page 181)
Grevillea (fear of speaking truth) (page 211)

T

Tenacity

Bamboo (determination) (page 133)

Tenderness

Bodhi Tree (devotional love) (page 159)
Hollyhock (softness) (page 215)
Nectarine Blossom (affection) (page 251)
Papaya Flower (receptivity) (page 263)
Rose (nurturing) (page 319)

Tension

Bird of Paradise (mental tension) (page 149)
Chocolate Daisy (tied up in knots, complication) (page 171)
Dandelion (physical tension) (page 177)

Timelessness

Banana Blossom (freedom from time constraints) (page 137)
Date Palm Flower (freedom from extremes) (page 181)
Passionflower (mindful awareness) (page 269)
White Magnolia (change, transition) (page 349)

Timidity

Banana Yucca (tentative) (page 141)
Jade Succulent (hesitation) (page 225)
Jasmine (aloof) (page 229)
Peony (shyness, shame) (page 273)
Royal Poinciana (feeling unworthy, undeserving) (page 325)

Tolerance

Fireweed (forgiveness) (page 197)
Nectarine Blossom (camaraderie) (page 251)

Transition

Arctic Lupine (steadiness) (page 129)
Lilac (flexibility) (page 235)
Mandevilla (nonattachment) (page 241)
Pink Primrose (growth) (page 291)
White Magnolia (acceptance of change) (page 349)

Trauma

Bee Balm (big changes or traumatic experiences) (page 145)

Fireweed (emotional wounds or scars) (page 197)
> Squash Blossom (past or current sexual abuse) (page 335)

Trust

> Banana Blossom (timing) (page 137)
> Brugmansia (delegation) (page 165)
> Euphrasia (intuition) (page 187)
> Hollyhock (relationships) (page 215)

U

Understanding

> Hollyhock (tenderness) (page 215)
> Night-Blooming Cereus (insights) (page 257)
> Pink Lotus (wisdom) (page 279)
> Rhododendron (compassion) (page 315)
> Trumpet Vine (communication) (page 345)

V

Violence

> Black Bat Flower (anger) (page 153)
> Bodhi Tree (aggression) (page 159)

Vitality

> Jade Succulent (expanded chi) (page 225)
> Jasmine (radiance) (page 229)
> Pomegranate Flower (reproductive) (page 301)
> Red Bird of Paradise (drive, motivation) (page 307)
> Yarrow (energy despite computer, phone, air travel) (page 357)

Vulnerability

> Brugmansia (hardened heart) (page 165)
> Hong Kong Orchid (fear of being exposed) (page 221)
> Jasmine (aloof) (page 229)
> Nectarine Blossom (under attack) (page 251)
> Papaya Flower (tenderness) (page 263)
> Pink Magnolia (self-sacrificing) (page 285)
> Rhododendron (feeling unloved or motherless child) (page 315)

W

Weakness

> Jade Succulent (low vitality) (page 225)
> Passionflower (frazzled) (page 269)
> Pink Lotus (dull) (page 279)
> Pomegranate Flower (reproductive, vulnerable to others' energy) (page 301)
> White Water Lily (distraction, out of tune) (page 353)
> Yarrow (excessive electronics, air travel) (page 357)

Wisdom

> Bodhi Tree (devotion) (page 159)
> Pink Lotus (insights) (page 279)
> White Magnolia (understanding) (page 349)

Worry

> Arctic Lupine (extreme stress) (page 129)
> Banana Blossom (running out of time) (page 137)
> Black Bat Flower (phobias, paranoia) (page 153)
> Grevillea (what others think) (page 211)
> Hollyhock (fear of betrayal) (page 215)
> Rhododendron (unreciprocated love) (page 315)
> White Magnolia (difficulty with change, transition) (page 349)

X

Y

Z

APPENDICES

APPENDIX A: EDIBLE FLOWERS

Another fun way to weave flowers into your daily life is to eat them! The easiest way to use edible flowers is to toss them into a salad or sprinkle them onto a fruit salad, but below you'll find my favorite plug-n-play recipes to enhance your dining experience with flower power magic. Of course, each flower has a different flavor, from sweet to herbal to spicy, so you'll want to experiment.

It's important to make sure you use fresh flowers and petals from organically grown flowers—or flowers from your garden or a local farm. Do not use flowers from a florist, as they likely contain harmful chemicals or pesticides. If you're using flowers from a local farm, make sure no manure has been applied to the soil in the last four months. Always rinse the flowers, remove any insects, and gently dry the flowers with a paper towel.

If you have ragweed allergies, avoid Chamomile and Carnation. If you have composite flower allergies, avoid Calendula, Chicory, Chrysanthemum, and Marigold. If you are pregnant, please do research and consult with your midwife/doctor.

Allium (Garlic, Onion)

Anise Hyssop

Basil

Bachelor's Button

Bee Balm

Borage

Calendula

Carnation

Chamomile

Chicory

Chives

Chrysanthemum

Cilantro

Citrus Blossoms (grapefruit, lemon, lime, orange)

Clover

Dandelion

Daylily

Dianthus

Dill

Dendrobium Orchid

Elderflower

Fennel

Fuchsia

Gardenia

Geranium

Gladiolus

Hibiscus *(Hibiscus rosa-sinensis)*

Hollyhock

Honeysuckle *(Lonicera japonica)*

Hyssop

Impatiens

Jasmine

Johnny-Jump-Up

Lavender

Lemon Verbena

Lilac

Marigold

Marjoram

Marshmallow

Mint

Mustard

Nasturtium

Okra

Oregano

Pansy

Passionflower

Plum Blossom

Radish

Red Clover

Rose

Roselle *(Hibiscus sabdariffa)*

Rosemary

Sage

Society Garlic

Squash Blossom

Sunflower

Thyme

Tulips

Violet

Violas

Flower Petal Butter

Pretty up your butter by adding a confetti of fresh flower petals!

Ingredients

Handful of fresh flowers/petals

One stick of butter, room temperature

Mash the butter using a fork. If you have large flowers like Roses or Nasturtiums, use a sharp knife to mince the flowers. When the butter is soft, fold the flowers into the butter with a rubber spatula. Store the floral butter in the refrigerator and use within one week.

Personal Favorites: Rose (floral), Lavender (herbal), Nasturtium (spicy), purple garlic, or chive flowers (savory).

Tips: If you're using flowers with a floral scent (Rose, Jasmine, Gardenia), you may want to sweeten the butter with a tablespoon of honey or maple syrup. If you avoid bread and pastries, try adding flower butter to a baked or mashed sweet potato!

Flower Petal Goat Cheese

The perfect way to add color and decadence to a salad or snack!

Ingredients

Handful of fresh flowers

4 ounces goat cheese

Pull each of the petals or florets off the flower head or stem and sprinkle them onto a plate. If using large flower petals, mince them. Unwrap the goat cheese and use a spoon to take out equal portions of goat cheese. Roll each piece into a ball, sprinkle some petals onto the ball, and use your hands to press the petals into the cheese. Throw the flower-petaled goat cheese into a decadent salad or drizzle local honey on top. This recipe makes 8 to 10 balls, enough for about 3 to 4 individual salads.

Flower Petal Shortbread Cookies

Gluten-free and easy to whip together with only a few ingredients, this recipe makes a simple shortbread cookie base to which you can add your favorite edible flowers and share with everyone! For this recipe, I like to use dried flower petals, lending to the cookie crunch. Rose petals blend especially well with the cherrylike flavor of the almond flour, but you can use any edible flower.

Ingredients

2 cups almond meal
6 tablespoons softened butter
2 tablespoons maple syrup
1 teaspoon vanilla extract
Handful of dried flowers/petals

Use a fork to mash the butter and blend all the ingredients together until well mixed. Place the cookie dough onto a piece of plastic wrap in a log shape about 2 inches in diameter. Wrap up your cookie log and refrigerate for 1 hour. When you're ready, preheat your oven to 350°F and remove the cookie dough from the refrigerator. If your log was a little bumpy before, now is your chance to roll it (remember making snakes with clay when you were a kid?). Then open up the plastic wrap and slice the log into cookie slices that are about 1/4 inch thick. Place the slices on aluminum foil or parchment paper on a cookie sheet. Bake the cookies for about 12 to 14 minutes, until golden and slightly browned. Let them cool on the pan for 10 minutes before transferring them. Makes about two dozen cookies.

Flower-Infused Liquors

Macerating—or soaking—flower petals in alcohol is the traditional way of making floral tinctures and infused alcohols. If you're interested in the physical therapeutic benefits from flowers, or you have a hankering for a handcrafted cocktail from time to time, here's the lowdown:

Fill a mason jar half full with flowers (see edible flowers list). Pour vodka, brandy, or whiskey over the flowers, fully submerging them so that the alcohol reaches about 1/4 inch over the top of the flowers. Close the jar by screwing on the lid so that it's airtight. Allow the flowers to soak in the alcohol for 2 to 4 weeks, picking up the jar daily and shaking it to infuse it with your good vibes. After 2 to 4 weeks, taste-test some of the alcohol. When the intensity of the flavor is to your liking, pour out the alcohol into a pretty bottle, leaving the plant material behind to discard.

Tip: Flowers like Hibiscus or Purple Basil will infuse a clear alcohol like vodka with a beautiful color.

Share your creations with us! #flowerevolution

APPENDIX B:
POISONOUS &
TOXIC FLOWERS

All flowers have a purpose for being, be it their incredible qualities or healing benefits; however, some are highly poisonous and toxic if you eat them or bathe with them. Below is a list of the flowers that should not be eaten or used in bathwater, oil infusions, extracts, perfumes, etc. They may be taken as flower elixirs, but require a skilled and trained practitioner to carefully collect the flowers and do the proper dilutions before their essence can be taken internally or applied to the skin.

Oftentimes our intuition is already working for us, even when we're not aware of it. I bet you've never thought of putting bleeding hearts or daffodils on a salad; it just doesn't occur to us, because some part of us knows they are not appropriate for eating. Our sixth sense can always be trusted. If you come across a flower that you are not familiar with or that you cannot identify, and you have a funny feeling about it, honor that feeling and steer clear of that plant.

Very Poisonous

Belladonna

Brugmansia

Datura

Hemlock

Oleander

Poisonous

Black Bat Flower	Hellebore	Morning Glory
Bleeding Heart	Hyacinth	Periwinkle
Calla Lily	Iris	Pride of Madeira
Chinese Lantern	Lantana	Rhododendron
Cyclamen	Larkspur	Star of Bethlehem
Daffodil	Lily of the Valley	Wolfsbane
Foxglove	Monkshood	

APPENDIX C: FLORAL DYES

Using flowers for dyeing fabric is fun, and it reminds us of the rich abundance of the world we live in! An alternative to using chemical dyes, using flowers for dyeing fabric creates a beautiful natural palette of colors that you can grow in your garden.

Cooking Method

This method works best for larger pieces of fabric like T-shirts and pillowcases. Pour water into a pot, bring to a boil, and then turn the heat down to a simmer. Cover the surface of the water with a thick layer of the flowers of your desired color. Simmer until the water is a rich color. Strain or scoop out the flowers/petals from the infusion. Place your fabric in the flower dye and soak it until it reaches the desired color saturation. Rinse the fabric in cold water and then soak in a bowl with a handful of sea salt for several hours to lock in the color. Alternatively, you can use mordants like iron (two-week infusion of rusty nails, 2 parts water, and 1 part white vinegar in a jar), acorns, vinegar, or other metals (simmer fabric in an iron, copper, or aluminum pot and soak overnight). Mordants can intensify, as well as alter, colors from natural dyes.

Sun Dyes

For smaller pieces of fabric (think Furoshiki: Japanese-style wrapping of presents), you can dye fabric with flowers in the sun. Similar to making sun tea, you can sun-dye your fabrics. Wrap up dried flowers of your choice inside a piece of fabric, and use a string to tie the fabric up, so the flowers stay inside the cloth. Use one variety of flower or several different kinds of fresh flowers. Place the fabric in a large jar full of water and leave out in the sun for two days. The water may begin to look dirty—that's okay. After two days of soaking it in the sun, remove the fabric and discard the flowers. Rinse the fabric with cold water. To maintain the same grade of color, soak it in salt water for several hours.

Pink

Bee Balm (red variety)—pink (page 145)

Dried Hibiscus flowers—bright pink (page 311)

Hollyhock petals (pink › yellow, darker colored › plum tones, red-purple) (page 215)

Roses (mix with lavender or lemon juice for bright pink) (page 319)

Strawberries (fruit, pink) (page 341)

Red

Bamboo (page 133)

Pomegranate, Fruit skins (page 301)

Yellow/Orange

Calendula

Crocus (saffron, with alum mordant)

Daffodil (dead, dried flowers with alum mordant)

Dahlia

Dandelion flowers (page 177)

Goldenrod

Lilac twigs (page 235)

Marigold

Mimosa

Red Clover (blossom, leaves, stem with alum mordant)

Safflower

St. John's Wort

Tansy

Green

Black-Eyed Susans

Chamomile leaves

Coneflower

Foxglove (poisonous)

Hydrangea flowers

Purple Milkweed

Queen Anne's Lace

Snapdragon flowers

Tea Tree flowers

Yarrow (yellow variety)

Blue/Purple

Black Iris

Hyacinth

Purple Iris

Queen Anne's Lace

FLOWERIFIC RESOURCES

Flower Elixirs

Special *Flowerevolution* bonus materials, print-outs & digital floral wallpapers: www.lotuswei.com/fun

Flower elixirs & holistic lifestyle blog: www.lotuswei.com

Flower Films

Inspirational Flower Films: www.movingart.com

Wings of Life, Disneynature—Shot by Louie Schwartzberg

TED Talks by Louie Schwartzberg

"The Hidden Beauty of Pollination"
"Nature. Beauty. Gratitude."
"Hidden Miracles of the Natural World"

Fantastic Fungi: www.fantasticfungi.com

Floral & Botanical Books

The Lost Language of Plants: The Ecological Importance of Plant Medicines to Life on Earth, by Stephen Harrod Buhner

Vibrational Medicine: The #1 Handbook of Subtle-Energy Therapies, by Dr. Richard Gerber

The Herbal Medicine-Maker's Handbook: A Home Manual, by James Green

Last Child in the Woods: Saving Our Children from Nature-Deficit Disorder, by Richard Louv

The Secret Life of Plants: A Fascinating Account of the Physical, Emotional, and Spiritual Relations between Plants and Man, by Peter Tompkins and Christopher Bird

The Hidden Messages in Water, by Dr. Masaru Emoto

Garden Anywhere, by Alys Fowler

Rosemary Gladstar's Medicinal Herbs: A Beginner's Guide: 33 Healing Herbs to Know, Grow, and Use, by Rosemary Gladstar

The Edible Flower Garden, by Rosalind Creasy

A Garden to Dye For: How to Use Plants from the Garden to Create Natural Colors for Fabrics & Fibers, by Chris McLaughlin

The Handbook of Natural Plant Dyes: Personalize Your Craft with Organic Colors from Acorns, Blackberries, Coffee, and Other Everyday Ingredients, by Sasha Duerr

Wild Color: The Complete Guide to Making and Using Natural Dyes, by Jenny Dean

Cooking with Flowers: Sweet and Savory Recipes with Rose Petals, Lilacs, Lavender, and Other Edible Flowers, by Miche Bacher

Miscellaneous Recommended Reading for a Happy, Healthy Life

Big Magic: Creative Living Beyond Fear, by Elizabeth Gilbert

Essentialism: The Disciplined Pursuit of Less, by Greg McKeown

The Life-Changing Magic of Tidying Up: The Japanese Art of Decluttering and Organizing, Marie Kondo

No More Dirty Looks: The Truth about Your Beauty Products—and the Ultimate Guide to Safe and Clean Cosmetics, by Siobhan O'Connor and Alexandra Spunt

The Art of Asking: How I Learned to Stop Worrying and Let People Help, by Amanda Palmer

Flower-Powered Music

LOTUSWEI Spotify station: http://bit.ly/musicwithflowers

Certified Organic Dried Flowers & Essential Oils

http://www.mountainroseherbs.com

Beautiful Botanical Gardens around the World

U.S.

Atlanta Botanical Garden, Atlanta, GA
Brooklyn Botanic Garden, Brooklyn, NY
Chicago Botanic Garden, IL
Denver Botanic Gardens, CO
Desert Botanical Garden, Phoenix, AZ
Longwood Gardens, Kennett Square, PA
Lotusland, Montecito, CA
Missouri Botanical Garden, St. Louis, MO
Na ʻAina Kai Botanical Gardens, Kilauea, HI
Naples Botanical Garden, Naples, FL
New York Botanical Garden, Bronx, NY
Pittsburgh Botanic Garden, Pittsburgh, PA
San Francisco Botanical Garden, San Francisco, CA

Worldwide

Acharya Jagadish Chandra Bose Indian Botanic Garden, Kolkata, India
Belmond Reid's Palace, Madeira, Portugal
Berlin-Dahlem Botanical Garden and Botanical
Museum, Berlin, Germany
The Butchart Gardens, British Columbia, Canada
Byodoin, Kyoto, Japan
Claude Monet's Garden, Giverny, France
Jardim Botânico, Rio de Janeiro, Brazil
Kirstenbosch National Botanical Garden, Cape Town, South Africa
Koishikawa Korakuen Gardens, Tokyo, Japan
Monte Palace Tropical Garden, Funchal, Portugal
Montreal Botanical Garden, Montreal, Canada
Nong Nooch Tropical Botanical Garden, Chonburi Province, Thailand
Royal Botanic Gardens, Kew, London, England
Royal Botanic Gardens Victoria, Melbourne, Australia
Royal Botanic Garden Sydney, Sydney, Australia
Seychelles National Botanical Gardens, Mahé, Seychelles
Singapore Botanic Gardens, Singapore

ENDNOTES

Chapter 1

1. Stephen Harrod Buhner, *The Lost Language of Plants: The Ecological Importance of Plant Medicines to Life on Earth* (White River Junction, VT: Chelsea Green Publishing, 2002), 224.

2. Roger Ulrich, O. Lundén, and J. L. Eltinge, "Effects of Exposure to Nature and Abstract Pictures on Patients Recovering from Heart Surgery." (paper presented at the Thirty-Third Meeting of the Society for Psychophysiological Research). Abstract published in *Psychophysiology* 30, supplement 1 (Rottach-Egern, Germany, 1993).

3. Neeta Weinstein, Dr. Richard M. Ryan, and Andrew K. Przybylski, "Can Nature Make Us More Caring? Effects of Immersion in Nature on Intrinsic Aspirations and Generosity," *Personality and Social Psychology Bulletin*. University of Rochester. (2009): 1316–1328," accessed October 15, 2015, http://selfdeterminationtheory.org/SDT/documents/2009_WeinsteinPrzybylskiRyan_Nature.pdf.

Chapter 2

1. Dominic Clarke, Heather Whitney, Gregory Sutton, and Daniel Eric, "Detection and Learning of Floral Electrical Fields by Bumblebees," *Science* 340, no. 6128 (2013): 66-69, doi: 10.1126/science.1230883.

2. "All-time Box Office: USA," Internet Movie Database, last modified October 14 2015, http://www.imdb.com/boxoffice/alltimegross.

3. Dr. Qing Li, "Forest Medicine," Nippon Medical School, accessed November 5, 2015, http://college.nms.ac.jp/en/research/topics/fm.

4. Cleve Backster, *Primary Perception: Biocommunication with Plants, Living Foods, and Human Cells* (Anza, CA: White Rose Millennium Press, 2003).

5. Paul Stamets, *Mycelium Running: How Mushrooms Can Help Save the World* (Berkeley, CA: Ten Speed Press, 2005).

6. "Water: The Great Mystery," Master Skaya Movie Company. Intention Media Inc. 2008, accessed July 5, 2015, https://vimeo.com/127630186.

Chapter 3

1. Stephen Harrod Buhner, *The Lost Language of Plants: The Ecological Importance of Plant Medicines to Life on Earth* (White River Junction, VT: Chelsea Green Publishing, 2002), 270–271.

2. Transcribed from a talk by Venerable Choden Rinpoche, "The Life of a Hidden Meditator: A Subtle Form of Revolution," *Mandala*, July/August 2000, http://cdn.fpmt.org/wp-content/uploads/mandala/archives/mandala-issues-for-2000/july/LIfe-of-a-HIdden-Meditator-Choden-Rinpoche-72dpi.pdf?b53e5e.

3. Stephen Harrod Buhner, *The Lost Language of Plants: The Ecological Importance of Plant Medicines to Life on Earth* (White River Junction, VT: Chelsea Green Publishing, 2002).

4. Masanobu Fukuoka, *The Road Back to Nature* (New York: Japan Publications, 1987).

Chapter 4

1. Ian C. G. Weaver, Nadia Cervoni, Frances A. Champagne, Ana C. D'Alessio, Shakti Sharma, Jonathan R. Seckl, Sergiy Dymov, Moshe Szyf, and Michael J. Meaney, "Epigenetic Programming by Maternal Behavior," *Nature Neuroscience* 7 (July 27 2004): 847–854; M. J. Meaney, "Maternal Care, Gene Expression, and the Transmission of Individual Differences in Stress Reactivity Across Generations," *Annual Review of Neuroscience* 24 (2001): 1161–1192; P. M. Plotsky and M. J. Meaney, "Early, Postnatal Experience Alters Hypothalamic Corticotropin-Releasing Factor (CRF) mRNA, Median Eminence CRF Content and Stress-Induced Release in Adult Rats," *Molecular Brain Research* 18, no. 3. (May 1993): 195–200; Dan Hurley, "Grandma's Experiences Leave a Mark on Your Genes," *Discover*, June 25, 2015, http://discovermagazine.com/2013/may/13-grandmas-experiences-leave-epigenetic-mark-on-your-genes; Chris Bell, "Epigenetics: How to Alter Your Genes," *The Telegraph*, October 16, 2013, http://www.telegraph.co.uk/news/science/10369861/Epigenetics-How-to-alter-your-genes.html.

Chapter 5

1. His Holiness the Dalai Lama, *Worlds in Harmony: Compassionate Action for a Better World* (Berkeley, CA: Parallax Press, 2004), 57, 66.

2. James H. Fowler and Nicholas A. Christakis, "Dynamic Spread of Happiness in a Large Social Network: Longitudinal Analysis Over 20 Years in the Framingham Heart Study," *The British Medical Journal*, December 5, 2008, doi: http://dx.doi.org/10.1136/bmj.a2338; Pam Belluck, "Strangers May Cheer You Up, Study Says," *The New York Times*, December 4, 2008, http://www.nytimes.com/2008/12/05/health/05happy-web.html?_r=1&.

Chapter 6

1. Dalai Lama XIV, *An Open Heart: Practicing Compassion in Everyday Life* (New York: Back Bay Books, 2002).

2. Rosita Arvigo and Nadine Epstein, *Spiritual Bathing: Healing Rituals and Traditions from around the World* (Berkeley, CA: Celestial Arts, 2004), 15.

3. Stephen Harrod Buhner, *The Lost Language of Plants: The Ecological Importance of Plant Medicines to Life on Earth* (White River Junction, VT: Chelsea Green Publishing, 2002), 227.

Chapter 7

1. Elizabeth Alexander, *The Light of the World: A Memoir* (New York: Grand Central Publishing, 2015), 147.

2. Weinstock, "The Potential Influence of Maternal Stress Hormones on Development and Mental Health of the Offspring," U.S. National Library of Medicine: *Brain, Behavior, and Immunity* (2005), http://www.ncbi.nlm.nih.gov/pubmed/15944068; P. D. Wadhwa, C. A. Sandman, and T. J. Garite, "The Neurobiology of Stress in Human Pregnancy: Implications for Prematurity and Development of the Fetal Central Nervous System," U.S. National Library of Medicine: *Progress in Brain Research* (2001), http://www.ncbi.nlm.nih.gov/pubmed/11589126; Rebecca M. Reynolds, Javier Labad, Claudia Buss, Pearl Ghaemmaghami, and Katri Räikkönen, "Transmitting Biological Effects of Stress in Utero: Implications for Mother and Offspring," *Psychoneuroendocrinology* 38, no. 9 (2013), doi: 10.1016/j.psyneuen.2013.05.018, www.sciencedirect.com.contentproxy.phoenix.edu/science/journal/03064530.

*"The developing fetus makes adaptations to an adverse in utero environment which may lead to permanent changes in structure and physiology, thus 'programming' the fetus to risk of ill health in later life. Epidemiological studies have shown associations between low birth weight, a surrogate marker of an adverse intrauterine environment, and a range of diseases in adult life including cardiometabolic and psychiatric disease. These associations do not apply exclusively to low birth weight babies but also to newborns within the normal birth weight range. Early life stress, including stressors in the prenatal and early postnatal period, is a key factor that can have long-term effects on offspring health."

Arctic Lupine

1. Gregory J. Sharam and Roy Turkington, "Diurnal Cycle of Sparteine Production in *Lupinus arcticus*," *Canadian Journal of Botany* 83, no. 10 (2005): 1345–48. Accessed May 7, 2015, doi: 10.1139/b05-104.

Banana Blossom

1. Dokrak Marod, Piya Pinyo, Prateep Duengkae, and Tanaka Hiroshi, "The Role of Wild Banana (*Musa acuminata Colla*) on Wildlife Diversity in Mixed Deciduous Forest," *National Science* 44 (2010): 35–43. http://t-fern.forest.ku.ac.th/iDocument/TFERN201202111446272.pdf.

Bee Balm

1. Green Deane, "Horsemint, Spotted Beebalm," *Eat the Weeds and Other Things, Too*, accessed October 5, 2015, http://www.eattheweeds.com/monarda-punctata-bergamot's-bud-2/.

Black Bat Flower

1. Dave Partington, "Tacca, the Black Bat Flower Plant," Daves Files, accessed May 7, 2015, http://davesfiles.com/Plants/Tacca/Tacca_Chantrieri_Black_Bat_Plant.htm; Dave Partington, "Bat Flower Frequently Asked Questions," Daves Files, accessed May 7, 2015, http://davesfiles.com/Plants/Tacca/Bat_Flower_FAQ.htm.

Bodhi Tree

1. Dr. Peter M. Brown, "Rocky Mountain Tree-Ring Research: Old List," Rocky Mountain Tree-Ring Research Inc., last modified January 2016, http://www.rmtrr.org/oldlist.htm.
2. J. B. Disanayaka, *Water in Culture: The Sri Lankan Heritage* (Colombo, Sri Lanka: Ministry of Environment & Parliamentary Affairs, 1992) 57–60.

Chocolate Daisy

1. Janice Tucker, "Chocolate Flower: Berlandiera lyrata," Santa Fe Botanical Garden, last modified August 2012, http://www.santafebotanicalgarden.org/august-2012/.

Dandelion

1. Rosemary Gladstar, *Family Herbal: A Guide to Living Life with Energy, Health and Vitality* (North Adams, MA: Storey Books, 2001), 19, 25.

Date Palm Flower

1. Susan Russo, "Medjool: A Date to Remember," NPR online, October 17, 2007, http://www.npr.org/templates/story/story.php?storyId=15282847.

Fire Star Orchid

1. Susan Heeger, "Poor Man's Orchid: Epidendrums Don't Cost a Fortune, and Even the Novice Gardener Will Find Them Forgiving," *Los Angeles Times*, June 9, 2002, http://articles.latimes.com/2002/jun/09/magazine/tm-45410.

Fireweed

1. Richard Mabey, *Flora Britannica: The Definitive New Guide to Wild Flowers, Plants and Trees* (London: Chatto & Windus, 1996).
2. Bob Brett, "Sea-to-Sky Fireweed," *Whistler Naturalists,* last modified September 15, 2000, http://www.whistlernaturalists.ca/?page_id=279.

Gardenia

1. Subhuti Dharmananda, Ph.D., "Gardenia: Key Herb for Dispelling Dampness and Heat Via the Triple Burner," Institute for Traditional Medicine online, last modified September 2003, www.itmonline.org/arts/gardenia.htm.

Giant Spider Lily

1. "Bakong, Spider Lily, Crinum Asiaticum: Philippine Medicinal Herbs/Philippine Alternative Medicine," StuartXchange online, last modified April 2013, http://www.stuartxchange.org/Bakong.html.

Grevillea

1. Selwyn L. Everist, *Poisonous Plants of Australia* (London; Sydney: Angus & Robertson, 1981).

Hollyhock

1. Michael Howard, *Traditional Folk Remedies* (London: Century, 1987) 155.

Jade Succulent

1. "Grin Taxonomy for Plants," USDA: Agricultural Research Service, National Genetic Resources Program—Germplasm Resources Information Network, last modified July, 20 2010, http://www.ars-grin.gov/cgi-bin/npgs/html/taxon.pl?404524.

Nectarine Blossom

1. Miklos Faust and Béla Timon, *Origin and Dissemination of Peach*, Horticultural Reviews 17 (1995): 331; R. A. Seelig, "Nectarines: Fruit & Vegetable Facts & Pointers," United Fresh Fruit and Vegetable Association, 3rd ed. (1971).

Passionflower

1. S. Akhondzadeh, H. R. Naghavi, M. Vazirian, A. Shayeganpour, H. Rashidi, and M. Khani, "Passionflower in the Treatment of Generalized Anxiety: A Pilot Double-Blind Randomized Controlled Trial with Oxazepam," *Journal of Clinical Pharmacy and Therapeutics* (October 26, 2001): 363–367, http://www.ncbi.nlm.nih.gov/pubmed/11679026.

Pink Lotus

1. Carol Kaesuk Yoon, "Heat of Lotus Attracts Insects and Scientists," *New York Times*, October 1, 1996, http://www.nytimes.com/1996/10/01/science/heat-of-lotus-attracts-insects-and-scientists.html.

Pink Magnolia

1. Mona Bourell, "In Bloom: Magnolia liliiflora," San Francisco Botanical Garden online, last modified March 2015, http://www.sfbotanicalgarden.org/garden/bloom_15_03.shtml.
2. Anthony Huxley and Mark Griffiths, *The New Royal Horticultural Society Dictionary of Gardening* (London, United Kingdom: Nature Publishing Group, 1999); "Magnolia liliiflora—Desr.," Plants for the Future, accessed July 14, 2015, http://www.pfaf.org/user/Plant.aspx?LatinName=Magnolia+liliiflora.

Pink Primrose

1. Mark "Merriwether" Vorderbruggen, "Pink Primrose," *Foraging Texas: Merriwether's Guide to Edible Wild Plants of Texas and the Southwest* (2016), http://www.foragingtexas.com/2008/04/primrose-pink.html.

Pink Spirea

1. Harvey Wickes Felter, M.D. and John Uri Lloyd, Phr., M., Ph.D., *King's American Dispensatory,* (Cinncinati, Ohio Valley Co., 1898, scanned version by Henriette Kress 1999–2014): http://henriettes-herb.com/eclectic/kings/index.html.

Pomegranate Flower

1. K. K. Jindal and R. C. Sharma, *Recent Trends in Horticulture in the Himalayas: Integrated Development Under the Mission Mode* (Tagore Garden, New Delhi: Indus Publishing Company, 2004), 139.
2. "Pomegranate: The Longevity Plant," Ayurvedam, accessed on October 12, 2015, http://www.ayurvedam.com/htm/leela/Pomegranate.htm.
3. Henry Dore, S.J., translated by M. Kennelly, S.J., "Researches into Chinese Superstitions," *Varietes Sinolojique or Miscellanies on China* (Shanghai: T'usewei Printing Press, 1914) 722, https://archive.org/stream/researchesintoch01dor/researchesintoch01dor_djvu.txt.

Silk Floss

1. Robin Booth, "Subtropical Growing in Kerikeri: A Slowly Accumulating, Descriptive Repository of Plants Growing in the Bay of Islands—*Ceiba speciosa*," accessed on October 7, 2015, http://netlist.co.nz/communities/Wharepuke/Feature.cfm?WPID=4399.

Strawberry Blossom

1. "FAOSTAT: Production of Top 5 Producers 2013," Food and Agriculture Organization of the United Nations: Statistics Division, accessed June 2015, http://faostat3.fao.org/browse/Q/QC/E.

Trumpet Vine

1. Dr. David Creech, "Campis grandiflora—Chinese Trumpet Creeper," Stephen F. Austin State University: Arthur Temple College of Forestry and Agriculture, accessed October 7, 2015,http://sfagardens.sfasu.edu/index.php/plant-index/115-campsis.

White Water Lily

1. "Floating Leaved Rooted Plants," State of Washington: Department of Ecology, accessed October 14, 2015, http://www.ecy.wa.gov/programs/wq/plants/plantid2/descriptions/nymodo.html.
2. Robin Dipasquale, "Numphaea odorata: White Pond Lily," Medical Herbalism: Materia Medica and Pharmacy, 2001, accessed October 15, 2015, http://medherb.com/Materia_Medica/Nymphaea_odorata.htm.

Yarrow

1. "Lookout: Mobile Mindset Study," Conducted by Harris Interactive on behalf of *Lookout*, June 2012, https://www.mylookout.com/img/images/lookout-mobile-mindset-2012.pdf; Victoria Wollaston, "How Often Do You Check Your Phone? The Average Person Does It 110 Times a DAY (and Up to Every 6 Seconds in the Evening)," *Daily Mail*, last modified October 8, 2013, http://www.dailymail.co.uk/sciencetech/article-2449632/How-check-phone-The-average-person-does-110-times-DAY-6-seconds-evening.html; Victoria Wollaston, "How Often Do YOU Look at Your Phone? The Average User Now Picks Up Their Device More than 1,500 Times a Week," *Daily Mail*, last modified October 7, 2014, http://www.dailymail.co.uk/sciencetech/article-2783677/How-YOU-look-phone-The-average-user-picks-device-1-500-times-day.html; Mary Meeker and Liang Wu, "Internet Trends: D11 Conference," Kleiner Perkins Caufield Byers (KPCB), last modified May 29, 2013, http://www.kpcb.com/blog/2013-internet-trends; Britney Fitzgerald, "Americans Addicted to Checking Smartphones, Would 'Panic' If They Lost Device (Study)," *Huffington Post*, last modified June 22, 2012, http://www.huffingtonpost.com/2012/06/21/americans-are-addicted-to-smartphones_n_1615293.html; David Hinckley, "Average American Watches 5 Hours of TV Per Day, Report Shows," *New York Daily News*, last modified March 5, 2014, http://www.nydailynews.com/life-style/average-american-watches-5-hours-tv-day-article-1.1711954.
2. Alma R. Hutchens, *Indian Herbalogy of North America: The Definitive Guide to Native Medicinal Plants and Their Uses* (Boulder, CO: Shambhala Publications, 1991).

INDEX

Note: Page numbers in *italics* indicate projects or recipes.

ACKNOWLEDGMENTS

A perfect illustration of our interconnectedness, this book arose from the love of many people.

Amy McDonald brought Louie Schwartzberg and me together, and Bonnie St. John planted the seed for the book when we were all in India. Scott James watered the seed and was instrumental in making this collaboration happen. Louie's vast love and appreciation of flowers, his ability to capture their beauty, and our mutual desire to save the world through flowers was the sunshine that made the seed sprout.

This book would not have blossomed without the loving coaching and editing of Morgan Farley, and Lisa Reinhardt's polishing and support. I'm grateful for the generous suggestions made by Sally Hess-Samuelson, Siobhan O'Connor, and Jana Hexter.

Deep bow to Sara Jeane for working her magic with Louie's spectacular photos, and heartfelt gratitude to Reid, Patty, Sally & the whole Hay House crew for welcoming this work into the world.

To all my clients & Flowerevolutionaries who teach me so much, I love you fiercely. A special thanks to Jen Paul for being so open to sharing.

Endless gratitude to my flower power team: Robbie Cohen, Taylor Rico, Jodi Upton, Darla Zavacky, Michon Javelosa, Lynn Dooher, and Frank Banuelos, for keeping the business flourishing and giving helpful feedback.

Thank you to my dearest family for supporting me in all the ways you do, and for your unconditional love & encouragement.

Last but not least, I want to express my undying devotion and deepest gratitude to Gyalwang Karmapa for his timeless blessings of this project, and especially to Karma Sangye Rapten for his relentless, fearless, and utterly supernatural love.

To all the flowers and Mother Earth herself for their vast waves of wisdom, as well as all the unseen supporters and guides of this project, I am forever grateful.

ABOUT KATIE AND LOUIE

Katie Hess is a flower alchemist and the founder of LOTUSWEI, one of the world's leading floral apothecaries. After 15 years of independent research of flower and plant-based healing, her flower-powered community is thriving in over 15 countries. She partners with premiere hotels and spas, naturopathic practices, and botanical gardens to instigate a revolution with the premise that you transform the world by transforming yourself (with a little help from flowers). Katie travels worldwide to seek out flowers that reduce stress, improve sleep, and accelerate personal growth. Her transformative elixirs having been featured in *O, The Oprah Magazine, The New York Times, Los Angeles Times, Sunset,* and *Organic Spa Magazine*. A lifelong spiritual seeker, Katie has studied meditation and mindful-awareness techniques with several Tibetan Buddhist masters, including the Dalai Lama and the Karmapa, Tibet's next generation leader. Discover what your favorite flower means about you at lotuswei.com.

Louie Schwartzberg is an award-winning filmmaker and photographer whose notable career spans more than four decades providing breathtaking imagery using his time-lapse, high-speed, and macro cinematography techniques. Louie's recent theatrical releases include the 3-D IMAX film *Mysteries of the Unseen World* with National Geographic, narrated by Forest Whitaker, and the pollination documentary feature *Wings of Life* for Disneynature, narrated by Meryl Streep. Louie also directed the popular theme park ride film *Soarin' Around the World*, now showing at Disney Theme Parks worldwide. As the only filmmaker in the world who has been shooting time-lapse flowers, 24/7 continuously for 40 years, Schwartzberg is a visual artist breaking barriers and telling stories that celebrate life and reveal the mysteries and wisdom of nature, people, and places. His three TED talks have 50 million combined views. He has received numerous awards, including one of his proudest, the Pollinator Protection Award from the North American Pollinator Protection Campaign. He is the first filmmaker to be inducted into the American Association for the Advancement of Science and the Lemelson Foundation's Invention Ambassadors Program. Website: www.movingart.com

Hay House Titles of Related Interest

YOU CAN HEAL YOUR LIFE, the movie, starring Louise Hay & Friends
(available as a 1-DVD program and an expanded 2-DVD set)
Watch the trailer at: www.LouiseHayMovie.com

THE SHIFT, the movie,
starring Dr. Wayne W. Dyer
(available as a 1-DVD program and an expanded 2-DVD set)
Watch the trailer at: www.DyerMovie.com

THE FUTURE IS NOW: Timely Advice for Creating a Better World, by His Holiness
the 17th Gyalwang Karmapa

LET IT OUT: A Journey Through Journaling, by Katie Dalebout

LIGHT IS THE NEW BLACK: A Guide to Answering Your Soul's Calling and Working Your Light,
by Rebecca Campbell

MINDFUL INTENTIONS, by Louie Schwartzberg

RADICAL SELF-LOVE: A Guide to Loving Yourself and Living Your Dreams, by Gala Darling

All of the above are available at your local bookstore,
or may be ordered by contacting Hay House (see next page).

We hope you enjoyed this Hay House book. If you'd like to receive our online catalog featuring additional information on Hay House books and products, or if you'd like to find out more about the Hay Foundation, please contact:

Hay House, Inc., P.O. Box 5100, Carlsbad, CA 92018-5100
(760) 431-7695 or (800) 654-5126
(760) 431-6948 (fax) or (800) 650-5115 (fax)
www.hayhouse.com® • www.hayfoundation.org

Published and distributed in Australia by: Hay House Australia Pty. Ltd., 18/36 Ralph St., Alexandria NSW 2015
Phone: 612-9669-4299 • Fax: 612-9669-4144 • www.hayhouse.com.au

Published and distributed in the United Kingdom by: Hay House UK, Ltd., Astley House, 33 Notting Hill Gate, London W11 3JQ • Phone: 44-20-3675-2450 • Fax: 44-20-3675-2451 • www.hayhouse.co.uk

Published and distributed in the Republic of South Africa by: Hay House SA (Pty), Ltd., P.O. Box 990, Witkoppen 2068
info@hayhouse.co.za • www.hayhouse.co.za

Published in India by: Hay House Publishers India, Muskaan Complex, Plot No. 3, B-2, Vasant Kunj, New Delhi 110 070 • Phone: 91-11-4176-1620 • Fax: 91-11-4176-1630 • www.hayhouse.co.in

Distributed in Canada by: Raincoast Books, 2440 Viking Way, Richmond, B.C. V6V 1N2
Phone: 1-800-663-5714 • Fax: 1-800-565-3770 • www.raincoast.com

Take Your Soul on a Vacation

Visit www.HealYourLife.com® to regroup, recharge, and reconnect with your own magnificence. Featuring blogs, mind-body-spirit news, and life-changing wisdom from Louise Hay and friends.

Visit www.HealYourLife.com today!

Free e-newsletters from Hay House, the Ultimate Resource for Inspiration

Be the first to know about Hay House's dollar deals, free downloads, special offers, affirmation cards, giveaways, contests, and more!

 Get exclusive excerpts from our latest releases and videos from *Hay House Present Moments*.

 Enjoy uplifting personal stories, how-to articles, and healing advice, along with videos and empowering quotes, within *Heal Your Life*.

 Have an inspirational story to tell and a passion for writing? Sharpen your writing skills with insider tips from *Your Writing Life*.

Sign Up Now!

Get inspired, educate yourself, get a complimentary gift, and share the wisdom!

http://www.hayhouse.com/newsletters.php

Visit www.hayhouse.com to sign up today!

 HAY HOUSE

 HAYHOUSE RADIO
radio for your soul

 HealYourLife.com

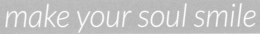